The Medieval Professional Reader at Work:
Evidence from Manuscripts of Chaucer, Langland, Kempe, and Gower

For

Denise L. Despres

*whose aesthetic, spiritual, and intellectual
gifts have enriched our own work over the years*

Edited by KATHRYN KERBY-FULTON and
MAIDIE HILMO

The Medieval Professional
Reader at Work:
Evidence from Manuscripts of
Chaucer, Langland, Kempe,
and Gower

English Literary Studies
University of Victoria
2001

ENGLISH LITERARY STUDIES

Published at the University of Victoria

Founding Editor

Samuel L. Macey

GENERAL EDITOR

Robert M. Schuler

EDITORIAL BOARD

Thomas R. Cleary

Evelyn M. Cobley

Kathryn Kerby-Fulton

Stephen A. C. Scobie

Nelson C. Smith

BUSINESS MANAGER

Hedy Miller

ISBN 0-920604-77-3

The ELS Monograph Series is published in consultation with members of the Department by ENGLISH LITERARY STUDIES, Department of English, Univeristy of Victoria, P.O. Box 3070, Victoria, B.C., Canada v8w 3w1.

ELS Monograph Series No. 85
©2001 by contributing authors, as indicated on Contents page.

Cover: The Squire, *The Canterbury Tales*, MS Ellesmere 26 C9, fol. 115v, by permission of The Huntington Library, San Marino, California.

Printed on acid-free paper, sewn, and bound by
MORRISS PRINTING COMPANY LTD.
Victoria, British Columbia

CONTENTS

Introduction

The Medieval Professional Reader and Reception History, 1292-1641

Kathryn Kerby-Fulton

Books go on making history long after their authors are dead, but in all except a few celebrated cases — Augustine's dramatic conversion upon opening Paul's Epistle to the Romans, or John Ball's canonization of Piers Plowman in the rebel letters of 1381 — the readers who make such history have been largely unknown or forgotten. This small collection of essays suggests some methods and approaches for the recovery of medieval reader response from manuscript evidence of a kind still too often ignored or undervalued. Until quite recently, for instance, marginal annotations to medieval literary texts were considered worthless unless they were demonstrably authorial, and pictorial cycles shared the same fate if they were not author-inspired, or, at the very least, submissively "faithful" to the text in character and detail. Fortunately, these attitudes toward reception evidence have begun to change. Today, living uneasily along the hermeneutic fault-line that Deconstruction left behind as it rumbled through the humanities in the 80s, scholars seem to find increasing comfort in the view that even if authors are dead, readers are not. But excavating reader response is still a relatively new enterprise: although Jauss long ago theorized a "horizon of expectations" in the study of reader reception,[1] such horizons still remain remote, abstractly peopled territories of theoretical vastness. Individual readers of the past, however, we can know in some important ways: from the late medieval period, their responses have been left to us in literally thousands of manuscripts, and they can be recovered by the kind of paleographical, linguistic, textual, and iconographic analysis which, however, has not been popular work, mainly because it is detailed and hard. It has also been maligned as the positivism which keeps medievalists hidebound, unresponsive, and unfashionable.[2]

Fortunately, these views are no longer tenable, but the work still remains hard, and much of it remains undone. It is work, we would suggest, that keeps us not in the past, but usefully connected to it. And while other approaches promise new perspectives, manuscript studies promise what has recently been called a "new erudition."[3] It is in this spirit that the essays in *The Professional Reader at Work* were collected together, to offer practical, manuscript-based studies of medieval reading habits in use. Our term "professional reader" may require a little glossing: we use it slightly differently from the way that Malcolm Parkes defined it in his classic essay on "The Literacy of the Laity."[4] For us a professional reader is someone whose job it is to prepare a text for the reading public, someone whose job description (supervisory scribe, corrector, annotator, editor, illustrator) allows him to filter the text for presentation to the patron or reading community. Professional readers wielded a great deal of power, and their impact on medieval culture should never be underestimated.[5]

The medieval reading process was unusually multi-faceted, and can surprise the modern reader by offering an alternative grid or map of a text we believe we know well — one that cuts across, or unsettles, familiar stereotypes we all hold. In *Iconography and the Professional Reader*, Denise Despres and I outlined five key functions of the medieval reading process, which can be: mnemonic, meditative, performative, self-reflexive, and sometimes dissenting (the latter used in its general rather than strictly theological sense). Perhaps these concepts might be best introduced by exemplification from one of the manuscripts studied here: British Library MS Additional 61823, *The Book of Margery Kempe*. This manuscript appears to have found its most avid professional reader well over a century after it was initially made (a fact which in itself unsettles our notions of book production). Known to modern scholars as the Red Ink Annotator, this reader in fact did much more than annotate the text: the evidence suggests, I would argue, that he also rubricated, punctuated, corrected, and even sporadically illustrated it, in order to heighten and develop its primitive *ordinatio*, and provide the maximum amount of reader guidance. All these jobs were done by one hand, working in red ink, though certainly not at one sitting, as the variety of ink-batches in use shows.[6] Two basic colours of red ink were used (as is quite common in the rubrication of other utility grade manuscripts like this one).[7] The Annotator went back over it several times, and at different sittings. This he did, in common with scribes of other such manuscripts where, as here, one professional reader wears many hats. And it is clear that he could not resist switching hats several times on the same page, pausing to catch a correction, then splash a letter, or repunctuate a phrase, and so on, all in the same stint. This rubricator was not a trained artist, but he was a scribe, familiar, at least by sight, with fashionable modes of book decoration and, most of all, passionately concerned to guide and enhance the reader's experience. He added informal illustrations in the margins (images of the fire of divine love [fol. 43v], a heart [fols. 102r, 106r], a pillar [fol. 15r], and so on) to stimulate affective meditation. These are also, like many of the written annotations, mnemonic devices, meant to enhance the laborious process of memorization. The *Book*, after all, appears to have been created for loaning out, as Nicholas Watson has suggested, and, as Kelly Parsons's essay so meticulously documents here, loaning largely to the laity associated with Mount Grace Abbey, many of whom were women. It was likely on behalf of these readers that he performed one of the functions of his reading that was not at all haphazard or spontaneous, his systematic "censoring" of (or filtering, or, indeed, dissenting from) some of Kempe's more extravagant imaginings, especially those sexually or otherwise sensationally marked. We know this because at a few of these points in which a section has been crossed through in red there is a marginal "d" (for "deleatur," fol. 98v), overlined in red — perhaps a note to himself made on an earlier pass through the manuscript?

From the study of other contemporary manuscripts we know that even the most (to the modern eye) casual-appearing annotations were often actually preplanned and executed by a professional reader, and the Kempe manuscript shows exactly this non-spontaneous sort of attention, as well. Spontaneity (or its absence) in the Red Ink Annotator's work, however, is balanced by a striking enhancement or encouragement of affective spontaneity in his readers — and indeed in himself ("trew it is blyssyd lord"; fol. 92v). This is where the performative and self-reflexive aspects of his reading, and the quality of reading he is modelling, are evident. Some of the now famous annotations, "father M. was wont so to doo" (fol. 85) or "So dyd prior Norton in hys excess" (fol. 51v), which bestow a kind of clerical authority on Kempe's own excesses, are actually, in the manuscript, just part of a larger visual tissue of markings encouraging the reader toward as dramatically performative and self-reflexive a reading as possible. The reader of the annotations in print does not see this tissue, nor the many visual details he painstakingly provided to sustain these responses and to encourage meditative and mnemonic reading simultaneously, such as his subtle system of drawing tiny, semi-decorative images, like the courtly fleur-de-lys over the word "dalyauns" (fol. 47v) or small tears falling from words like "wepyng" (fol. 25r). He repeats the little tears thereafter in spots even where the word itself is not mentioned, but he wants the feeling evoked—and the performance of the action, the weeping itself, or at

9

the very least meditation on these things, and memory of passages so linked. What he is after is the stimulation of "interiority" or "internal progress," to use Linda Olson's terminology,[8] and the Kempe manuscript shows brilliantly not only how this self-reflexivity is fostered through readerly performance, but also how an autobiographical text inspires layers of readerly autobiographical annotation, and, once in a while, a kind of respectful censorship, where the reader dissents from the author whose text cost him untold hours of painstaking penwork.

The fascinating details of how others among these tiny, roughly but meticulously executed features of the manuscript operate I leave in the capable hands of Kelly Parsons's reading. The appendix accompanying her study provides the first entirely complete transcription of the annotations, correcting and augmenting Meech and Allen's original transcriptions.

It remains to briefly introduce the four essays printed here for the first time. Previewing Parsons's study, Nicholas Watson writes:[9]

Kelly Parsons's study of "The Red Ink Annotator of *The Book of Margery Kempe* and His Lay Audience" looks afresh at a text Middle English scholars know well, through the eyes of a medieval reader whose understanding of the book had already — or so I had assumed — been well analyzed by earlier scholars, most recently Karma Lochrie. Margery Kempe's autohagiography survives for us only in a manuscript owned by the late fifteenth-century Carthusians of Mount Grace, a group of "devotional specialists" whose milieu, still imperfectly understood, has interested two generations of modern English scholar-monks, from David Knowles to Edmund Colledge and James Hogg. Since Knowles and Colledge are among those who were most condescending about Kempe when she erupted onto the scholarly landscape in the 1940s and 1950s, it has always seemed surprising that their medieval alter egos should have seen so much to interest them in her book: not simply preserving it but annotating it extensively, even comparing her experiences to those of two of their religious virtuosos, the mystical writers Richard Methley and John Norton.

Lochrie used this interest to dignify Kempe by associating her with a group she understands in the terms suggested by Knowles. But Parsons takes the discussion several stages further by arguing that the red ink annotations in the Kempe manuscript show us a side of the Mount Grace Carthusians that has largely been ignored: their commitment to the pastoral care of their lay associates, both men and women. Whereas early in the century the monastery produced two outstanding works of vernacular theology for lay consumption, Nicholas Love's *Mirror of the Blessed Life of Jesus Christ* and the paraphrase of Henry Suso, the *Tretyse of the Seven Poyntes of Trewe Love and Everlastynge Wisdom*, late fifteenth-century Mount Grace was self-conscious about Latinity. Not only did Methley and Norton write almost exclusively in

10

Latin, but Methley devoted much energy to translating and annotating *The Cloud of Unknowing* and the Middle English version of Marguerite Porete's *Mirror of Simple Souls* into Latin for his associate Thurstan Watson. Parsons shows how at least one of the few vernacular texts that survive from the last decades of Mount Grace's history was carefully prepared for use outside the monastery, by a monk or group of monks who clearly considered Kempe's idiosyncratic life and devotions a suitable model for the women and men in their spiritual charge.

Besides making us think again about the way the transmission and reception history of medieval texts so often seem almost designed to baffle our modern preconceptions about how reading and religious experience is gendered, Parsons's article opens for us what is virtually a whole new approach to *The Book of Margery Kempe* as a pastoral treatise. Since this is exactly how the book's prologue, written by its priest scribe, frames Kempe's narrative, this is an approach that is going to need to be taken very seriously indeed.

A different approach, and a different set of medieval readers, is examined in Maidie Hilmo's essay on the Ellesmere Chaucer. As Derek Pearsall writes of her study,[10] "Maidie Hilmo reads the miniatures in the Ellesmere manuscript of *The Canterbury Tales* not so much as evidence of the responses of an early reader as evidence of their role as an aspect of text-production. For her, they are part of the shaping and preparation of the manuscript for aristocratic viewing, and they function in important ways as what she calls a 'visual guide to the reading process.'" Her analysis captures an aristocratic audience mirroring its heroes to themselves while mocking its social inferiors, and is the first study of the Ellesmere cycle to show Ellesmere's production team at work to stylize, elevate, decorate, and sometimes even sanitize Chaucer's text. "Hilmo peels back the layers of pictorial evidence to reveal the complex cultural and political agenda that these professional readers set themselves — or, perhaps, that was set for them in relation to the person for whom the manuscript was intended, upon whose identity she speculates."

A third approach to the excavation of readership is Carl Grindley's comprehensive system of classification for manuscript marginalia, a system that illuminates both medieval understanding of narrative (through the examination of marginal reading aids), and the ethical and polemical response of readers. As Derek Pearsall writes about Grindley's essay, "reception-theory does not have to confess itself defeated if authorial intention cannot be proved: the way a text was understood, the way it came to be understood, are all part of the complexly incremental process of interpretation that we inherit, add to, and hand on. No text is clean of these processes, except one that has never

11

been read. The essay by Carl Grindley, on marginalia, is based on extensive work on two *Piers Plowman* manuscripts, Huntington Library MS HM 143 and British Library MS Additional 35157, set in context with further work on a representative range of annotated manuscripts containing Middle English in the Hunterian Library at Glasgow. It is an ambitious attempt at a taxonomy of marginalia in late medieval English manuscripts, and will be extremely useful as a first and much-needed step towards classification; perhaps equally useful will be the complete list it provides of annotations in these two key manuscripts of *Piers Plowman*."

The final essay in this volume, by Kathryn Kerby-Fulton and Steven Justice, is on Scribe D's marketing of Gower for a particularly politically engaged audience, demonstrating that D was concerned both with the currency of the Gower text and its topicality. It also suggests that illustrations were consciously used in the production of his Gowers to enhance the authority of the vernacular text, and that Scribe D, like his colleague on the Trinity Gower, Scribe B (responsible for both the Hengwrt and the Ellesmere Canterbury Tales manuscripts) pursued a "look" for the marketing of vernacular English poetry. These manuscripts suggest increasingly positive perceptions of the capacity of the vernacular at this time, and do not reflect a condescension to the non-latinate texts, both in script and in decoration. Moreover, the fact that many of Scribe D's clients had some kind of Westminster association is surely relevant to this felicitous reflection of the vernacular's increased status by the late fourteenth and early fifteenth centuries. It makes, we hope, a happy note on which to close this collection of studies of professional readers at work upon some of the most important literary texts extant in Middle English.

Maidie Hilmo and I wish to thank the other contributors for their exceptional patience and cheerfulness, Darlene Hollingsworth for her meticulous and dedicated work on the manuscript, and most especially to thank Robert Schuler, the editor of English Literary Studies, for his exemplary professionalism, generosity and willingness in the service of a worthy cause.

NOTES

[1] Hans Robert Jauss, "Literary History as a Challenge to Literary Theory," in *Toward an Aesthetic of Reception*, trans. Timothy Bahti (Minneapolis, 1982), 25.

[2] See Lee Patterson, "On the Margin: Postmodernism, Ironic History, and Medieval Studies," *Speculum* 65 (1990), 106.

[3] For the concept, see the special issue of *Representations* (1997) entitled *The New Erudition*.

4 For Parkes, "the literacy of the professional reader" is that of "the scholar or professional man of letters," which he distinguished from the cultivated reader and the pragmatic reader; see "The Literacy of the Laity," in *The Medieval World*, ed. David Daiches and A. Thorlby (London, 1973), 555.

5 For a discussion of how the concept is used here, see Kathryn Kerby-Fulton and Denise Despres, *Iconography and the Professional Reader: The Politics of Book Production in the Douce "Piers Plowman"* (Minneapolis, 1999).

6 The *capitulum* paraphs are consistently done in orange-red, inserted at a different sitting, and using a different ink batch from the red annotations themselves. These in turn, though less consistently, appear to have been done at a different time from the red initials which introduce each chapter, many of which are decorated in rough imitation of contemporary "strapwork" rubrication: see for instance the initial "O" on fol. 11v, which should be compared to the (again roughly) historiated "O" in which Kelly Parsons has noted the image of the Five Wounds (see her fig. 3, below) or to the "O" on folios 14 and 19, which contain the sacred monogram, and a face, respectively.

7 See the example of Bodleian Library MS Douce 104, discussed in Kerby-Fulton and Despres.

8 Linda Olson, "Untangling the Thread of Internal Progress in a Benedictine Community: An Abridgement of Augustine's *Confessiones* from Medieval Norwich," in K. Kerby-Fulton and M. Hilmo, eds., *The Medieval Reader: Reception and Cultural History in the Late Medieval English Manuscript*, special issue of *Studies in Medieval and Renaissance History*, Third Series, vol. 1 (2001), forthcoming.

9 Quoted by permission from Watson's reader's report.

10 Comments on Maidie Hilmo's and Carl Grindley's articles are from Derek Pearsall's reader's reports, and quoted by permission.

Framing the Canterbury Pilgrims for the Aristocratic Readers of the Ellesmere Manuscript

Maidie Hilmo

Introduction

That the Middle English word for *border,* "bordure," can also mean sto-ryteller or mocker[1] is uniquely appropriate in its various applications to the design of the Ellesmere Manuscript of Geoffrey Chaucer's *Canterbury Tales.*[2] Framing the beginnings of the relevant tales, each of the illus-trated pilgrim storytellers either enters the enclosure defined by the demivinet border from the left margin on the verso folios or (except for the Miller) approaches the text from the open right side on the recto folios. The borders often serve as flourished serifs or supports for the large decorated initials, forming an organic transition into the field of the text which is to be imagined as being voiced by the respective tellers. While mimicking the pilgrims' spatial and temporal movement towards Canterbury, this progression of open-sided frames not only marks the divisions and transitions within and between tales but also provides authority, coherence, and continuity to the succession of diverse tales arranged by the Ellesmere literary editor to make the frag-ments seem as if Chaucer had finished ordering and compiling them.[3]

The embellished borders, especially where they include the pilgrim portraits, serve at least three functions, which I shall outline briefly before examining them with respect to the intended audience. First they declare that, in this manuscript, the fictional domain of the text is an aristocratic preserve, as indicated particularly by the portrait page of the Knight who enters first and sets the compass for the rest of the illustrations. Although Chaucer's pilgrims ride along the road to Canterbury, the ornamental trellis-work of the Ellesmere borders visu-ally summons forth movement through an aristocratic pleasure garden comparable to those laid out, for instance, by John of Gaunt and Henry V.[4] Emphasizing the "extent of the owner's holdings and his wealth," such large gardens, enclosing up to a dozen or so acres, might include rows of various fruit trees and exotic trees, flowers in rectangular beds and growing up trellises, turf benches, walks, labyrinths, tunnels, fish

14

ponds, and buildings or bowers for "solitary or social pleasures."[5] The available ornamental vocabulary selected for the framework includes stylized motifs suggestive of plants that could be found within such an English *pleasance*: roses, daisy buds, trumpet and thimble flowers, barbed cinquefoils and marigolds, as well as oak leaves, vines and ivy.[6] Traditional Hiberno-Saxon interlace clusters conjure knot gardens and mazes evocative of magical divinition, infinity, and interiority.[7] The kinetic potential of the border emphasizes movement with elements that twist, turn, straighten, push in, enfold, and then reverse direction and alternate the flow of energy in an ongoing fantasy of endless variation. The viewer is required to follow along at different speeds, pausing when the forms group together before being released. Adding interest at the bottom of the horizontal border on the first folio (fig. 1) is the dragon with one wing pointing backwards to the spiky zig-zag serations which seem like a continuation of his tail, and which connote snakiness on other borders even without his presence there, while the other wing points forward to the bottom terminal of the spiraling border as he looks in the direction of the next folio. Just as a tour through a pleasure garden could lead to delightful and surprising discoveries, so a journey through the Ellesmere Manuscript becomes a transformative experience often signaled by the decorative paraphernalia.

Secondly, and related to the first function since the pleasure gardens were often inspired by literary descriptions,[8] they serve metaphorically to define the enclosed text as a garden of verse, a concept popularized since the *Roman de la Rose*[9] and having special application to the works of Chaucer, praised by his contemporary Eustache Deschamps (who called a compilation of his own work a "garden") for having established an English "orchard of poetry."[10] While the designation applies more particularly to Chaucer's early works, especially those actually set in gardens,[11] the visual presentation of the *Canterbury Tales* as a literary garden in the Ellesmere minimizes the originality of much of its content. The richness of the border embellishment itself supports the status quo, affirming that the text is not revisionist.[12] This is important for its acceptance during a period of conservative orthodoxy when the new Lancastrian dynasty itself needed to be viewed within the continuum of traditional English values. Related to this ideological objective is the literary aim of presenting Chaucer as a poet of "rhetorical finesse (aureate)"[13] suitable for the refined tastes presumed in his audience. That the borders serve as a visual analogue of Chaucer's rhetorical dexterity is demonstrated, for example, on the Franklin's portrait page (fig. 2). This pilgrim's punning denial of the knowledge of "colours" (ProFranT

15

724)[14] in the main text is visually played up and contradicted by the embellished border sprays which enclose the Latin source of this rhetorical disclaimer, proving the Franklin's expertise. This sort of virtuosity and responsiveness to the text might have been displayed by a sophisticated and experienced master artist reacting sensitively and working closely with a literary editor in order to "illuminate" the intended English audience,[15] while simultaneously effecting a visual laureation, or political sanction, of its poet.[16]

Thirdly, the aristocratic and poetical gardens are transformed into intimations of a paradisal garden at the *Parson's Tale*, which commands an impressive profusion of 16 out of a total of 71 borders — just under a quarter in the entire manuscript — supporting the likelihood that the program was designed by someone familiar with preparing expensively produced religious manuscripts.[17] A floriated embellishment springing from the border at the top of the last page of the *Parson's Tale* (fig. 3) underlines the annotation "what the fruyt of penance is" beside his conclusion describing the joys of heaven. Like an ongoing series of open-ended square brackets, the demivinet borders that frame this manuscript from the first to the last pages imply that the real pilgrimage is, as the Parson proposes, "Of thilke parfit glorious pilgrymage / That highte Ierusalem celestial" (ProParsT 50-51).[18] In following along the Parson's penitential "wey in this viage" (49), made palatable by those lush borders and culminating in the "confession" which inscribes Chaucer's salvation (in addition to ensuring his reputation for posterity regarding the works mentioned), the aristocratic reader of the Ellesmere Manuscript is led to a privileged sense of sharing in the spiritual fruits.

This essay will concentrate on the first function of the ornamental borders as emphasized by the representations of the Knight and of some of the other pilgrims whose social status has been adjusted. That this manuscript is intended for an aristocratic audience is, of course, immediately seen in its sheer size, which is close to four times that of two relatively contemporary illustrated manuscripts of poetry, the Douce 104 version of *Piers Plowman* and the *Pearl-Gawain* manuscript.[19] The luxury of unfilled space on every page marks one of the prerogatives of wealth. Further, it is too heavy to be held in one's lap for meditative purposes; the size of the open codex resting on some support allows, in addition to its perusal by a solitary reader, for the possibility that a small courtly audience might gather around it. During the delivery process, the principal reader or a member of the audience might point out pertinent visual details that help establish the tone of the narrative. The quality of the vellum, the pigments, the gold leaf and, above all, the organization necessary for carrying the ambitious plan through to completion, testify to the physical and human resources made available for its construction.

Previous studies have already classified and described the Ellesmere pictures in relation to their accuracy as visual translations of the text.[20] However, in applying their own analytical categories these modern studies have largely missed what the illustrative program really contributes to its aristocratic readership's understanding of the *Canterbury Tales.* To be open to the ways the pictorial elements actually function is to study each page with all its interacting components in relation to every other page, and thereby gain a sense of the purpose of the whole endeavor. This study confirms the general observation by Doyle and Parkes that the illustrations "were designed as an adjunct to the apparatus, and not merely as an afterthought of decoration";[21] indeed, they are a principal and active part of the apparatus. The vocabulary of representation includes facial expression, gesture, posture, movement, dress, color, size, and attribute. First the Knight's portrait will be examined, followed by some of the other portraits that are elevated to make them suitable models for an aristocratic family circle; finally, those of inferiors who are mocked will be shown to confirm the social attitudes of this elite audience.

"and at a knyght than wol I first bigynne"

On the framed page beginning the *Knight's Tale* (fig. 4) the text occupies less than half the page. A sense of stability is assured for the audience by the suggested rectangular structure of the demivinet border and by the regular rows of script anchored to it a hair's breadth from its bars, the effect softened by the embellishments and the horizontal curves at the top and bottom. Visually balancing the illustration of the rider opposite, the large initial "W" with its background of scrolling plant motifs extends from the frame into the block of script, as if their planar dimensions were co-extensive. Because it also functions as the first letter of a word, this champ, like the others of various sizes, transfers to the rest of the script something of its decorative character as calligraphy to be enjoyed for its contribution to the pictorial field. As the first letter of "Whilom," it initiates the narrative and transports the audience back to the tale's pagan past.

Recalling the General Prologue, it repeats, in its design and size, the large "W" introducing the *Canterbury Tales* on the first folio (fig. 1). There the border is an exuberant floriated outgrowth of this letter, seemingly propelled by the bursting energy of spring: "Whan that Aprill . . ." The border and the text have become identified as co-extensive, making of

17

this manuscript a literary garden and accentuating the images of flowers, spring breezes, and melodious birds in the first verses of the General Prologue.[22] Indicative of the designer's conception of the structure of the *Canterbury Tales*, these two decorated letters are the two largest in the manuscript, demonstrating that the General Prologue and the body of the tales were considered two separate sections. Along with the smaller champs in this manuscript, they mark divisions in the text, a practice not utilized in the nearly contemporary Hengwrt Manuscript of the *Canterbury Tales* which, although copied by the same scribe,[23] has only parafs, showing that these divisions in Ellesmere were the result of thoughtful editorial planning.[24] Despite the equality in size of the two largest initials, however, the addition of an illustrated figure to the page beginning the tales indicates that the tales themselves were privileged over the General Prologue. Further, as Kathleen Scott observes, the border of this illustrated page "shows a somewhat greater mass of decoration than the rest" of the borders in this manuscript,[25] confirming its preeminence in the total scheme.

In coloring, the interlocking "V" shapes of the "W" at the beginning of the *Knight's Tale* are a mirror image of their antecedent at the beginning of the General Prologue, mnemonically tightening still further the narrative link between both parts. The audience is reminded that the description of the Knight, the highest ranking pilgrim, comes first and that he is to be the first storyteller. Finally, the large decorated "W," like the first one in the Ellesmere Manuscript it echoes, is part of the ornamental architecture of the demivinet border and so not only defines the enclosed "large feeld" of the text (KnT 885) as a cultivated space, but also appropriates it and, in the process, approves this vernacular poetic garden for its privileged audience.[26] Pleasure is intensified by confirming to its readership their social rank. While the non-aristocratic pilgrims might have told their tales for their mutual "myrthe" (GP 766) within Chaucer's narration, in this *manuscript* the text of the tales and the portraits of the tellers are as artfully constructed for the delectation of aristocratic eyes as are the courtly garden and amphitheater described in the *Knight's Tale* itself. What V. A. Kolve calls "garden values"[27] predominate, not only in the *Knight's Tale*, but throughout the manuscript. Just as the chain of love binds all the elements and the successions of species, as Theseus states in his final speech (KnT 2987-3016), so the repetition of borders controls the reception of the narratives in an almost ritualistic manner.

Movement and imaginative scope, on the other hand, are fostered on the right side of the illustrated pages where there is no marginal restraint at the irregular edges of the script. Because of the extent of space, it is an area in the visual field which allows for a transition from the hieratic frontality of the ornamentally framed script on the left to the entry of the unframed illustration of the rider. Charging the blank space with atmosphere and three-dimensionality, the mounted Knight approaches at a slight angle as his horse turns toward the text. As Meyer Schapiro has shown, the three-quarter profile is ideally suited to movement into the narrative mode,[28] as is confirmed at this juncture where the first of the tales begins. With respect to Chaucer's use of convention in affirming *auctoritas*, as Laura Howes observes in connection with the *Book of the Duchess*, the entrance of the narrator to the garden indicates that the beginning of an organized story is about to begin.[29] In the Ellesmere Manuscript, the entrance of the first illustrated narrator to the garden of verse signals the introduction of the first tale. Below the illustration, about four-fifths of the way down the page, the word *narrat(io)* confirms verbally to the audience the place where the immediate story begins. The unframed space on the right half of the recto page further allows the viewer, who is not separated from the narrator by seeing him through a framed aperture, to participate in the dynamic process of the narration. Within this extravagance of space which encourages leisurely viewing, each member of the audience, according to personal capacity, experience, and attentiveness, can fill in such imaginative details as might be prompted by the reading or stimulated by the visual features of the page. That such was actual practice is suggested by the little scene Chaucer added to the story of *Troilus and Criseyde* in which Criseyde and her ladies, read to by a "mayden," stopped reading and listening in order to pause over and repeat aloud rubricated lines from the *Thebaid* describing the fall of a Greek soothsayer to hell: "we stynten at thise lettres rede."[30] It is clear that the Ellesmere, with its further addition of floral frames and figural illustrations, was "meant to be seen when read."[31] If the red letters caused Criseyde and her ladies to linger, how much more would an illustration have piqued their interest!

The decision by the manuscript's creators to leave an amplitude of space on the right side of the recto pages on which tales begin also allows for considerable flexibility and critical discernment in the exact placement of the illustrated figure. In the case of the Knight, there is further room for movement, but the horse has been halted in midstride at the threshold of the ornamental enclosure. This gracious entry allows maximum scope for the gestural vocabulary of the mounted rider. Since this is the first illustrated figure in the manuscript and the first tale, the sweeping open-handed gesture of this "master of cere-monies" serves as a formal greeting to the audience and as a courteous introduction to the text. His raised arm is an authoritative gesture, con-veying good will, indicating wisdom, and demanding silence prepara-tive to speaking, according to the analysis of similar gestures in John Bulwer's mid-seventeenth-century *Chirologia* which relies primarily on classical sources and art works.[32] In Roman art "one of the best-known images," as Moshe Barasch remarks, was the *adlocutio* or emperor's address to his army, portrayed with just this speaking gesture "request-ing quiet and attention."[33] A modern discussion on body language sug-gests that the original purpose of the hailing gesture with the open hand "was to show that individuals were unarmed,"[34] emphasizing trust-worthiness. On this manuscript page, the Knight gesturally calls attention to the narrative just as the marginal annotation below does verbally. Further, as if the visualized authoritative and authorizing figure does indeed generate the story, his eyes also direct the gaze back to the script which is to be imagined as being voiced by him, inviting the reader to emulate the process. The title confirms the text as the "knyghtes tale" and, by proximity, identifies him.

Since there is no author portrait of Chaucer at the beginning of the Prologue to the *Canterbury Tales* in the Ellesmere,[35] this deferment and displacement of authorial responsibility represents a different strategy on the part of the designer. The playful yet defensive apology of the pil-grim Chaucer in the Prologue to the *Canterbury Tales* that "I speke hir wordes" (729), meaning that he is only repeating the stories of the pil-grims in their own words, is confirmed by the successive illustrated por-traits of the pilgrim authors and by the editorial colophon of the Ellesmere Manuscript that indicates the compilation of the stories is at an end. By spreading the attribution among the several pilgrims, both Chaucer and this manuscript's designer attempt to emphasize the unity of the tales while at the same time deflecting any criticism these diverse tales in the vernacular might attract. Both also offer a double-take on the presumed orality of the tales. The absence of an authorial portrait of Chaucer at the beginning of the General Prologue in the Ellesmere Manuscript, like the pictorial absence of Chrétien from the corpus of his works, "harks back to oral culture."[36] The presence of a knight on horseback, on the other hand, as in many of the manuscript openings of Chrétien's Arthurian romances, serves as an author portrait, signals the genre of chivalric romance, and evokes its performative function of oral delivery.[37] Chaucer's authorship has, in a sense, been temporarily subsumed into that of the Knight.

20

The blank space around the rider allows not only the strategic placement of the portrait but also permits overlapping interpretations of his identity. Most obviously, he is the Knight of the Prologue who, as one of a group of pilgrims on the way to the shrine of Thomas Becket, has agreed to tell a tale. As that Knight, he is mature in years and campaigns, as shown by his grey hair and beard, "worthy" as indicated by his serious expression, and "meeke" (GP 68-69), as projected, in part, by the seemly and non-aggressive stance of his horse. When the details of the pictured horse and rider are examined, it becomes apparent that the illustration is no mere translation into visual form of the General Prologue's description. In his recent study, Richard Emmerson has laid to rest the assumption the portraits are primarily intended to illustrate the General Prologue.[38] The Prologue is recalled, certainly, but important modifications and transformations have taken place.

Since the horses are also part of the visual reinterpretations in the Ellesmere, a close look at the Knight's horse yields some significant clues as to what the designer strove to present. In the General Prologue, Chaucer the pilgrim says the Knight's "hors weren goode but he was nat gay" (74). The illustration shows a horse that is by far the best specimen of any in the Ellesmere, its well-muscled body exuding power and the pride of breeding. Care seems to have been taken even in the rendering of his noble mane, the curls being underlined in black and highlighted with white. Not only is the horse better than "goode," but the trappings of his harness are rather splendid, adorned at every interval with an abundance of gold bosses, hinges, and tips. Only five other horses in the manuscript are painted with decorative straps over the haunches, evidently an indication of the wealth or status of the rider, or an aspiration to them.[39]

The horse's haunch is inscribed with an "M" which Terry Jones guesses is intended as a brand to stand for "Milano," the city-state which employed English mercenaries such as the famous John Hawkwood.[40] It is true that Ucello's 1436 portrait of the mounted John Hawkwood, which Jones analyzes, depicts a similar horse, but it shows no evidence of a brand. Further, Hawkwood is clearly shown in armor beneath his surcoat in this fresco, unlike the Ellesmere Knight.[41] The squiggle on the Ellesmere horse's neck, which Jones (p. 29) postulates is a "y" (although it is horizontally rather than vertically displayed and is more rounded than the angular "y" of "ffemenye," the last word in line with the illustrated horse's left leg, 866), is more competently rendered than the "M" and might be an abbreviation, showing through the brown paint, indicating an instruction to the illustrator. The "M" could, however, stand

21

for "miles" with respect to the knights in the Drury family mentioned in the first flyleaf addition to the Ellesmere Manuscript — "Robertus Drury miles. William Drury miles. Robertus Drury miles" — who may have been its early sixteenth-century owners, but it is unlikely to have been a mark made by the professional book artisans of this production since they left no other signs of such amateurish, shaky lettering.[42]

Just as the mount is richly appointed and more than "goode," so the rider is considerably more than an ordinary knight. He is pictured with understated elegance. Particularly striking is his proud bearing. He sits straight and tall in his saddle, yet it seems to cause him no strain, as if it were a posture to which he had become long accustomed. The General Prologue describes the Knight's array: "Of ffustian he wered a gypon / al bismotered with his habergeon" (75-76). This portrait of a knight unostentatiously dressed in a "gypon," a tight-fitting, padded garment of coarse fustian worn over his "habergeon" or short type of mail shirt,[43] has been discarded. Instead, with only echoes of the text, the Ellesmere Knight displays a color-coordinated ensemble. He wears a knee-length, high-necked, and wide-sleeved houpelande which, because of the extreme slenderness of his illustrated body profile, is unlikely to cover a gypon over a habergeon. It is made of long panels carefully stitched together, producing scalloped edging. Restrained in color and thereby deflecting the criticism of estates satire against ostentation,[44] it appears to be sober grey, although it seems to have a violet shimmer or iridescence characteristic of some silks, a fabric worn by the richest knights.[45] A detail not previously noticed is that he wears not full rust-brown gloves, but fingerless mittens. They are like those worn by the dreamer, the Pearl Maiden, knights and royalty, as well as by the hand of God in the miniatures of the *Pearl-Gawain* manuscript.[46] His other accessories, also in rust-brown, include a chaperon, a gold-tipped scabbard, and what may be the remains of fashionable gold-tipped arming points on his chest."[47] As Martin Stevens comments, the "long points" of his shoes indicate his rank more significantly than any other part of his attire.[48] He is also the only pilgrim illustrated with a gold rowel spur, a spiked wheel introduced at the end of the thirteenth century.[49] All the gold decoration of this portrait is painted on by hand, the first use of this method in the manuscript, unlike the gold-leaf applied to the border bar with its ornamentation and the decorated initials.[50] His outfit reflects the mode of the early fifteenth century as pictured, for example, on the riders in the first of May festivities in the *Très Riches Heures* of Jean, Duke of Berry[51] and in the headgear, houpelande, and gold rowel spurs of the first rider in the "Riding Party," one of the illustrations in the *Collected Works of Christine de Pizan* (fig. 5),[52] both contemporary manuscripts. The Ellesmere Knight could easily be assimilated into one of these royal riding parties.

Were the Knight not placed at the beginning of his tale, the viewing audience might well identify him as a great lord rather than simply as a knight. As it is, like the other mounted pilgrims, he has the potential for affecting the reading of the tale and for being affected (i.e. being reinterpreted) by the tale itself. That this kind of enriching cross-reference was encouraged is indicated by the dynamics of the layout. First of all, the horse's respectful gaze is directed at the first sentence, especially at the identification of Theseus:

> Whilom as olde stories tellen us
> There was a duc þat highte Theseus
> Of Atthenes he was lord and gou*er*nour
> And in his tyme swich a Conquerour
> That gretter was ther noon under the sonne.
>
> (859-63)

The emphasis of the text is clearly on power, and the words nearest the horse — "gou*er*nour," "conquerour," and "sonne" — heighten this effect.

As if that alone were not enough, the two decorated gold-leaf initials, secondary in size to the "W" of the opening, both point to Theseus. The first is the "I" at the top of the page beginning the Latin quotation from the *Thebaid* of Statius referring to the approach of Theseus to his native land after fighting with the Scythians (xii, 519-20): *Iamq(ue) domos patrias Scithice post aspera gentis prelia laurigero.*[53] Placed strategically under the vegetal decoration of the border instead of in the margin, this quotation permits the symbolism of the laurel, which as a garland crowns the mounted Theseus of Chaucer's *Knight's Tale* (1026-27), to be transferred instead to the border of the garden of verse.[54] The reference to *patrias* in the inscription at the top of the Knight's page also connects the idea of the laureation of conquerors (and their recording poets) with an emerging nationalism.[55] The Latin itself lends authority to the tale and teller, and flatters the learned reader who must supply the name Theseus from memory, adding a further *cachet* to the principal reader if a translation into the vernacular is to be part of the performance. Upon first glance, it leads to the assumption that it is the inscription for the illustrated figure whose open-handed gesture points up towards it. It also provides a cultural, if not actual, genealogy for the Knight who is then identified by the title below which, in effect, supercedes it as an inscription for the mounted figure. The second gold initial, a "I," occurs near the bottom of the page, beside the *narrat(io)* already mentioned, calling attention back to:

> This duc of whom I make mencioun
> Whan he was come almoost unto the toun
> In al his wele and in his mooste pride . . .
>
> (893-95)

Both decorated gold-leaf initials, then, call attention to the approach of the proud conqueror, Theseus.

In these ways, the dynamics of the page allow for a multilevel interpretation of the approaching mounted rider. As storyteller, he is the Knight of the Prologue; as subject of the story, he is Theseus. As the latter, he lends additional status to the Knight, with the result that the audience sees the Knight as a powerful, worldly lord and so is prepared to respond to him and to his tale accordingly. Those features held in common reflect both ways, ferrying additional details from one portrayal to the other. For example, preceding his Boethian speech near the end of the tale, Theseus exhibits a "sad visage" before "any word cam fram his wise brest" (2985 and 2983). This description could apply equally to the countenance and attitude of the illustrated figure, an elaboration of the wisdom attributed to the Knight in the General Prologue. Subsequent viewings of the mounted rider would be enriched with such details accrued consciously or unconsciously from previous reading.[56] The visual portrait shows evidence of the selection of those features which are consistent with the presentation of the Knight as a lord whose pronouncements have authoritative weight. This sort of conflation functions as yet another unifying device which, like the decorated "W," pulls together more tightly the threads from the General Prologue and the *Knight's Tale.*

What the portrait of the mounted rider does not feature is quite striking with respect both to the Knight of the General Prologue and to Theseus — any evidence of a martial life! The first two-thirds of the General Prologue describes more than two decades of military feats. The Knight served worthily in "his lordes werre" both in "cristendom" and in "Hethenesse" (47, 49). The General Prologue stresses the Knight as a crusader, which Jill Mann says is a role the Church envisaged for chivalry, mentioned as a duty in the dubbing ceremony.[57] It is interesting that the illustrated Knight in the Douce 104 Manuscript of *Piers Plowman* also lacks any evidence of armor. There this omission — along with the portrayal of his rueful expression, the gesture of immobility indicated by his crossed arms, and his stance in which his feet point ambivalently in opposite directions — manifests his failure as a secular authority whose role is to guard the Church against wastrels and evil men.[58] The *Pearl-Gawain* manuscript does show Gawain and the Green Knight in armor and with a full complement of sharp weapons in two of the scenes, but there are spiritual overtones in the illustrative program of that manuscript.[59]

In the General Prologue, Chaucer verbally frames the list of the Knight's previous military expeditions with a description of his noble qualities. His love of the chivalric virtues precedes this sanitized list, while mention of his wisdom and gentility follow it, casting a moral tone over this Knight's military career. The violence inherent in such a life is suppressed by the omission of grisly details. The only reminder of the Knight's military role is that his "gypon" is "al bismotered" (GP 75-76). This is usually taken as indicating that it is soiled or stained by rust[60] from his iron mail shirt dampened by perspiration. But another meaning of "bismotered" is bespattered,[61] suggesting that bloodstains, whether his own or heathens', might have mingled with the sweat of his own martial exertions, bespattering his mail shirt. Chaucer turns even this small detail in favor of the Knight's religious piety, implying that he is anxious to do the right thing spiritually by going on pilgrimage right after coming from his last "viage" (77), thereby overriding any desire for worldly approval when he does not change out of his "bismotered" habergeoun first.

On another level, Theseus too has just come from his latest conquest, that of the Amazons. The predominant image the audience has of Theseus at the beginning of the tale is his approach to Athens, which the narrator mentions three times (873, 894, and 1026-27) as a means of advancing the narrative while sketching in background information. The return procession follows the defeat of the "regne of ffemenye" (866). This victory prefaces the story of Palamon and Arcite, the young knights whose object of desire is the sister of the conquered queen. Voice is not given to the defeated warrior women; instead, sympathy is accorded to the weeping women Theseus meets on the way home. The Amazons' suffering is, as it were, transferred to the latter, finding emotional release and moral approval in this recasting of acceptable gender roles. At the same time, "this worthy duc, this Theseus" (1001) who "up hente" (957) the lamenting women is allowed to appear in a favorable light vis-à-vis women, rushing off as he does to defeat the tyrant who would not allow them to bury their slain husbands. The actual violence of both battle accounts occurs offstage.

25

While in the *Knight's Tale* violence, the expected means by which victory in warfare is effected, occurs only at the periphery of the events just referred to, in the Ellesmere portrait of the mounted rider there is no evidence of it at all. In contrast, for example, to the "extraordinary mixture of bloodthirstiness and piety" that is found in MS Advocates 19.3.1, a fifteenth-century North Midland manuscript,[62] violence in the Ellesmere has been visually concealed, canceled even, certainly denied entry to the safe and beautiful surface space enclosed by the decorated border. There are no rust or blood stains anywhere on the Knight's person. Nor has he weapons. Hindman observes that "the granting of arms, with the sword the principal emblem of power, had long been associated with the knightly function."[63] This Knight has not even a serviceable sword such as is worn for self-protection by the illustrated figures of the Miller, the Reeve, and the Summoner in the same manuscript. Even his tiny dagger, with its gold pommel, guard, and scabbard chape, is more an accessorizing ornament than weapon, unlike the more lethal dagger by which the illustrated Shipman (fol. 143v) presumably dispatched "hem hoom to euery lond" (GP 400). The illustrated Knight does not wear any armor that is visible and he carries no shield; nor is his horse protected by any covering.[64]

The reason the Knight was portrayed not as a warrior, as the General Prologue would have it, but as a lord or *seignor*,[65] likely relates directly to the person commissioning this manuscript or its intended recipient. It may well be that the first portrait in the Ellesmere, having accrued the noble aura of Theseus, provided a flattering mirror in which a noble patron might have cared to see himself.[66] Further, by identification with the Gothic milieu of the lordly Knight, the pagan matter of the Theseus story is made familiar and acceptable to the patron and his family.[67] Charges of idolatry are deflected in the scenes in which the pagan deities of Venus, Diana, and Mars are prayed to by Palamon, Emily, and Arcite respectively not only by Chaucer, who introduces oratories for each of them,[68] but by the Ellesmere scribe, who adds annotations which place them in a courtly love context as the embodiments of love, chastity, and chivalry.[69] The Ellesmere portrait of the Knight as lord rather than as warrior excludes open signs of violence as inappropriate, not only in the cultivated garden of verse so carefully set up by the frame, but also within the pleasure gardens at the reader's home, the latter projected as a calm place indicative of order and stability, prosperity, and good government. Violence has been effectively aestheticized.

Finally, the mounted Knight becomes the guide who initiates the literary pilgrimage for privileged readers.[70] He invites them to see from his perspective, temporarily merging their identity with his. The rest of the page itself reinforces this perspective in the orderliness of its coordinated ornamentation which colors and guides the reading process. Further, it is an active zone across which the illustrated figure relates to the text and within which the audience has imaginative room to recreate the scenes under the subtle guidance of decoration and illustration. In the case of the illustrated portraits, the absence of a specific setting permits multiple and conflated interpretations. In this instance, the mounted rider functions alternately or simultaneously as the storytelling Knight from the General Prologue, as Theseus, as patron of the manuscript and, being the first portrait illustrated, as surrogate authorial guide to the *Canterbury Tales* generally as well as to the *Knight's Tale* specifically.

The imagined setting could be the road to Canterbury, the road to Athens, the grounds of the patron's estates, or an extension of any future viewer's own richly appointed space. Perhaps most interesting in the absence of a pictured setting, for which there was certainly room, is the preservation of an element of mystery concerning the identity of the illustrated figure. The placement of these figures means that the storytellers, with the exception of the Miller, approach the text from the unknown space beyond the lateral sides of the open manuscript book. This design feature, where the illustrated figures ride toward the text from the outer margins, stresses the enigmatic nature of the pilgrims' origins and identity. Not only is the "present" setting undefined, but the past venue exists only in the uncontrolled space beyond the page. There, for instance, the blood of heathens or Amazons may stain the earth, but it does not mark the ordered surface of the manuscript.[71]

While the pilgrim portraits visually guide the reading process, they themselves resist a single interpretation and are thus as elusive as Chaucer, whose own style is often intriguingly ambiguous. The mounted Knight as lord introduces this visually embellished romance, the first of the ongoing and open-ended sequence of tales. All that is congruent with his perspective regulates the experience of his audience for this tale and defines the attitude to be assumed toward pilgrims of lesser rank. His portrayal frames and overarches the reading of subsequent tales, as do the other elements of the ordinatio. At the same time, the viewing audience is encouraged to become actively and creatively engaged in filling in the "blank" spaces and in re-visioning both the tellers and the tales from an aristocratic viewpoint.

Recasting Selected Pilgrims for Aristocratic Family Viewing

If the Knight were the only illustrated figure to be raised in status, he would be out of place since noble lords are seldom found alone, especially within such an aristocratic space as that defined by the decorated border. This means that some of the other pilgrims needed to be elevated to present a suitable inner circle for this Knight in the Ellesmere Manuscript, thereby also providing entry into the exclusive society of the viewing audience.

After describing the small retinue of the Knight, the General Prologue turns to the person next in status, who happens to be the Prioress (fig. 6). Rather than depicting her as a woman with only pretensions to the speech and manner of her social superiors, as Chaucer does, Ellesmere's designer has raised her to the level of her aspirations. Nevertheless, the essence of the presentation on the page beginning the *Prioress's Tale* is religious. In the border above the illustration, visual weight is given to the floral bouquet appended to the bars beside one of the stanzas in her Prologue concerning the Virgin's bounty and her anticipation of people's needs. While this sort of bouquet with two flowers extending from the main mass might seem coincidental at this point, its recurrence in other passages dealing with women makes it less so.[72] This shows the designing artist's flexibility in using the available ornamental vocabulary, often just that, but on occasion achieving specific effects which support the overall presentation, in this case one possibly derived from previous work on religious manuscripts, especially Marian devotions. While the Prioress as illustrated adds a sober religious tone, she does not, however maternal she may be as indicated by her tale about the child, complete a possible family circle with the Knight and his son or visually present a model for a chatelaine in the audience.[73] Since, for similar reasons, the Second Nun also presents an unlikely candidate for these purposes, the choice had to fall on the Wife of Bath. By happy coincidence, it proved possible to assimilate details from her narrative in order to adjust her social rank by the placement of her portrait near the tale her illustration frames.

The Wife of Bath's gaze (fig. 7) is directed to the line: "The Elf queene with her ioly compaignye" (WBT 860). The extremes of the General Prologue's description are modified in this rendering or are suppressed entirely. There Chaucer describes her face as "Boold . . . and fair and reed of hewe" (GP 458). Instead of displaying outright boldness, her expression appears goal-directed and purposeful. Her fairness is played up, but her redness of hue is modified to a blush on her modeled cheeks, making her portrayal seem consonant with that of the "Elf queene" of her story. Her horse looks intently at the line referring to the time of the Elf queen's reign — "manye hundred yeres ago" (863) — as if to emphasize the time factor which is so critical to her and to her tale of a magical transformation from age to youth. The illustration portrays the Wife as a young woman, and she is gratuitously given a high forehead. She is "ywympled wel" but her "couerchiefs," while elaborate, do not seem to weigh quite "ten pound" (GP 453-54). Her hat, while broad, is yet not quite as large as a "bokeler" (GP 471); rather, it is the size of a suitable traveling hat such as that worn, for example, by Mary in the "Flight to Egypt" in a somewhat later miniature now in Vienna.[74]

Most notably, her *overt* sexuality is played down: if she is "Gat tothed" (GP 468), this is concealed by her closed mouth; likewise, if she is wearing "scarlet reed" hose (GP 456), this is concealed by her *foot mantel* (GP 472), as are her new shoes. Her "hipes large" (GP 472) accentuate her fashionably small high waist.[75] The use of gold for her belt is a striking addition to the portrait placing her, like the Knight, in the same milieu of early fifteenth-century aristocratic fashion as that shown by the highborn lady with the high gold belt in "The Riding Party" (fig. 5) and also by the one who picks flowers in the April scene of the *Très Riches Heures* of Jean, Duke of Berry.[76] The trappings of her horse are also gold, and hers is the only horse except the Knight's which is fitted with gold stirrups. Her horse and its trappings seem to be a more modest, feminine version of the Knight's in its style of gear and in the position of its legs and body. Unlike the two nuns in this manuscript who ride side-saddle, but like the illustrated Penthesilea in *Des Cleres femmes*,[77] she sits "esily" (GP 469) astride her horse, suggesting an experienced traveler.[78] The Wife of Bath's small riding whip, not mentioned in the text, adds complexity and ambiguity to her illustrated portrait, emphasizing her attempt to control her destiny while injecting, perhaps, a touch of humor for the reader who remembers her Prologue.[79] This illustration, unaccompanied by marginal glosses, dominates the page by its medial position. As Susan Schibanoff has shown, where there are any glosses, whether for her Prologue or Tale, the Ellesmere supports or augments the Wife of Bath's text, unlike the glosses of MS Egerton 2864 later in the century, which challenge it and denounce her immorality.[80] With the intended audience obviously in mind, the scribe changed the more conventional *no(ta) bene* in the margin of the Hengwrt manuscript beside the Wife's discussion about gentility to *De gen(er)ositate*[81] (WBT 1109), as if emphasizing the desired behavior for people of noble rank, and added *exemplum* (WBT 1146) beside her discussion showing that a lord's son is not naturally free of villainy, emphasizing to the highborn young reader the behavior to be avoided. The Wife is allowed to present herself as she would recreate herself if she could. By conflation with the Fairy Queen of her tale and without the sexual innuendo accorded her in the text, downplayed also by the glosses, the Wife has been sufficiently elevated in status to provide a female counterpart to the portrait of the Knight in the Ellesmere Manuscript, making her suitable as his partner and a model for an aristocratic female reader.

The General Prologue furnishes one pilgrim by way of a direct familial relationship to the Knight in the person of his "sone a yong squier" (79). The placement of his tale within the manuscript may have had repercussions on an audience attuned to subtle signs of differences in social importance. Just as the Knight is given authoritative status not only by coming first in the General Prologue and in the order in which his tale is related, but also by being illustrated first and accorded an enhanced status, so the *Squire's Tale* itself is given a special distinction in the Ellesmere order. Unlike the jumbled arrangement of the earlier Hengwrt manuscript, probably the result of the copyist "working with exemplars that were arriving on his desk in fragmentary form and unpredictable sequence," as Pearsall speculates, the Ellesmere arrangement was "the best that could be arrived at" because the same scribe, or his editors, now had time "for a more leisured scrutiny of the papers, and a more reasoned ordering of them."[82] In this reorganization, Fragment V (Group F), containing the *Squire's Tale* and the *Franklin's Tale*, was placed in the center of the Ellesmere Manuscript, following the *Merchant's Tale* (whose illustration, as I will show, plays off the Squire's portrait) in Fragment IV (Group E). That there might have been a special distinction in the *Squire's Tale* being placed in the exact center of the Ellesmere is indicated by analogy with the organization of some other fifteenth-century manuscript compilations, as mentioned by Seth Lerer (following the lead of Sylvia Huot), who notes that a work placed in the centre of a manuscript can refract meaning backwards and forwards. He refers specifically to Oxford, Bodleian Library, MS Tanner 346 in which the attempt to frame the compilation as Chaucerian is strengthened by mention of Chaucer's name right at the middle, serving as "a central authorizing figure."[83]

If, indeed, intelligent compilers at the time favored such a location as a way of showcasing a subject, then increased attention might be accorded to a medial illustration if the details warrant it. The placement of the fragment containing, in this case, the *Squire's Tale* and the *Franklin's Tale* — both self-consciously demonstrating rhetorical finesse, a skill for which Chaucer himself was most admired in the fifteenth century[84] — supports those other features of the Ellesmere's presentation

30

which combine to celebrate Chaucer's art. In the *Squire's Tale*, Chaucer seems to parody self-conscious rhetorical delivery when he shows the Squire more concerned with style than with the story itself, which he never gets to finish. This rhetorical focus is enhanced by the design of the page (fig. 8), whereby the last two lines of the Squire's Prologue serve as an inscription, reminiscent of the Latin preceding the *Knight's Tale*:

> Haue me excused if I speke amys
> my wyl is good and lo my tale is this.[85]

It is the same rhetorical trick of denying rhetorical accomplishment that is given visual prominence on the Franklin's page. The effect of these lines at the top of the page, which the illustrated Squire's self-referential gesture seems to express, was not possible in the earlier Hengwrt version because there, completely out of place, the Squire's Prologue or Head-link comes after the *Merchant's Tale* but before the *Franklin's Tale*. As with the Franklin's page in Ellesmere, the ornament enhances the effect; in this case the entire upper border serves as a wavy, flourished serif for the top bar of the squared decorated "A" beginning the tale, while the left oblique stroke of the "A" descends into a flourished vegetal scroll below the portrait of the Squire, causing his horse to jump.

The likelihood that the placement of the Squire might have had contemporary political relevance is reinforced by the details advancing the status of the illustrated Squire. Confirming an awareness of the notion of centrality is the annotation set off, in this manuscript, by scrolls in the border just below the illustration: *centru(m) circuli*. This Boethian idea of a stable center within a circle draws attention to one of the qualities of the ideal ruler mentioned in Chaucer's text: "Of his corage as any centre stable" (SqT 22).[86] Given the addition of the illustration, a young aristocratic reader of this manuscript, likewise "yong fressh strong" (23), might find this exemplary. With its philosophical underpinnings recalling the Knight's speech concerning the First Mover who "stable is and eterne" (KnT 3004), and within the larger context of this manuscript's successive open-ended borders suggesting the progression of the religious pilgrimage, this integrated design helps confer a Boethian and divine sanction to the ruling faction, which the elevated status of the Squire represents. The interest in the qualities of a good ruler which this manuscript displays is supported, for example, by the expansion of Hengwrt's annotation *No(ta)* to *No(ta)te do(mi)ni* (KnT 1774) beside Theseus's reminder to himself not to be like a merciless

31

lion when he decides to reduce to imprisonment the death sentence he formerly gave to Palamon and Arcite.[87] Further, in the change from the singular to the plural form of the imperative, the intended readership of the Ellesmere is also defined.

The Squire (fig. 8) is attired in a manner which might well suit the "roial estat" (SqT 26) of the young Cambyuskan of his tale: he has ermine leggings, certainly not mentioned in the General Prologue description. With the exception of the illustration of the ambitious Merchant, the pictured Squire has the longest points on his shoes next to the Knight in this manuscript. Much of the white paint has flaked off the point, making this less obvious to a modern viewer.[88] He wears white gloves, like the victorious Arcite in the *Knight's Tale* who is clothed in them on his funeral bier (KnT 2874). Not previously noticed, but clear from an enlargement (fig. 9), is that the self-referential position of his hand displays a ring under his glove, carefully outlined and so distinguishing it from the flowers on his garment, near the top of his ring finger. It mirrors the fashion of Henry V (fig. 10) who is portrayed "in a black capp"[89] and wears one of his rings near the top of his ring finger.[90] The position of the ring near the top of the Squire's finger calls attention to it, stressing its relevance with respect to the tale which mentions a magic ring given by the strange knight to Canace, the king's young daughter, enabling her to understand the language of birds (SqT 146-55). Particular attention is called to the properties of the ring in the marginal annotation adjacent to this description: "of the vertu of the ryng" (fol. 116v). The ring's narrative importance is featured later when the peregrine falcon tells the princess the heart-rending story of being jilted in love by her false mate given to "peynted" words (SqT 560).

While the Squire's ring has ample relevance to the story alone, other features of the illustrated Squire allude to fashions in excess of the description in the General Prologue. One such is the belt with clapper bells hanging by chains or cords from it, all in accessorizing white (which may be of silver, like the rowel spurs he wears). Such bells became fashionable in England after 1393-94 when Richard II, borrowing from a German vogue, had two gold bells fitted to his belt.[91] They reached the height of fashion in the first third of the fifteenth century as shown, for example, in the slightly later *Troilus* and *Criseyde* frontispiece, where a man in a blue garment has a profusion of them dangling from an elaborate collar and from a belt.[92] Dangling from longer cords or chains, the illustrated Squire's are very like the rumbler bells worn by Henry V in another early fifteenth-century miniature.[93] A different view by way of social commentary on the fashion of suspended bells is that offered in the Douce 104 manuscript of *Piers Plowman* in the illustration of Pride (fol. 24r), who is shown with gold rumbler bells. The Ellesmere portrayal, however, has no satiric edge.

The Squire's high hat, which is broad at the top and in a slightly different blue from the border leaf nearest it, is in the same style as that of the black hat worn by Henry Bolingbroke (shortly to be Henry IV) in the *Histoire du Richard* by Jean Creton.[94] The "white embroidered insignia"[95] on the Squire's hat may be suggestive of the white swan, the device of the wealthy family of Henry V's mother, Mary de Bohun, which Henry IV customarily wore in the form of a pendant.[96] The hat itself is also comparable to that with a gold medallion worn by the second noble rider in the contemporary French manuscript, "The Riding Party" (fig. 5), and the gold medallion on the dark green (?) hat worn by one of the parents in the betrothal scene in the April picture of *Très Riches Heures* of Jean, Duke of Berry.[97] In the latter the adjacent figure of the prospective groom wears a red chaperon similar to the one with the dagged gorgets of the other rider in the "Riding Party," confirming that both the tall hat of the Squire and the headgear of the Knight belong to the same early fifteenth-century aristocratic fashion. This suggests that the illustrator, if not actually influenced by the fashions favored by the royal court, may have been aware of a manuscript illustration in which these two forms of hats were likewise paired,[98] perhaps a calendar picture of April or May showing aristocratic outdoor pleasures with which the Squire, "as fressh as is the monthe of may" (GP 92), is associated.[99]

The spirit of spring informs the illustration of the Squire. In the General Prologue, his short gown is embroidered like a meadow with "fresshe floures whyte and reede" (89-90); in the illustration, his short dark green houpelande is decorated with some small white four-petalled florets and with red-petalled flowers with white centers. It is lined with a red-brown (probably silk) lining, the same color as the reins, and is edged with ermine. Everything seems caught at the moment of take-off. The flowing sleeves of the rider (GP 93), the horse's swinging tail and saddle straps accentuate the upward thrusting arc of the powerful horse.[100] For the reader who approaches this tale more than once, this illustrated horse recalls and so anticipates the magical flying horse in the narrative which the Squire compares to the best Lombardian and Apulian horses and associates with the mythical winged horse Pegasus (SqT 193, 207). Given the extended ekphrasis or rhetorical description in the narrative, and the two marginal annotations — "of the vertu of the steede of / bras" and *.i. equs pegaseus*

(SqT 115, 207) — it would be difficult for the reader, especially one as knowledgeable about horses as many aristocrats would be, not to linger over this illustration and even come back to it during the reading process. This magnificent horse's eyes and ears seem intently focused on the title "Heere bigynneth the Squieres tale," as if prompting the narrative to begin forthwith. In relation to the rider, the proportions of this horse are quite large by Ellesmere standards (and more realistic to the modern eye), engaging the viewer's particular attention. The portrait of the Squire on his horse is granted ample personal space for a verso illustration, emphasizing the rider's status. Like his father, the Squire sits high in the saddle, in this case displaying his straight shapely leg of "euene lengthe" (GP 83).[101]

While the General Prologue describes him as being "of greet strengthe" and having been "somtyme in chyuachie" (84-85), this illustrated Squire scarcely looks "twenty yeer of age" (82). Certainly this weaponless youth does not call up violent battle scenes any more than did the Knight, although he does sit on his horse most elegantly (94). His serious facial expression is, rather deliberately, one of innocence. Like the quintessential squire and the picture of the youth in the Ages of Man iconography,[102] he does have hair with "lokkes crulle" (81), recalling the miniature of Henry IV's coronation in which his adolescent son holding the sword of justice has crimped-looking light brown hair (before he had his hair cut short as in his later portraits) and wears wide, slashed sleeves.[103] Unlike the portrait of the young Prince Henry, the Ellesmere Squire has no weapons, nor are there symbolic floral shapes in the decorated initial or demivinet border as there are on folio 57v concerning the god of love in the only surviving copy of Chaucer's translation of the *Romance of the Rose*.[104] Rather, his serious expression resembles that of the illustration of Langland's *liberum arbitrium* in the Douce 104 manuscript who, as Kathryn Kerby-Fulton and Steven Justice have demonstrated, is depicted as a combination of spiritual and courtly lover, dressed as he is in "tight hose and a red floral jacket, holding . . . a mirror (emblematic of self-reflectiveness)."[105] If the Ellesmere Squire seems too modest to love so "hoote" all night that he scarcely sleeps (GP 97-98), his delicate features and deferential gaze do confirm his courtesy as demonstrated in his attendance upon his father's table (99-100). In the text of his tale what the Squire admires about the mounted knight who enters the court is his courtesy which could not be faulted even by Gawain if "he were comen ayeyn out of ffairye" (96). What is perhaps most extraordinary about the illustration of the Ellesmere Squire is that he is portrayed neither as a squire attendant upon a warrior nor as a lover, according to conventional iconography, but as the epitome of an innocent and courteous young noble. As Greg Walker has pointed out with respect to Gawain's response to the Green Knight in the *Pearl-Gawain* manuscript, "courtesy does not simply demarcate the battlefield, it explicitly offers an alternative to it — a means . . . of re-negotiating honor and courtliness in terms of his own choosing, in order that the direct, warrior-code challenge of the Knight might be deflected and neutralized."[106] This same observation is appropriate to the illustrated Ellesmere Squire whose portrait models, as it were, an alternative to violence and licentious sexuality. The General Prologue does present him as an educated son who could both "purtr-eye" and write (96), accomplishments not accorded his father. Courteous and literate, he is visually presented on the Ellesmere page as representing the ideal young nobleman. Like the Gawain to whom he refers in his tale, "accordant to hise wordes was his cheere" (103). He is "stylish and polite" with a "taste for fancy," as Seth Lerer argues in regard to "the ways in which the Squire's persona and performance shaped the literary values of the fifteenth century."[107]

Mocking Social Inferiors

While some of the pilgrims are pictorially elevated in status to suit the aristocratic space defined by the floriated borders, others are permitted entry by neutralizing through satiric representation — sometimes mild but occasionally to the point of demonization — any threat they might pose to social power. The superiority of the knightly class and their right to the privileged life are reaffirmed, while the aspirations of other classes to wealth, as well as their claims to culturally exclusive romantic, rhetorical, and chivalric attainments, are frequently mocked.

Of this there is no better demonstration than the Merchant's portrait (fig. 11). The artist has exploited the potential of its placement on the page and in relation to that of the Squire which follows it in the Ellesmere order. If everything about the illustration of the Squire, placed at the top of the page, implies ascent, everything about the Merchant, placed at the bottom of the page, implies an unseemly upward mobility. Nothing could inscribe his ambitions more explicitly than his attempt to ape the Squire. Every lineament of man and horse can be viewed as a reflection of his social superior—from his own posture to that of his leaping horse. That the imitation is excessive, and therefore deserving of mockery, is apparent not only from his forked beard (GP 270) and his expensive Flemish beaver hat (GP 272), but also from his expression which is like that of the illustration of Covetousness

35

in the Douce version of *Piers Plowman* who looks "so hungrily and holow" (VI:197, fol. 27r). Whereas the elegant Squire's ensemble is restrained in color, the Merchant's red coat, slashed at the sides and embroidered with flowers like that of the God of Love in the *Roman de la Rose*,[108] is entirely inappropriate to his position. His clothes reveal that he would like to become culturally assimilated with the class described in contemporary chivalric romances, but he is not in any position to play such a lover since he is in debt (GP 280), reassuring the aristocratic reader that all this show is without substance. The extremely long, thin points on his feet, perhaps even longer than those of the Knight, not only violate all sumptuary laws but demonstrate how he overreaches himself. Even his horse strains to reach one of the leaves he sees in the border ornament above him.

As the coming man in the socio-political scene in the late medieval world, the Merchant is portrayed as young, there being nothing in the text to suggest his age even though his story is about a January-May marriage.[109] The nature of the illustration recognizes this new force in society without approving or allowing its unchallenged entry and acceptance into the space occupied by the feudal aristocracy. As Sylvia Thrupp has shown, the boundaries between merchants and gentlemen at this time was permeable but fraught and complex.[110] Merchants and their children could climb the social ladder by such means as their wealth allowed, not restricted from rising by service to the powerful, especially the royal household as in the case of Chaucer himself, by education and the professions, by blood relationship to those advanced in ecclesiastical office, by military service, by taking up knighthood with all its burdens, by acquiring high positions such as that of mayor in urban administration, by purchasing a country house and living the life of a gentleman and, as in the case of the Wife of Bath who at least advanced her financial situation (leaving further ascent to the fantasy of her fiction), by marriage. Nor, at the other end, were those of gentle rank entirely aloof from the activities of trade, provided it did not involve manual labor and was in wholesale rather than retail engagement, often by way of silent partnerships. The practice of charging interest, which underpins capitalist growth and expansion, did not, however, gain moral acceptance easily.[111] In the Ellesmere, a visual response to the usurious practices of merchants, over which both church and state claimed jurisdictional authority,[112] is expressed in the illustration of the Prioress (fig. 6). She shrinks back disapprovingly, as if responding to the annotation in the inner margin *t(ur)pe lucrum* beside the main text (PrT 491). Her horse, exhibiting an attitude that is even more severe, has seemingly dislodged the bar border with its decorative capital from its normal alignment.[113] The precarious spiritual position of merchants is indicated in *Piers Plowman* when the merchants weep for joy because Truth gives them a secret seal to the effect that, if they used their profits for charitable public works, no devil would harm them when they died.[114] That there was social force to this conception about acquired wealth is evident in the number of contemporary merchants' wills which left substantial amounts to charity for the good of their souls.[115] The illustration of the Merchant in the Douce 104 version of Langland's work shows a merchant, also in red, counting his coins (fol. 102v), a fairly stereotyped image. He is placed not beside the line referring to those engaged in legitimate buying and selling (XXI:238), but a few lines further down, beside the extended list of God's gifts to various professions and trades, including those who have to do with numbers, whom the illustrator represents as a merchant rather than as a diviner (240-41). As indicated by the Douce illustrator on other folios, it is the excessive concern for coins, implied by the number of them in the merchant's lap, that perverts the utilization of God's gifts and thereby threatens Piers's efforts to cultivate truth.

The innovation of the Ellesmere portrayal is therefore the more striking in having the Merchant shown, not counting his coins or even carrying a money bag (like the illustrated Covetousness in Douce 104), but as a parodied version of the Squire whose place in the social hierarchy he attempts to emulate and, in a sense, displace. As in the Douce illustrations, it is not gold *per se* that is bad. The Ellesmere illustrator, cultivating an aristocratic audience, implies that the display of gold is appropriate to that estate, as shown in the illustration of the Knight wearing gilded spurs denoting his status,[116] but should be restricted among the emerging middle class, never mind clergy or greedy peasants: a conservative attitude not unlike that of Christine de Pizan concerning the dress appropriate to bourgeois women.[117] A similar conservatism is reflected in the Ellesmere portrayal of the Prioress who does not have the gold brooch at the end of her rosary as disclosed by Chaucer's text. The attitude reflected elsewhere in Ellesmere to the subject of gold and the new moneyed economy is indicated in the long, extended flourishes in the border bracketing the Latin source in the *Liber parabolarum* by Alanus de Insulis which serves as an annotation to the Canon Yeoman's reflection in his tale that everything which shines is not gold, and that every apple fair to the eye is not good (962-65). The illustrated Merchant looks like a squire, but his clothes do not make him an aristocrat.

The unruly Miller's gold thumb, strikingly painted in the illustration (fig. 12), calls attention to his dishonesty in weighing corn (GP 561-62). Stout, thick-necked, drunk, weaponed, and entirely lacking in courtesy,

37

this Miller is everything the Knight and the Squire are not, both in the text and in the illustrations. Since his "cherles tale" (ProMLT 3169) is a direct challenge to Knight's — he even employs the same metaphor of literary creation used by the Knight when he mentions the "oxen in my plogh" (3159) — it is interesting to note how the Ellesmere designer registers that opposition. The unique placement of the illustration of Robin the Miller on the inside of the gutter margin near the binding can be considered an accident of the manuscript's production process. Alternatively, in view of the Miller's insistence on paying back the Knight with a "noble" story of his own (ProMLT 3126-27),[118] and the fact that this tale also begins with a "W," perhaps the illustration reflects his attempt to answer the Knight since he also approaches his tale, as does the Knight, from the top right. This positioning would imply that the designer might also have been deliberately playing with the idea of a border, suggested by one or more punning comments in the General Prologue as to the Miller's being a "janglere and a goliardeys" (560) or teller of dirty stories since *border* meant "a storyteller, a mocker, a minstrel or jester." The comparison of his beard to that of a "sowe" (552) which, together with his other boorish characteristics, calls up the image of a boar (*bor*), and his playing of a bagpipe (565) might be associated with the French *Bordon*, a "bagpipe . . . or a mule." The portrayal conjures up the association of playing at hitting a mark, as in *border* or *behorder*, which is what the Miller does in relation to the Knight and his story.[119] The Miller is allowed into the aristocratic space of the page as a fool or mocker (*border*), the role played by the other churls or churlish pilgrims.

Because the Miller insists on contesting the Knight's storytelling, the *Monk's Tale*, which should have followed the Knight's according to the Host's request, is judiciously delayed. The Monk's challenge to the Knight's position is evidently more serious than the Miller's bawdy parody of courtly love and the whole romance genre. Exaggerating his role as a narrator of tragedies, specifically one who tells about the fall of those in high degree — hence the Knight's "disese" when he calls for an end to so much heaviness (ProNPT 2771)—is his attire which, in the illustration, is funereal black from head to toe (fig. 13). The illustrator resisted the impulse to portray his shiny bald head, emphasized in the General Prologue (198). This "blackening" of the Monk, whose narration concerning the tragic fall of those in power reminds the audience that the Knight's status is not necessarily secure, represents a different sort of portrayal, quite devoid of humor, on the part of the designer. Although Lucifer is the tale's first example of a fall, the annotation "lucifer" in the space ruled for annotations nearly touches the base of the Monk's illustration. One of his greyhounds sniffs at the word "twynne" (2005), referring to the fallen angel who became Satan and could not escape from his misery in hell, further connecting the Monk with tragedies and black Satan. His facial expression is neutral (more evident in the original manuscript than in the photograph) and while his eyes do not seem to protrude or roll in his head, as described by the General Prologue (201-02), they do look at the first line of text ending in the word "Tragedie." His horse and greyhounds are festooned with elaborate gold bells and collar ornaments, demonstrating the impropriety of "daun Piers" (ProNPT 2792) who favors hunting and worldly, rather than spiritual, wealth.[120] Although it is not immediately apparent, because the black pigment on his clothes has been smudged,[121] there may have been a suggestion of the gold pin under his chin to fasten his hood (195-97).

Presented less soberly and more in the mode of low comedy is the portrait of the Cook (fig. 14). As David N. DeVries remarks with respect to the ways in which customers were cheated, fraud threatened "to destabilize the body politic" just as the rotten and unclean food sold by Roger of Ware threatened to "destabilize the body gastronomic."[122] DeVries also points out (393) that "the Host's admonition specifically links fraudulent business practice to fraudulent narrative practice." This connection makes all the more interesting the illustration of the Cook whose right hand offers up a steaming (stinking?) plate in the direction of the text describing the apprentice Perkyn Revelour who was a "short felwe / with lokkes blake" (CkT 4368-69), very like the illustrated Cook himself. His left hand carries as an attribute a large black meat hook, not mentioned in connection with the Cook but declaring his identification with the very devil, as in the Summoner's description of the damned being clawed with fleshhooks (SumT 1730-31).[123] The illustration of the Cook confirms for the aristocratic audience what the most obnoxious and repulsive churls look like — and this is one par excellence with his large thick peasant's foot so unlike the Knight's long, thin elegant one. This association of the illustrated Cook with the lowest class caters to the Ellesmere audience's sense of superiority in a way that the illustration in the Cambridge manuscript, showing him instead as a member of the professional middle class whose clothes cover his leg, does not.[124] In the Ellesmere, it is impossible to ignore the exaggerated bloody spots illustrating the unappetizing "mormal" (GP 386) on his bandaged leg. He is depicted in his underpants (not mentioned in the text), apparently to show the sores, but there is a similar presentation of peasants in their "working clothes" in the September scene for the grape harvest in the lavish *Très Riches Heures* of Jean, Duke of Berry. One such worker in his underpants is displayed near the middle of the lower third of that painting, exposing his buttocks to the viewer and showing his thick, hairy legs as he bends down performing his task.[125] In the case of the Ellesmere Cook, the dirty bandage and apron draw further attention to his lack of cleanliness, signalling disease and moral degeneracy to medieval audiences.[126] Both the calendar picture and the Ellesmere's rendition of the Cook show, for their respective aristocratic owners, a view of manual laborers that is demeaning.

The Cook's horse intensifies the negative impression of the portrait. The droll expression of the illustrated "capul" or nag, with his head turned back and his front leg raised and curved expressively in a manner unique within this manuscript, is perfectly explained when seen as anticipating the fall of the drunken Cook whose horsemanship or "chyuachee" is ridiculed in the Prologue to the *Manciple's Tale* (50).[127] There the Manciple also charges the Cook with nightwalking (16-19),[128] connecting him with thieves and prostitutes. This entire visual presentation would provide amusement to upper-class viewers confident of their own equestrian — and ethical — superiority. Of course, any laughter might be tinged with some queasiness concerning the quality of the food prepared, on occasion, for them!

Vying with the Cook in being the most revolting of the illustrated pilgrims is the puny Summoner (fig. 15), with a face to scare children (GP 624-28) that also associates him with the devil (SumT 1622). Whereas the illustrated Wife of Bath does not have red hose (contrary to GP 456), indicative of her sexuality, the lecherous Summoner does: a graphic example of the recasting of the pilgrims to suit the prejudices of an aristocratic audience. The placement of the angry Summoner so close to the lines about the friar who preached to get money for "hooly houses" (SumT 1718) emphasizes the quarrel between them in the text. The annotation on the facing page (fig. 16) may also have affected the placement of the Summoner. Adjacent to the lines concerning the lion who sits in wait to slay the innocent (FrT 1657-58), this Latin annotation gives the biblical source for the simile of the wicked man who lies in wait to ambush the poor man (Psalm 10.8-9), contextualizing the Summoner's attempt to cheat the poor widow (FrT 1376-77).[129] The placement of the illustration of the Summoner, so close to the text that his horse's head is surrounded by it and touches it, is more comprehensible if he is viewed in relation to the annotation opposite, as if he too were lying in ambush, ready to serve his summons.

Dominating the portrait of the Summoner is his overly large garland (GP 666) of red and white flowers, the colors duplicating the red and white splotches on his face. If the flowery coat is inappropriate for the not-so-courtly Merchant, this garland on the head of the obscene Summoner is a complete travesty of the image of a courtly or divine personage, as found, e.g., in the *Knight's Tale*. There, Emily makes a "subtil gerland" from the "white and rede" flowers she gathers (1053-54) and wears a garland of oak leaves to the altar of Diana (2290); the statue of Venus is garlanded with roses (1960-61) like the God of Love in Chaucer's *Romaunt of the Rose* (907-08); and Arcite (2175-76), like Theseus (1027), wears one of laurel.

Within the format of this folio, the configuration of the Summoner visually balances the block of the decorated letter "L" with its scrolling serifs on the same horizontal level in the demivinet border as the illustration. The garlanded Summoner seems to have been thrust out of the bracketing vegetal scrolls on the left as if his presence there is inappropriate. The pimply Summoner waits to pounce, his garland serving not to crown him as conqueror, lover, or poet, but to camouflage his intent, whether with respect to young people (GP 664) or to the bribable recipients of his summons. The garland, however, is too obvious and therefore *déclassé*, unlike the subtle inferences which the perceptive reader might tease out of the visual apparatus in a leisurely viewing and reviewing of the manuscript.

Conclusion

The supertextual richness of such pages as those beginning the Knight's and Squire's tales is professionally designed to please the Ellesmere Manuscript's aristocratic, or even royal, owners who might thereby lay claim to rhetorical expertise.[130] In making the portrait of the Squire nobler and younger than called for by the Prologue's description, in picturing him as a suitable riding companion to the lordly Knight, and in refining the Wife of Bath, the artistic designer doubtless had in mind the sort of family circle for whom this manuscript was destined. Sustaining this intention is the layout and decoration: even the more vulgar pilgrims bordering the tales are introduced into the ornamental enclosure, which serves metaphorically as a garden of verse and also reflects the ambience of the aristocratic reader, in a way that reinforces the latter's self-perception of superiority.[131]

Less certain is the exact identity of the projected readers. Was the Ellesmere Manuscript commissioned by someone like Thomas Beaufort, Duke of Exeter, or John, Duke of Bedford, as a gift for a youth like John de Vere, twelfth earl of Oxford, its first recorded owner later in the century?[132] Or, in view of the suggestive visual allusions, perhaps including the small dragon on the bottom of folio 1v (fig. 1), was the Ellesmere Manuscript made with Henry, Prince of Wales, in mind?[133] The Knight's portrait might then refer to Henry IV himself — also portrayed with a mustache and beard, albeit as a slightly younger man, holding a red rose (one of the decorative motifs in the Ellesmere), in the portrait now in St. James Palace[134] — or to one of the young prince's relatives or supporters? If such a scenario has credibility, then the book itself becomes a kind of seal[135] of the relationship of guardian and young charge. The question then becomes: why are there not more direct signs of patronage? At present this is difficult to assess. If there was a perception, during the planning stages, that there might be an imminent change of power, then it was the better part of discretion not to be too direct.

Or was the focus, after all, to present an aureate Chaucer to an unidentified, albeit aristocratic, posterity? The only other border creature, the more worm-like dragon with the washed-out face on the bottom border of the Prologue to the *Clerk's Tale*, occurs just below the stanza concerning "deeth" who has slain "ffraunceys petrak the lauriat poete" (fol. 87v). Chaucer, in the voice of the Clerk, says "alle shul we dye" (31-38). The Ellesmere artist adds a kind of visual "Amen" by means of the backward-looking dragon who has also "slayn" Chaucer, implying that this manuscript was made after Chaucer's death, thereby beginning the process of posthumous laureation and fulfilling his own sense of planting a literary garden "for posterity."[136]

All that can be said with any kind of certainty is that, given the care with which the text of the *Canterbury Tales* has been framed to provide every kind of visual guide to stimulate a conservative reading of Chaucer, and, considering the conscious censorship of overt signs of violence and sexuality in the portraits elevated in status, the Ellesmere Manuscript presents to its readers a social vision of orderly control by a refined and courteous ruling class. The ornamental sugar-coating framing endless passages of edification in the *Parson's Tale* even offers this ruling class an aesthetics of salvation that is altogether agreeable.

NOTES

[1] This French loan word in Middle English contexts is explored in Laura Kendrick, "The Jesting Borders of Chaucer's *Canterbury Tales* and of Late Medieval Manuscript Art," *Animating the Letter: The Figurative Embodiment of Writing from Late Antiquity to the Renaissance* (Columbus, OH, 1999), pp. 217-25,

especially 223. She suggests that Gothic marginalia may have provided a model for the structure of Chaucer's *Canterbury Tales* with its connective links and even for the relationship of some tales to others as bordering. I am grateful to Laura Kendrick for providing me with an earlier version of this.

2 San Marino, Huntington Library, MS Ellesmere 26 C9, made in London probably within the first decade of the fifteenth century (see discussions in *The Ellesmere Chaucer*, cited below). I would like to thank Mary Robertson, the Chief Curator of Manuscripts, for granting me access to the precious original, which made possible many insights, both technical and conceptual. This manuscript has been published in a new facsimile, "a covetable object in its own right" (in the words of Jill Mann in the information brochure), by the Huntington Library and Yushodo Co. of Tokyo as *The Ellesmere Chaucer* in 1995. A companion volume, *The Ellesmere Chaucer: Essays in Interpretation*, eds. Martin Stevens and Daniel Woodward (San Marino and Tokyo, 1995), contains the most extensive studies of individual aspects of this manuscript to date. It includes bibliographical references, as does Kathleen Scott's catalogue entry no. 42 for the Ellesmere in her *Later Gothic Manuscripts: 1390-1490*, 2 vols. (London, 1996), 2:140-43. In my transcriptions from the Ellesmere Manuscript, all Middle English expansions of abbreviations have been italicized, while expansions of Latin abbreviations have been enclosed in brackets. Citations of Chaucer's literary works are from Larry Benson, ed., *The Riverside Chaucer*, 3rd ed. (Oxford, 1990). References are given parenthetically, employing standard abbreviations for the tales. Prologues are designated by "Pro," so that "ProFrT," e.g., indicates the Prologue to the *Friar's Tale*.

3 See the discussion by Derek Pearsall in *The Life of Geoffrey Chaucer: A Critical Biography* (Oxford and Cambridge, MA, 1992), pp. 234-35.

4 Laura L. Howes, *Chaucer's Gardens and the Language of Convention* (Gainesville, FL, 1997), pp. 24, 29, and 31.

5 Howes, *Chaucer's Gardens*, pp. 26 and 30; and chapter 1, "Gardens Chaucer Knew," for the general information.

6 As described by Margaret Rickert's chapter on "Illuminations," in John M. Manly and Edith Rickert, *The Text of the Canterbury Tales Studied on the Basis of All Known Manuscripts*, 1 (Chicago, 1940), pp. 565-66, and by Kathleen L. Scott, "An Hours and Psalter by Two Ellesmere Illuminators," in *The Ellesmere Chaucer*, pp. 92-94. Because of the stylization, it is difficult to determine the exact identity of all the floral and leaf forms.

7 I am deeply indebted to Leonard A. Woods for his invaluable suggestions concerning the ornamental vocabulary of the Ellesmere border.

8 Derek Pearsall and Elizabeth Salter, *Landscapes and Seasons of the Medieval World* (London, 1973), p. 110, concerning the illustrations to Boccaccio's *Decameron* which "were actually used for gardening treatises"; and Howes, *Chaucer's Gardens*, pp. 22-23.

9 Even in the poem itself there are hints that the garden is one of artifice, evidently understood as such in Chaucer's translation describing the plenitude of colorful flowers which "grew there never in mede" and which adorned the ground as if "men had it peynt" (Fragment A, 1434 and 1436). Howes discusses Chaucer's use of literary gardens in connection with the conventions of courtly love to point out the tragedy that results when social and political realities intrude for

lovers like Troilus and Criseyde (*Chaucer's Gardens*, pp. 64-82). Terry Comito speaks of the "gardens of the *Roman de la Rose* flourishing in verse and floral motifs proliferated [on] tapestries, manuscripts and cathedrals," in the late Middle Ages; see *The Idea of the Garden in the Renaissance* (New Brunswick, NJ, 1978), p. 152.

[10] This is mentioned in a letter-poem or "plant" for the orchard, evidently in reply to one by Chaucer to Deschamps. From Deschamps' response, Chaucer seems to have referred to his own poetic ambitions in this metaphoric way: "*Et un vergier, ou du plant demandas / De ceuls qui font pour eulx auctorisier, / A ja longtemps que tu edifas* [and long since you established an orchard and asked for plants from those who write poetry for posterity]," edited and translated in J. A. Burrow, *Geoffrey Chaucer: A Critical Anthology* (Baltimore, 1969), pp. 26, 28. See also D. S. Brewer, *Chaucer and Chaucerians: Critical Studies in Middle English Literature* (London, 1966), p. 243. In her comment on these lines from Deschamps, Laura Howes, in *Chaucer's Gardens*, pp. 5-6, says that the "metaphoric resonance of gardens was firmly established by the fourteenth century." As Laura Kendrick observes, Deschamps refers to a compilation of his own work as a garden in which he has sown "flowers" from various authors, possibly a "*florilegium* of extracts" or translations; see "The *Canterbury Tales* in the Context of Contemporary Vernacular Translations and Compilations," *The Ellesmere Chaucer*, pp. 286-87.

[11] See Howes, *Chaucer's Gardens*, on the *Book of the Duchess* and the *Parliament of Fowls*, pp. 35-63, and on "*Troilus and Criseyde*, pp. 64-82.

[12] Contrast the way in which the text was viewed in Oxford, Bodleian Library, MS Douce 104. See Kathryn Kerby-Fulton and Denise Despres, *Iconography and the Professional Reader: The Politics of Book Production in the Douce "Piers Plowman,"* Medieval Cultures 15 (Minneapolis, 1999).

[13] Seth Lerer, "Writing Like the Clerk: Laureate Poets and the Aureate World," in *Chaucer and His Readers* (Princeton, 1993), pp. 24, 48-49, and 239, no. 57.

[14] From the Latin *colores* which Phyllis Hodgson reminds us is "a technical term for rhetorical embellishments"; "Notes," *Chaucer: "The Franklin's Tale"* (London, 1961), p. 74.

[15] This also manifests Chaucer's verbal-visual interplay in passages which self-consciously refer to the act of artistic creation such as that in the Clerk's Prologue where, in declaring obedience to the Host's request to speak plainly, the Clerk does the very opposite by relating a tale of "ffraunceys Petrak, the lauriat poete, / . . . whos rethorike sweete / Enlumyned al ytaile of poeterie" (ProClT 18, 31-33). The Ellesmere Manuscript fulfills the self-promotional analogy.

[16] Lerer, "Writing Like the Clerk," pp. 24 and 49. See also the discussion by Derek Pearsall concerning Hoccleve's effective creation of Chaucer as poet laureate in "Hoccleve's *Regement of Princes*: The Poetics of Royal Self-Representation," *Speculum* 69 (1994), 400.

[17] Kathleen Scott has identified two of the Ellesmere border artists as having worked on Oxford, Bodleian Library, MS Hatton 4, which "contains an Hours of the Virgin interworked with an Hours of the Cross, a Sarum Calendar, and a Psalter"; see "An Hours and Psalter," p. 87 and the discussion on pp. 101-04. Previously, Margaret Rickert had observed comparable styles in seven English

manuscripts including a missal, two Wycliffite Bibles, and two Psalters in "Illuminations," p. 566. That two of these manuscripts comparable to the Ellesmere are Wycliffite Bibles is interesting because of the exclusion in the former of any representations of the deity, the Virgin, or the saints, subjects which became anathema to the Lollards and like-minded followers of Wycliffe. In a bid to ensure the acceptance and preservation of this manuscript for the future, this may have been but one factor influencing the decision to portray the pilgrim storytellers, but not the subjects of their stories, and also to utilize the symbolic suggestiveness of the frames rather than any direct sacred imagery which might have been considered idolatrous. The portrayal of the pilgrims in Ellesmere represents a middle ground between orthodoxy and the opposite extreme that "none ymages shuld imaked be" (*Regement of Princes*, 5007, as quoted by Pearsall in "Hoccleve's *Regement of Princes*," 403). Perhaps it is one of the ironies of the times or a deliberate intention that the portrait of Chaucer on fol. 153v be considered as a "kind of icon . . . with writerly instead of saintly attributes," as Pearsall remarks with respect to the virtual mirror image of this portrait in the margin of Hoccleve's *Regement of Princes* in London, British Library, MS Harley 4866, fol. 88r, possibly made for Prince Henry ("Hoccleve's *Regement of Princes*," p. 403). An addendum to Pearsall's discussion regarding Hoccleve's commissioned Chaucer portrait is that it strengthens the possibility that he may have been involved in some advisory capacity in the making of the Ellesmere. As a scribe, Hoccleve would have known the best artistic designers available for this project. He himself did not work on the Ellesmere as a scribe, even though he worked as Scribe E with the Ellesmere scribe, Scribe B, on a Gower manuscript, as indicated by A. I. Doyle and M. B. Parkes, "The Production of Copies of the *Canterbury Tales* and the *Confessio Amantis* in the Early Fifteenth Century," *Medieval Scribes, Manuscripts and Libraries* (London, 1978), p. 185.

[18] The Ellesmere borders prepare the reader for the idea of the pilgrimage as a "figure for the journey of man's life through the world," which the *Parson's Tale* makes explicit (Pearsall, *The Life of Geoffrey Chaucer*, p. 240). Upon subsequent viewings and within such a pious context, this would become part of the rich, multi-layered way the audience would appreciate their personal version of the *Tales* as being for "oure doctrine" (see Pearsall's discussion, *The Life of Geoffrey Chaucer*, p. 270).

[19] The Ellesmere Manuscript's present size is about 400 by 284 mm; see Daniel Woodward, "The New Ellesmere Chaucer Facsimile," p. 3. The Douce 104 MS (Anglo-Irish, 1427), is 213-217 by 146-151 mm, according to Derek Pearsall, "Introduction," *Piers Plowman: A Facsimile of Bodleian Library, Oxford, MS Douce 104* (Cambridge, 1992), p. xii. The *Pearl-Gawain* manuscript, London, British Library, MS Cotton Nero A.X, Art. 3 (English, illustrated c. 1400) is about 171 by 123 mm, according to Kathleen Scott, cat. no. 12, *Later Gothic Manuscripts*, 2:66. See also Israel Gollancz, ed. *Pearl, Cleanness, Patience, and Sir Gawain: Reproduced in Facsimile from the Unique MS. Cotton Nero A.x in the British Museum*, EETS 162 (1923; repr. London, 1955).

[20] See note 2 for references to bibliographical sources.

[21] Doyle and Parkes, "The Production of Copies," p. 190.

[22] Compare Chaucer's description in *The Book of the Duchess*, ll. 291-320. See *The Riverside Chaucer*, p. 334.

[23] Aberystwyth, National Library of Wales, MS Peniarth 392D, copied by "Scribe B"; see Doyle and Parkes, "The Production of Copies," p. 185.

[24] Ralph Hanna III, "(The) Editing (of) the Ellesmere Text," *The Ellesmere Chaucer*, p. 234. For a list of the occurrences of decorated letters and champs in the manuscript, see Martin Stevens, "Appendix A," in *The Ellesmere Chaucer*, p. 340.

[25] Scott, "An Hours and Psalter," p. 90.

[26] This metaphor of verbal creation, fortuitously mentioned further down on the same illustrated page (886-87), is reflected by the calligraphic rows of the letters. The plowing analogy is based on Matt. 13.24 which compares the kingdom of heaven to a man who sowed good seed in his field. In this manuscript, the agricultural image with its paradisal associations offers a variant to the literary garden image derived from the French romance tradition. In effect, it implies that the ensuing narrative, although set in pre-Christian times, is "good seed" within a larger cosmic framework. See also the discussion of the plowing image in Michael Camille, "Labouring for the Lord: The Ploughman and the Social Order in the Luttrell Psalter," *Art History* 10 (December, 1987), 434. V. A. Kolve astutely observes that the "larger design" of the *Canterbury Tales* is "self-reflexive, concerned with the nature of poetry itself"; see *Chaucer and the Imagery of Narrative: The First Five Canterbury Tales* (Stanford, 1984), p. 85. The artistic designer of the Ellesmere, in kindred fashion, clearly responded to and elaborated upon this exploration of the creative process, not only in specific instances but in the larger design of the codex itself, obviously taking particular pleasure in exploiting any potential for interplay between the sister arts.

[27] Kolve, *Chaucer*, p. 103.

[28] Meyer Schapiro, *Words and Pictures: On the Literal and the Symbolic in the Illustration of a Text* (The Hague and Paris, 1973), throughout.

[29] Howes, *Chaucer's Gardens*, pp. 36-38 and 41-42. She refers specifically to the *Book of the Duchess* in which the first "tale" (designated as such at l. 710 and used again for the second account at l. 1034) begins with the entrance of the man in black to the garden. She also points out that the description of the garden lies between the two sections of the story.

[30] *Troilus and Criseyde* II. 83 and 103 (see also the "Explanatory Notes" by Stephen A. Barney, p. 1031). Criseyde's use of the plural appears to refer to the maiden, the two ladies, and herself as being engaged in reading, listening, and pausing (100-03). Presumably, Criseyde quotes these rubricated words in the following lines (104-05; as Barney, p. 1032, points out). See also Howes, *Chaucer's Gardens*, pp. 68-70, on the arrival of Pandarus who interrupts this reading scene to tell of the lovesick Troilus in the palace garden, a situation which he assumes the literate Criseyde will know indicates that "Troilus is a conventional courtly lover."

[31] Sandra Hindman, *Sealed in Parchment: Rereadings of Knighthood in the Illuminated Manuscripts of Chrétien de Troyes* (Chicago, 1994), p. 162, speaking of the illustrated Chrétien romances.

[32] John Bulwer, *Chirologia: or the Natural Language of the Hand and Chironomia: or the Art of Manual Rhetoric* (1644, 1654), ed. James W. Cleary (London, 1974); esp. Gestus XIV (pp. 42-45, illus. "O" on p. 115 of the *Chirologia*), and Canons II, III and XIX (pp. 173-74, 180, and illus. "C" and "E" on p. 193 of the section titled "The Canons of Rhetoricians Touching The Artificial Managing of the Hand in Speaking").

46

[33] Moshe Barasch, *Giotto and the Language of Gesture* (Cambridge, 1987), p. 17.

[34] David Lambert et al., *Body Language* (Glasgow, 1996), p. 240.

[35] This is not the case within the inhabited "W" of London, British Library, MS Lansdowne 851, c. 1425 where Chaucer holds a book of the *Canterbury Tales*, and in Oxford, Bodleian Library, MS 686, c. 1435, where Chaucer points to the text.

[36] For the pictorial absence of Chrétien see Hindman, *Sealed in Parchment*, p. 197; for her discussions of oral culture see p. 162.

[37] Hindman, *Sealed in Parchment*, pp. 78, 83, and 162.

[38] Richard K. Emmerson, "Text and Image in the Ellesmere Portraits of the Tale-Tellers," in *The Ellesmere Chaucer*, pp. 143-70. He suggests that this "alternate set of portraits, now visual rather than verbal," serves to "facilitate reading by making explicit and visible the manuscript's *ordinatio*" (p. 144).

[39] See those of the Wife of Bath, the Squire, the Prioress, the Monk, and surprisingly, the Nun's (i.e., Prioress's) Priest, which adds further status to the Prioress.

[40] Terry Jones, *Chaucer's Knight: The Portrait of a Medieval Mercenary* (London, 1980), pp. 29-30.

[41] See Jones's illustration (*Chaucer's Knight*, p. 214) and his speculation that Chaucer may have based some of the elements of his characterization on Hawkwood. That may or may not have been the case, but it does not follow that the Ellesmere artist's illustration is based on a portrait of Hawkwood, the one mentioned by Jones being in any case later in date.

[42] For the "miles" reading and the Drury connection, see John M. Manly and Edith Rickert, *The Text of the Canterbury Tales: Studied on the Basis of all Known Manuscripts* (Chicago, 1940) 1: 152-55; also Herbert C. Schulz, *The Ellesmere Manuscript of Chaucer's Canterbury Tales* (San Marino, Calif., 1966), p. 19; Ralph Hanna III, "Introduction," *The Ellesmere Manuscript of Chaucer's Canterbury Tales: A Working Facsimile* (Cambridge, 1989), pp. 1-2 ; and Ralph Hanna III, "Rotheley, the De Vere Circle, and the Ellesmere Chaucer," *Huntington Library Quarterly* 58.1 (1996), 14-19.

[43] David Edge and John Miles Paddock, *Arms and Armour of the Medieval Knight* (London, 1988), pp. 185-86. Fustian was "a cloth of wool and linen or latterly cotton, with a raised nap, giving the effect of velveteen" worn by poorer knights (p. 86). Gawain, in the *Pearl* manuscript, fols. 95v, 129r, and 130r, appears to wear such a garment.

[44] Jill Mann, *Chaucer and Medieval Estates Satire: The Literature of the Social Classes and the "General Prologue" to the "Canterbury Tales"* (Cambridge, 1973), pp. 108-09.

[45] Edge and Paddock, *Arms and Armour*, pp. 85-86.

[46] This form of covering for the hand, excluding the fingers, is not immediately apparent in reproductions of the Knight because his fingers are darker than his face, but the shape is clearly noticeable once the image is enlarged on the computer screen. There is a cuff-like band at the edge where his fingers protrude. In the *Pearl-Gawain* manuscript, see especially fols. 41v, 42r, 42v, 60v, and 95v.

[47] These are ties "by which armor was secured in place"; see Edge and Paddock, *Arms and Armour*, p. 185.

[48] Martin Stevens, "The Ellesmere Miniatures as Illustrations of *Chaucer's Canterbury Tales*," *Studies in Iconography* 7-8 (1981-82), 124.

49 Edge and Paddock, *Arms and Armour*, p. 85. Some of the other pilgrims seem to have silver rowel spurs (the Squire, the Merchant, the Wife of Bath, the Monk, the Franklin, the Pardoner, the Summoner, the Manciple, the Clerk, and the Parson).

50 There are four other instances of gold paint in this manuscript: on Chaucer's "penner" (fol. 153v), on the Wife of Bath's belt (fol. 72r), on the bells and ornaments of the Monk's hounds (fol. 169r), and on the Miller's finger (fol. 34v). As will become apparent, this application of gold paint serves to raise the status of the pilgrim, to satirize inappropriate behavior, or to provide some humor.

51 Chantilly, Musée Condé, MS 65, fol. 5v, before 1416. See also the figure wearing red headgear in the April scene, fol. 4r.

52 London, British Library, MS Harley 4431, fol. 81r.

53 The full quotation from the *Thebaid* (xii, 519-20) is translated in *The Riverside Chaucer* note, p. 37: "And now (Theseus, drawing nigh his) native land in laurelled car after fierce battling with the Scithian folk, etc. [is heralded by glad applause and the heaven-flung shout of the populace and the merry trump of warfare ended]." The chariot was abandoned for the horse in Chaucer's version.

54 See also the garland given to the victorious Arcite on his bier (2875). J. B. Trapp, in "The Owl's Ivy and the Poet's Bays," *Journal of the Warburg and Courtaud Institutes* 21 (1958), 227-55, traces the classical association of crowning both conquerors and poets, pointing out that Boccaccio and Antonio Pucci refer to the crowning of Dante at his funeral in 1321. Trapp also mentions that Petrarch, who was himself crowned poet laureate, took the trouble to marginate his Vergil, "against Servius' comment on *Eclogues* 8. 13, the information, buttressed by the line from Status . . . that poets also were entitled to the laurel," 236-37. With these literary precedents, there may already have been a hint on the Knight's page that the Ellesmere border would take on something of this function even before the Franklin's page makes explicit that the enclosed garden is poetical and also before Chaucer's portrait (fol. 153v) suggests itself as a literary icon, all of which point to this manuscript having been "intended as a commemorative volume," to use Kathleen Scott's words in *Later Gothic Manuscripts*, 2:142. It celebrates the "flour of eloquence" by whose passing England was deprived of "the swettnesse / of retoryke" (Hoccleve, *Regement of Princes*, 1962 and 2084-85 respectively), a preliminary confirmation of Chaucer as the poet laureate effectively created by Hoccleve, as suggested by Derek Pearsall, "Hoccleve's *Regement*," 400.

55 For a discussion of Prince Henry's promotion of poetry in the vernacular, or the translation of such tales of martial chivalry into English "to create a stronger sense of nationhood," see Pearsall, "Hoccleve's *Regement*," 397-98.

56 Stevens, "The Ellesmere Miniatures," 124.

57 Mann, *Chaucer and Medieval Estates*, p. 113.

58 See my discussion of this illustrated Knight (fol. 35v) in "Retributive Violence and the Reformist Agenda in the Illustrated Douce 104 MS of *Piers Plowman*," *Fifteenth-Century Studies* 23 (1997), 17-19; also VIII:18-44 in Derek Pearsall's edition of *Piers Plowman*, pp. 147-48.

59 Fols. 95v, 129r, and 130r. For a discussion of the *Pearl* miniatures see my article, "The Image Controversies in Late Medieval England and the Visual Prefaces and Epilogues in the *Pearl* Manuscript: Creating a Meta-Narrative of the Spiritual Journey to the New Jerusalem," *SMRH*, 3rd series, vol. 1 (forthcoming).

[60] *The Riverside Chaucer*, p. 24. As Timothy Haskett pointed out to me, this is interesting because one of the main jobs of a knight's squire (or other manservant) would have been to clean and oil the mail, precisely because it was important that such a crucial and expensive piece of equipment not deteriorate and rust.

[61] *A Chaucer Glossary*, compiled by Norman Davis, et al. (Oxford, 1989), p. 15.

[62] Now in Edinburgh in the National Library of Scotland. Philippa Hardman, "A Medieval 'Library *In Parvo*,'" *Medium Ævum* 47.2 (1978), 268, points out that, in this manuscript, the *Gowther* romance has had extra details of military violence added, making it "more like a ballad or folk-tale . . . brutal, frank, racy and bloodthirsty," in contrast to another version of this tale in London, British Library, MS Royal 17.B.xliii, which includes more aspects of courtly observance. Similarly, the Ellesmere designer has amplified the courtly aspects of Chaucer's verse to suit a like-minded audience. Depicting the seige of Jerusalem in terrifying detail are the last two miniatures (fols. 190r and 190v) of a Book of Hours which also contains a "near-encyclopedia of devotional iconography," London, British Library, MS Egerton 2781, 1440-50; see Lucy Freeman Sandler, *Gothic Manuscripts: 1285-1385*, 2 (London, 1986), cat. no. 115, pp. 127-28. I am grateful to Denise Despres for calling my attention to this manuscript in the de Bohun group. The Ellesmere Manuscript tends to shy away from punitive violence also, unlike the Douce 104 MS of *Piers Plowman*; see my "Retributive Violence," 13-48.

[63] Hindman, *Sealed in Parchment*, p. 93.

[64] This was not the case in the other depictions of the Knight as printed by Caxton and De Worde later in the century. For a discussion of these armored knights see Betsy Bowden, "Visual Portraits of the Canterbury Pilgrims: 1484(?)-1809," in *The Ellesmere Chaucer*, p. 177. Chaucer's text does not mention the Knight's weapons, but as these other depictions indicate, weapons were as much part of a knight's assumed accouterments as the *gypon*, which Chaucer does mention, but only because he makes the point that it is *bismotered*.

[65] Hindman, *Sealed in Parchment*, p. 82, uses this term to describe a knight as "head of the household" to distinguish this status from that, for instance, of a knight as a "bacheler."

[66] The merging of the Knight and Theseus was observed by Martin Stevens who says that the miniaturist, with "his own audience in mind," created an image "which summons up the role of Theseus" ("The Ellesmere Miniatures," 124). The other design features of the layout of the page encourage this dual application.

[67] See the discussion on this process in Michael Camille, *The Gothic Idol: Ideology and Image-making in Medieval Art* (1989; repr. Cambridge, 1995), p. 102.

[68] *The Riverside Chaucer*, p. 834, n. 1884; compare the late Gothic temple created for Diana in Brussels, Bibliothèque Royale, MS 9242, fol. 174v, which is reproduced in Michael Camille, *The Gothic Idol*, p. 113.

[69] They are as follows: "The preyere of Palamon to Venus goddesse of loue," "The preyere of Emelye to dyane goddesse of Maydens," "The answere of dyane to Emelye," and "The orisoun of Arcite to Mars god of Armes" (KnT 2221-22, 2297-98, 2349-50, and 2373-74 respectively).

[70] Subsequent illustrated versions of the *Canterbury Tales* portrayed not the tales, but the storytellers, the precedent having been established in this manuscript.

Made within a decade or two after the Ellesmere, the only other manuscript with a program of illustrations for the *Canterbury Tales* is Cambridge, University Library, MS Gg. 4. 27 (1), which now contains only six remaining pictures of the pilgrims at the beginnings of their tales, plus four remaining pictures of the personified Deadly Sins added to the *Parson's Tale*, reinforcing the latter's importance for a late medieval audience. The other miniatures of pilgrims and Sins have been cut out. Scott considers the "idea of using a sequence of mounted Pilgrims" as deriving from the Ellesmere Chaucer "or from a similar lost manuscript" (*Later Gothic Manuscripts* 2:144). Scott incorrectly, however, distinguishes the Ellesmere placement of the pilgrims from that of Gg. 4. 27 (1) when she says that the latter's designer "did not understand the subtlety of placing the Pilgrims at their Prologues" in the Ellesmere manner (p. 145). In no case where there is a Prologue to a tale in the Ellesmere is the illustration placed there; rather, it is always placed within lines of the titles "here bigynneth . . ." announcing whose tale (not prologue) follows. Betsy Bowden, in "Visual Portraits of the Canterbury Pilgrims," traces early printed books and the first painted versions of the *Canterbury Tales*, all illustrated with pilgrim portraits.

[71] Contrast, for example, the two-page spread illustrating the battle with the Amazons in a French manuscript of Boccassio's *Teseida* now in Vienna, Österreichische Nationalbibliothek, MS 2617, c. 1455, fols. 18v-19. See Kolve, *Chaucer*, p. 409, n. 4.

[72] See, for example, that on the Knight's page beside the reference to Ypolita and the Amazons (KnT 880-83) and on the Squire's page beside mention of the king's beautiful daughter, Canace (SqT 33-35). On the Miller's page, fol. 34v, there may be some suggestion that a small floral bouquet with a rosette medallion and sprouting daisies is used ironically beside the Miller's description of the chamber of the maid-like clerk at Oxford that was adorned with sweet herbs, while he himself was as sweet as a licorice root (3205-07). Some irony may also be intended on the Shipman's page where a rosette medallion occurs beside the mention of the fair, young monk (25-28).

[73] It may be that she is portrayed as a widow since her pinched wimple (GP 151), worn over the chin in the illustration, was an important feature of widows' attire until the sixteenth century; see Margaret Scott, *A Visual History of Costume: The Fourteenth and Fifteenth Centuries* (London, 1986), p. 32, Illus. 16. The illustration shows a freestone effigy of a widow from the Church of St. Mary, Sprotborough, Yorks., now at Batsford, made by an anonymous English sculptor working after 1340. The wimple is meticulously crimped.

[74] Österreichische Nationalbibliothek, Cod. Ser. N. 2844, fol. 124v. This miniature from the Rothschild Prayer Book, Gent-Brüger School, c. 1510, is reproduced as a post card available at the Nationalbibliothek in Vienna.

[75] Wide, high belts were worn above the waistline in fifteenth-century fashion according to Geoff Egan and Frances Pritchard, *Dress Accessories c. 1150-c. 1450*, in Medieval Finds from Excavations in London 3 (London, 1991), p. 35. See also the next note.

[76] Chantilly, Musée Condé, MS 65, fol. 4v. While it is unlikely (unless the crusades brought some knowledge of this), there is a remote possibility that it may have some reference to the Byzantine gold marriage belt, adding an interesting

resonance in view of the Wife's many marriages. On an early Syrian example, see Edwin Hall, *The Arnolfini Betrothal: Medieval Marriage and the Enigma of Van Eyck's Double Portrait* (London, 1994), p. 21.

[77] Paris, Bibliothèque Nationale, MS fr. 12420, fol. 46r; reproduced in Sandra L. Hindman, *Christine de Pizan's "Epistre Othea": Painting and Politics at the Court of Charles VI* (Toronto, 1986) as fig. 81.

[78] Blanche M. A. Ellis, "Spurs and Spur Fittings," in *The Medieval Horse and Its Equipment c. 1150-c. 1450*, Medieval Finds from Excavations in London 5 (London, 1995), p. 124.

[79] Nicole Green, "Variant Interpretations," unpublished essay (Victoria, B.C., 1998), pp. 14-15, develops the implications of the whip, seeing it in terms of the Wife's need for control and yet her lack of control, her use of "Auctoritee" being "a verbal whip."

[80] Susan Schibanoff, "The New Reader and Female Textuality in Two Early Commentaries on Chaucer," *Studies in the Age of Chaucer* 13 (1991), 71-108.

[81] The importance of generosity as a characteristic of those in power is heavily supplemented by the mass of marginalia on poverty (WBT 1177-1206), not found in Hengwrt, and so is possibly of more than passing relevance to the scribe or editor.

[82] Pearsall, *The Life of Geoffrey Chaucer*, pp. 234-35.

[83] Seth Lerer, "Reading Like the Squire: Chaucer, Lydgate, Clanvowe, and the Fifteenth-Century Anthology," in *Chaucer and His Readers: Imagining the Author in Late-Medieval England* (Princeton, 1993), pp. 62, 69. Sylvia Huot comments on the organization of Old French poetic anthologies in *From Song to Book* (Ithaca, 1987), pp. 11-45.

[84] Carl Lindahl says that in the ninety years between 1385 and 1475, next to "master" used 23 times, Chaucer is referred to as "rhetor" 14 times, followed by "eloquent" 8 times, revealing "an elite cultural view"; see *Earnest Games: Folkloric Patterns in the "Canterbury Tales"* (Bloomington and Indianapolis, 1989), p. 166.

[85] In *The Riverside Chaucer* these are lines 7-8 of "Introduction to the Squire's Tale," but in the Ellesmere, they are lines 29-30 of "The prologe of the Squieres tale."

[86] The same annotation is present in Hengwrt. *The Riverside Chaucer* (pp. 452 and 891, n. 22) cites Boethius 4.pr.6.116-29.

[87] This follows as his compassionate response to the cries of the weeping ladies of his court and to his own reasoning concerning men's natural behavior in the matter of love (KnT 1748-72).

[88] A dark outline distinguishes his shoe from the leg of the horse which it overlaps; however, it is not continued to the point, where it was not required for articulation when the paint was intact. This sort of interrupted outlining for purposes of clarification and emphasis is also evident on later figures. Compare, for instance, the outline on the right leg of the horse of the Canon's Yeoman where, once again, the rider's leg is distinguished from the horse's by an outline. What this suggests is that someone looked over all the figures when they were finished, outlining where necessary. It is one technical aspect implying more collaboration and less separation of duties than previously recognized.

[89] As described in the record of the collections of Henry VII and Edward VI (1542, 1547 [49]) as quoted in Oliver Millar, *The Tudor, Stuart and Early Georgian Pictures in the Collection of Her Majesty The Queen* (London, 1963), cat. no. 6, p. 50. I am grateful to Sue Fletcher, Picture Library Assistant, Royal Collections Enterprises, for this information. It is possible that the short hair style Henry adopted was misunderstood and taken as a cap by the copyist (see note below). That this is likely is indicated by the cap-like hairstyle of Henry who has light brown hair in a miniature made during his lifetime and showing Hoccleve presenting him with the *Regement of Princes* in London, British Library, MS Arundel 38, c. 1411-13, fol. 37r, reproduced in color in Elizabeth Hallam, ed., *The Chronicles of the Wars of the Roses* (Godalming, Surrey, 1997), p. 123.

[90] There are at least six copies of this late fifteenth- or early sixteenth-century panel portrait of Henry V besides the one at Eton College. According to Millar, *The Tudor, Stuart and Early Georgian Pictures*, p. 50, "The source of the portrait may have been a medal, the effigy of the King in Westminster Abbey (from which the head was stolen in 1546) or a votive portrait in miniature or on the scale of life in which the King appeared as a donor." The position of Henry's open hand, shown from the back, also displays a ring on his little finger and on his index finger, both in the usual position. The artist would seem to have painted the hand in this position for the purpose of showing off these rings. In the Squire's portrait, only one ring is relevant to the story. A distinguishing facial feature in the portrait is Henry's nose, shown similarly in Arundel 38 (see preceding note), which might be compared to that of the illustrated Ellesmere Squire.

[91] Geoff Egan and Frances Pritchard, *Dress Accessories*, p. 336.

[92] Cambridge, Corpus Christi College, MS 61, fol. 1v.

[93] Cambridge, Corpus Christi College, MS 213, fol. 1r. Jean de Galopes is shown presenting Henry with his translation ("in a rather current French hand") of Bonaventure's meditations on the life of Christ and on the psalms. According to a couple of inscriptions, the book belonged to Henry V; see Montague Rhodes James, *A Descriptive Catalogue of the Manuscripts in the Library of Corpus Christi College Cambridge* (Cambridge, 1912), pp. 213-14. The chain around Henry's neck also resembles that of the Ellesmere Squire. It is reproduced in R. B. Mowat, *Henry V* (London, 1919), facing p. 46.

[94] London, British Library, MS Harley 1319, fols. 30v, 53v, and 57r. As stated by Gervase Mathew, *The Court of Richard II* (London, 1968), p. 209, Creton was "a 'valet' of Charles VI of France who had joined Richard's court in 1398, had accompanied him to Ireland in June 1399 and who had the Earl of Salisbury as his patron." This work, which is prejudiced in Richard's favor, is "crowded with realistic detail and there are attempts at portraiture." Fols. 53v and 57r are reproduced opposite p. 164.

[95] Emmerson, "Text and Image in the Ellesmere Portraits of the Tale-Tellers," p. 161.

[96] Hallam, ed., *The Chronicles of the Wars of the Roses*, p. 98. On this same page is a photograph of the Dunstable swan, now in the British Museum in London, an enameled version of this badge. On the evolution of badges which came to have political significance, see Joan Evans, *A History of Jewellery: 1100-1870* (1953; repr. London, 1970), pp. 64-67. Evans points out that "John Gower the poet on

his effigy in Southwark Cathedral wears . . . the swan pendant used by Henry in virtue of his first wife Mary Bohun," p. 65.

[97] Musée Condé, MS 65, fol. 4v.

[98] The gold medallions worn by some of the figures in the betrothal scene suggest that perhaps this is the insignia of a particular family. Jean Longnon and Raymond Cazelles, The "Très Riches Heures" of Jean, Duke of Berry (1969; rpt. New York, 1989), p. 175, speculate that the betrothal is that of the Duke's grand-daughter, Bonne, to Charles d'Orléans (April, 1410). The betrothal takes place on the castle grounds outside the walled orchard garden.

[99] On the association of the spring months in calendar pictures with courtly activi-ties, see Pearsall and Salter, Landscapes and Seasons, p. 140.

[100] In 1402 Parliament attempted to restrict anyone under "the rank of knight ban-neret" from wearing such wide sleeves; see Hallam, ed., The Chronicles of the Wars of the Roses, p. 98. Terry Jones, in Chaucer's Knight, p. 29, says the Squire is exe-cuting "a 'high school air' known as the capriole."

[101] Jill Mann, Chaucer and Medieval Estates Satire, p. 120, draws a comparison between Chaucer's Squire and the "unmarried gallant" described in Matheolus' Lamentations: "He sings, leaps or rides; he makes himself taller than he is. He has his hair often washed, curled, combed and parted. He wears well-soled shoes and gowns that are tight or flowing."

[102] See for example the picture of the youth combing his hair in the medallion on the wheel showing the Ages of Man in the De Lisle Psalter, London, British Library, MS Arundel 83, c. 1308-10, fol. 126v.

[103] London, British Library, MS Harley 4380, fol. 186v. This is reproduced in color in Elizabeth Hallam, ed., The Chronicles of the Wars of the Roses, p. 94, and in Peter Earle, The Life and Times of Henry V (London, 1972), p. 52. Henry, about to become Prince of Wales, as mentioned by Peter Earle, had been knighted by his father the day before the coronation (p. 39). Subsequently when he became king, Henry liked to present himself to his people as "the embodiment of justice"; see The Chronicles (above), p. 123. This Ellesmere visualization accords with the description of the young Prince Henry by one chronicler: "he was taller than most men, his face fair and set on a longish neck, his body graceful, his limbs slender but marvelously strong," while another chronicler draws attention to him as being "tall, clean-shaven, tight-lipped, sinewy and agile, more clerical than military in appearance"; see Hallam, The Chronicles, pp. 119 and 122 respectively.

[104] Glasgow, University Library, MS Hunter 409, English, c. 1440-1450. This is reproduced in color in Nigel Thorp, The Glory of the Page: Medieval and Renaissance Illuminated Manuscripts from Glasgow University Library (London, 1987), Plate 10. Thorp refers to the "exuberant play" of the "floral designs, chiefly of Lords-and-Ladies or Cuckoo Plant" on this page; see cat. no. 36, p. 89. For an extensive list of alternate English names, including "Knights-and-Ladies" see Cecil T. Prime, Lords and Ladies (London, 1960), pp. 216-17. Prime observes that during the medieval period it was thought that a plant's appearance revealed its uses to man; consequently, this plant was used as an aphrodisiac as well as one of the ingredients in love philters, p. 2.

[105] Kathryn Kerby-Fulton and Steven Justice, "Langlandian Reading Circles and the Civil service in London and Dublin, 1380-1427," New Medieval Literatures 1 (1998), 68 and plate on the facing page for the illustration on fol. 74r.

[106] Greg Walker, "The Green Knight's Challenge: Heroism and Courtliness in Fitt I of *Sir Gawain and the Green Knight*," *The Chaucer Review* 32.2 (1997), 120.

[107] Lerer, "Reading Like the Squire," pp. 68, 59, and 58 respectively.

[108] In Chaucer's translation, ll. 891-906; see *The Riverside Chaucer*, p. 696.

[109] Stevens, "The Ellesmere Miniatures," 125-26. Stevens has noted the similarities between the portraits of the Merchant and the Squire. He sees the Merchant as being rendered with "a spirit of joyfulness and play." The only qualification I would make is that this is how the Merchant would have liked to appear, but his avaricious facial expression betrays him.

[110] Sylvia L. Thrupp, "Trade and Gentility," in *The Merchant Class of Medieval London (1300-1500)* (Chicago, 1948), pp. 234-87. The information in the following sentences is summarized from this chapter.

[111] For a fuller discussion see Jacques Le Goff, "Trades and Professions as Represented in Medieval Confessors' Manuals," *Time, Work, and Culture in the Middle Ages* (Chicago, 1982), pp. 107-21.

[112] Thrupp, *The Merchant Class*, p. 175.

[113] See also the indentation of the bar border of the Chaucer illustration, fol. 153v.

[114] George Kane and E. Talbot Donaldson, eds. *Piers Plowman: The B Version, Will's Visions of Piers Plowman, Do-Well, Do-Better and Do-Best* (London, 1975), pp. 370-71, VII:18-38. Merchants were not given an absolute pardon in the margin of Piers's pardon because they would not keep holy days and because they swore.

[115] Thrupp, *The Merchant Class*, pp. 174-80.

[116] Ellis, "Spurs and Spur Fittings," p. 125.

[117] Christine de Pizan, *A Medieval Woman's Mirror of Honor: The Treasury of the City of Ladies*, trans. and introd. Charity Cannon Willard (New York, 1989), pp. 189-90. She particularly warns against extravagance in dress by women of property who seek to "inflate" their status by wearing garments appropriate "for a gentlewoman."

[118] See also 3110-13 concerning the pilgrims' response to the *Knight's Tale*.

[119] See Laura Kendrick's discussion of this wordplay in "The Jesting Borders of Chaucer's *Canterbury Tales*," *Animating the Letter*, pp. 217-25.

[120] The absence of pets in the case of the illustration of the Prioress shows that her portrayal has, by contrast, no ironic overtones.

[121] As it not infrequently is in this manuscript, perhaps due to damp and/or the placing of pages on top of each other before the black, evidently added last, was completely dry.

[122] David N. DeVries, "Chaucer and the Idols of the Market," *The Chaucer Review* 32.4 (1998), 394. See ProCkT 4343-48 in response to the Cook's offer to tell a "litel jape."

[123] Devils in medieval art are often portrayed with this attribute. As far as I am aware, the earliest western depictions occur in the influential Carolingian Utrecht Psalter, Utrecht, Bibliothek der Rijksuniversiteit, Cat. Cod., MS Bibl. Rhenotraiectinae, 1, Nr. 32.

[124] Cambridge, University Library, MS Gg. 4. 27(1), c. 1420-30, fol. 192v. See the discussion and reproduction in Kolve, *Chaucer*, pp. 264-67, fig. 126.

[125] This part of the painting (fol. 9v) was completed some seventy years later near the end of the fifteenth century by Jean Colombe, presumably working over the sketch by the Limbourgs, according to Jean Longnon and Raymond Cazelles, The "Très Riches Heures" of Jean, Duke of Berry, p. 178.

[126] Kolve, Chaucer, p. 258.

[127] That the designer was familiar with the Manciple's Prologue is apparent from the fact that the Manciple is illustrated with the gourd of wine (mentioned in ProMancT 82-83 and 91).

[128] Kolve, Chaucer, p. 259.

[129] See The Riverside Chaucer, p. 876 re. Jerome, who interprets the psalm image as a reference to the devil.

[130] Pearsall, The Life of Geoffrey Chaucer, pp. 234-35.

[131] See Pearsall's observations about Chaucer's innovative way of finding a place for the churl narrators of the fabliaux by "making the familiar equation between social class and moral behaviour"; The Life of Geoffrey Chaucer, p. 239.

[132] This is on the basis of a poem added to the head of the manuscript "copied by a hand probably trained in the third quarter of the century"; see Hanna and Edwards, "Rotheley, the De Vere Circle, and the Ellesmere Chaucer," 13. The Duke of Exeter (legitimized son of John of Gaunt) and the Duke of Bedford (Henry IV's third son) were the successive guardians of John de Vere; see Hanna, "Introduction," p. 1.

[133] This assumes that it may be more than a pointer for the reader to turn the page, being instead an indirect hint of the Welsh dragon. There is also a possibility that, since dragons appear throughout London, British Library, MS Egerton 3277, a Psalter and Hours that was probably made for Henry V's mother, Mary de Bohun, as pointed out to me by Denise Despres, there was a family interest in the dragon as a design element.

[134] Acc. 256596; like the panel portrait of Henry V, there are a number of copies, including a 1618 version. See Millar, The Tudor, Stuart and Early Georgian Pictures, cat. no. 4, p. 49.

[135] To use a term from Sandra Hindman, Sealed in Parchment, p. 127.

[136] See the quotation from the letter by Deschamps in note 10, above.

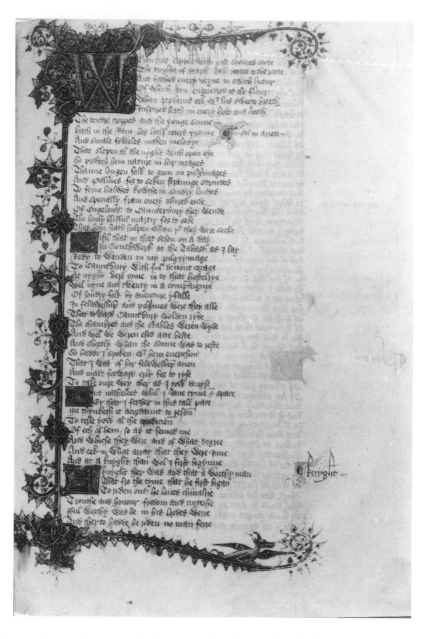

FIG. 1.   General Prologue, *The Canterbury Tales*, San Marino, Calif., Huntington Library, MS Ellesmere 26 C9, fol. 1r (by permission of The Huntington Library, San Marino, California).

56

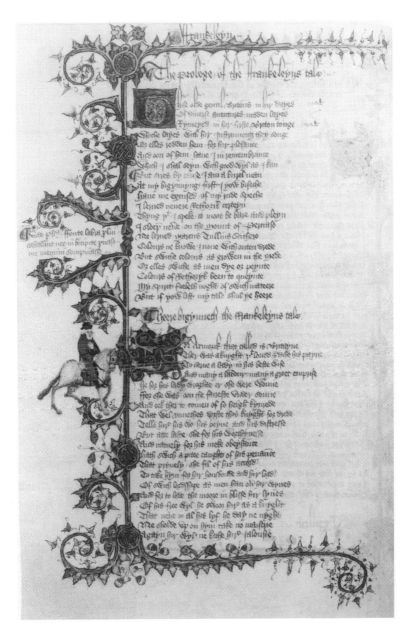

FIG. 2. The Franklin, *The Canterbury Tales*, San Marino, Calif., Huntington Library, MS Ellesmere 26 C9, fol. 123v (by permission of The Huntington Library, San Marino, California).

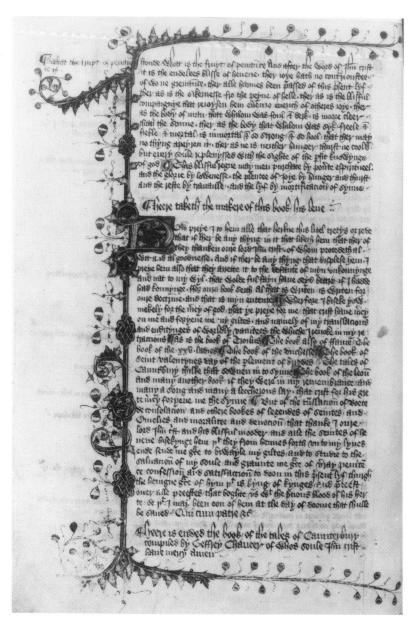

FIG. 3.   End of Parson's Tale and Chaucer's "leue," *The Canterbury Tales*, San Marino,
Calif., Huntington Library, MS Ellesmere 26 C9, fol. 232v (by permission of The
Huntington Library, San Marino, California).

FIG. 4. The Knight, *The Canterbury Tales*, San Marino, Calif., Huntington Library, MS Ellesmere 26 C9, fol. 10r (by permission of The Huntington Library, San Marino, California).

FIG. 5   The Riding Party, *The Collected Works of Christine de Pizan*, London, British Library, MS Harley 4431, fol. 81r (by permission of The British Library).

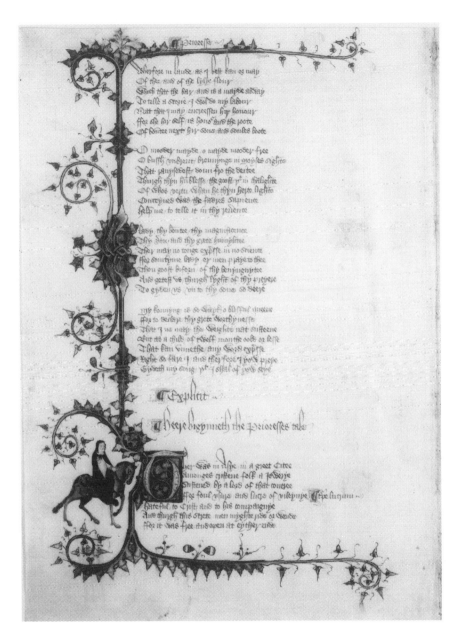

FIG. 6. The Prioress, *The Canterbury Tales*, San Marino, Calif., Huntington Library, MS Ellesmere 26 C9, fol. 148v (by permission of The Huntington Library, San Marino, California).

61

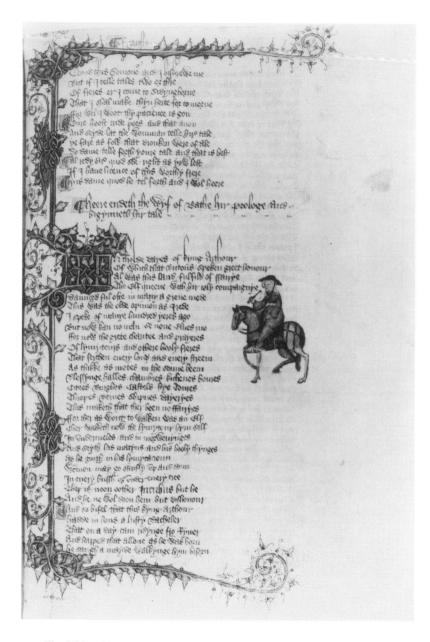

FIG. 7.   The Wife of Bath, *The Canterbury Tales*, San Marino, Calif., Huntington Library, MS Ellesmere 26 C9, fol. 72r (by permission of The Huntington Library, San Marino, California).

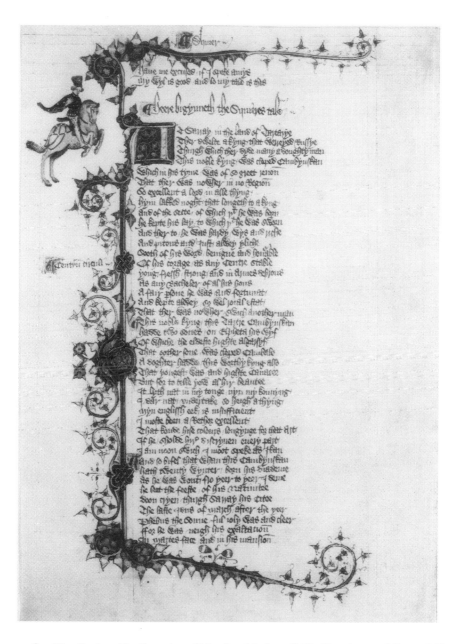

FIG. 8. The Squire, *The Canterbury Tales*, San Marino, Calif., Huntington Library, MS Ellesmere 26 C9, fol. 115v (by permission of The Huntington Library, San Marino, California).

FIG. 9. The Squire, detail, *The Canterbury Tales*, San Marino, Calif., Huntington Library, MS Ellesmere 26 C9, fol. 115v (by permission of The Huntington Library, San Marino, California).

64

FIG. 10. Henry V, panel portrait, Eton College, late fifteenth- or early sixteenth-century copy of lost original (by permission of Eton College Library; photograph Courtauld Institute of Art).

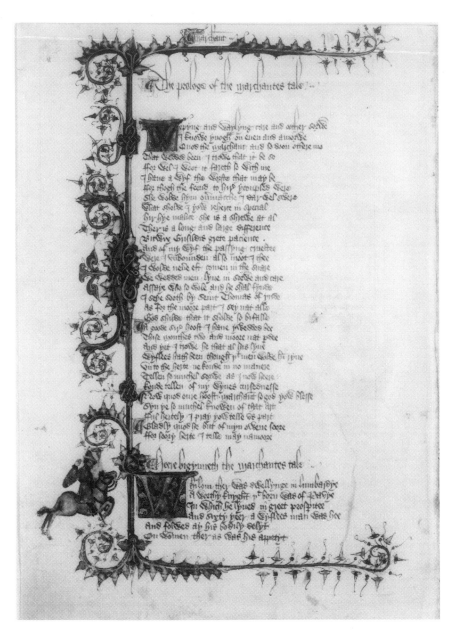

FIG. 11. The Merchant, *The Canterbury Tales*, San Marino, Calif., Huntington Library, MS Ellesmere 26 C9, fol. 102v (by permission of The Huntington Library, San Marino, California).

FIG. 12. The Miller, *The Canterbury Tales*, San Marino, Calif., Huntington Library, MS Ellesmere 26 C9, fol. 34v (by permission of The Huntington Library, San Marino, California).

FIG. 13. The Monk, *The Canterbury Tales*, San Marino, Calif., Huntington Library, MS Ellesmere 26 C9, fol. 169r (by permission of The Huntington Library, San Marino, California).

68

FIG. 14. The Cook, *The Canterbury Tales*, San Marino, Calif., Huntington Library, MS Ellesmere 26 C9, fol. 47r (by permission of The Huntington Library, San Marino, California).

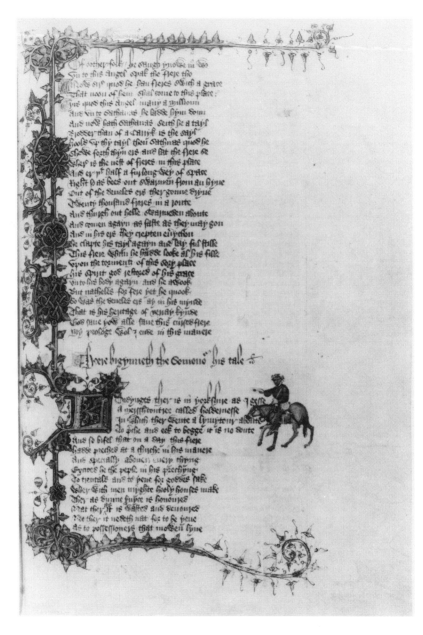

FIG. 15. The Summoner, *The Canterbury Tales*, San Marino, Calif., Huntington Library, MS Ellesmere 26 C9, fol. 81r (by permission of The Huntington Library, San Marino, California).

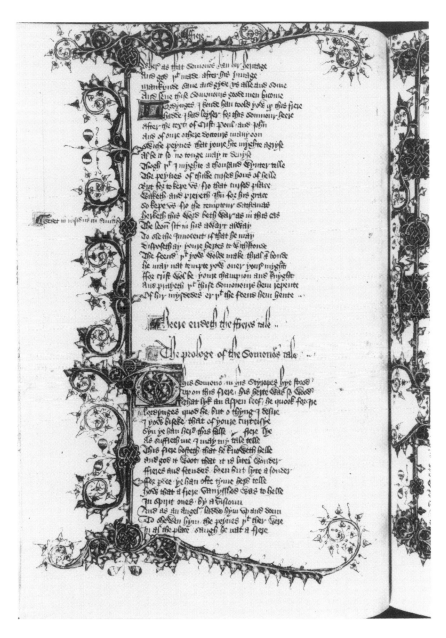

FIG. 16. Annotation from Psalm 10.8-9 at the end of the Friar's Tale, *The Canterbury Tales*, San Marino, Calif., Huntington Library, MS Ellesmere 26 C9, fol. 80v (by permission of The Huntington Library, San Marino, California).

Reading *Piers Plowman* C-Text Annotations: Notes toward the Classification of Printed and Written Marginalia in Texts from the British Isles 1300-1641

Carl James Grindley

Preface

In 1991 I was able to write, apparently with some degree of confidence, that "although many medieval manuscripts contain marginalia contemporary to their creation, very little research has been conducted on their content. In particular, it seems that the marginalia of *Piers Plowman* texts have been somewhat neglected."[1] In recent years, however, the study of late medieval insular marginalia has obtained a kind of academic cachet,[2] which unfortunately has not contributed much to the establishment of either a standard theory, or even a terminology, for describing marginal texts.[3] These shortcomings are due primarily to the historical neglect of marginal texts by cataloguers and by some textual scholars. Robin C. Alston — who entered the field from the more developed world of Coleridge marginalia study — claims that "the failure of librarians to appreciate the relevance of an important aspect of the post-publication history of books and [their] readers" has impeded the study of marginalia.[4] The study of medieval marginalia in particular is under-developed because of the relative newness of the field as a whole and the complex inter-relatedness of its constituent elements.

As far as manuscript catalogues are concerned, it is unlikely that the mistakes of the past will ever be repeated. For example, the British Library now actively understands the importance of what it used to call a "Few MS notes," and with its publication of Alston's book has helped to identify over 25,000 books containing marginal texts, including some 900 annotated incunabula.[5] Other catalogues also clearly indicate the presence of marginal texts, and some work has been done in publishing complete marginal texts for entire works.[6]

The greater issue, however, that of terminology and theory, requires effort even to begin to resolve. The problem may be approached from three separate angles. One, marginal texts may be analyzed according to medieval literary theory and the literary conventions of their day. Two, marginal texts may be analyzed according to contemporary literary theory. Three — the process I favor — marginal texts may be approached as descriptively as possible, with an eye to the future integration of different theoretical schools and the discovery of yet unknown historical data.

I think the only way to approach the sorts of marginal texts which appear in books from the late Middle Ages is pragmatically. I advocate that the greater theoretical concerns of contemporary critical thought be at least partially suspended until a significant, statistically meaningful sample of marginal texts is available to researchers. Unfortunately, very few marginal texts have been transcribed, and the process of transcribing and sorting marginal data lacks a clear methodology and a repeatable descriptive taxonomy. What follows, therefore, is a general discussion of manuscript marginalia; a proposed classification system for marks made in books, with examples from Huntington Library, MS HM 143 (MS X of the *Piers Plowman* C-Text, hereafter HM 143) and British Library, MS Additional 35157 (MS U of the *Piers Plowman* C-Text, hereafter Add. 35157); and complete transcriptions of both manuscripts' marginal texts.[7]

Introduction

The following system for classifying marginalia developed out of four major considerations and influences:

1) Certain paleographical assumptions and standards of presentation;
2) Limitation of the overall subject area to insular manuscripts written in Middle and Early Modern English;
3) A comparison of some of my suggested types of marginalia with medieval theories of textual reception and textual modes;
4) A comparison of marginalia in previously studied *Piers Plowman* manuscripts with those found other manuscripts of the late medieval and early modern periods.

First, the paleographical ground-rules used in the transcription of the marginalia have been adapted from the various writings of Malcolm Parkes, as follows:[8]

• The marginal texts have been re-lineated.
• Capital letters are used only where they occur.

- Latin abbreviations have been silently expanded.
- Expansions of Middle English and Early Modern English abbreviations, including superscripts, have been underlined.
- Spellings supplied in expansions relate to the standard expansion of the brevigraph, even where such expansions contradict the scribe's usual unabbreviated usage elsewhere in the same text.[9]
- The distinctions between "u" and "v," and "i" and "j" have been preserved;
- The double "s" ligature has not been preserved.
- The double "f" ligature has been standardized as "F."

The following symbols, modified from Parkes, have been used:

[ ]   Enclose words and letters which have been deleted by the scribe by means of crossing out, erasure, or expunctuation

| Indicates a line break

< >   Enclose letters which have been supplied in the transcription where the manuscript is deficient through damage, or where letters have been hidden by the binding. Where traces of the letter are still visible in the manuscript, the supplied letter has been printed in roman type. Where no traces of the letter remain, the supplied letter has been printed in italics. Where it is not possible to determine the nature of the missing letters from the context, dots have been supplied to indicate the number of letters which would fit into the space available. Underlines have been used to indicate either the expansion of partially recoverable abbreviation, or, when used with dots, an unrecoverable abbreviation.

⌋ ⌊   Enclose letters which have been added by a different hand

( )   Enclose letters which have been supplied either where the scribe has omitted them by mistake, or where he has omitted them on purpose but has failed to use the appropriate mark of abbreviation. They also enclose insertions of my own.

With special regard to the marginalia of HM 143, the following symbols also apply:

//   Indicates the presence of double virgules

|_   Indicates the presence of a combination bracket and underline

Second, although only two manuscripts of *Piers Plowman* are cited here, in arriving at the proposed classification system, I have minutely examined many diverse manuscripts from the British Isles where the main text was written in Middle or Early Modern English and where vernacular comment was supplied sometime between the years 1300 and 1641. The year 1300 was selected to coincide with the earliest datable and locatable manuscripts classified by the *Linguistic Atlas of Late Mediaeval English*. The terminal date of 1641 was deliberately chosen to reflect the continuity of marginalia found across the entire range of printed books covered by the *Short Title Catalogue* and the *Registers of the Company of Stationers*. All manner of texts were consulted: medical texts, poetry, dialogues, grammars, chronicles and legal documents.[10] Foreign language texts, manuscripts whose marginal texts were *entirely* written in Latin, and manuscripts of dubious origin in Middle or Early Modern English were excluded. Ideally, I would have included data and observations from continental or insular Latin texts, but I simply have not had the chance to conduct very much research in those areas. Therefore, it is pointless at this juncture to speculate whether or not the resulting observations hold true for other language traditions.[11]

Third, and as previously noted, I make no claim for any prescriptive pattern of annotation used either by scribes, printers, authors, or book owners. In my opinion, it seems that certain types of annotation relate to the tenets of medieval literary theory, but it is unclear whether annotators deliberately applied coherent theories to their marginalia, randomly or accidentally applied such theories, or if the resultant similarities between annotations and some aspects of medieval literary theory are entirely coincidental. I strongly suspect that most marginal comment is an echo of general medieval literary culture, a product of a particular understanding of texts, which was so common as to be nearly subconscious in its application.[12] When one compares marginal texts, even across a great range of books, the same basic types of marginalia appear again and again. Although the formal legitimacy of the parentage is in doubt, the likely ancestors of almost all of my proposed types and sub-types of manuscript marginalia may be found in two basic areas of medieval literary theory: the *ars grammaticae*, and scriptural hermeneutics. Of these two areas, the first is perhaps of greater importance, and is worth briefly describing.

The *ars grammaticae*, whose early medieval history has been documented by Martin Irvine in *The Making of Textual Culture*, may serve as an anchoring point for clues toward the reconstruction of the medieval understanding of texts. As Irvine points out, these grammatical arts go well beyond grammar *per se*:[13]

> *Grammatica* was responsible for some of the important features of manuscript format. For example, grammatical *lectio*, the rules for reading a text aloud and establishing the primary level of intelligibility, was linking methodologically to

the physical and visual format of the manuscript page. . . . Similarly, grammatical *enarratio* is methodologically connected to the development of the text and gloss format of literary and grammatical manuscripts in which the pages of a book were designed to include a gloss or commentary transcribed in the margins simultaneously with the main text.

As will be demonstrated, many of the most important sub-types of what I call Type III marginalia function directly as a manifestation of *enarratio*. As to scriptural hermeneutics, A. J. Minnis's *Medieval Theory of Authorship*[14] provided much useful historical information; influenced by his discussion and commentary, Kathryn Kerby-Fulton and Denise Despres have successfully linked medieval literary theory with specific *Piers Plowman* C-Text annotations.[15]

Fourth, much of the data and many of the examples in this paper have been taken from my earlier work on HM 143 and Add. 35157.[16] Although the classification systems presented in my master's and doctoral work have been subject to much revision, many of the original subtypes of marginalia remain unchanged.

The remainder of this essay proposes a working system wherein different types of manuscript marginalia are described and subjected to classification. This system is still under development and will no doubt continue to be refined with further research.

The Classification of Marks Made in Books

There is some confusion over exactly what is meant by "marginalia." The term is not satisfactory, mostly because the usual definition of a "margin" is too narrow. There are many types of margins, some of which are not necessarily found beyond the bounding lines of bifolio. Flyleaves, for example, are the *ur*-margins of books, and it is equally easy to recognize that the blank leaves which separate texts are marginal to other logical structures and so on. At least within the sphere of insular Middle English and Early Modern English manuscripts and printed books, three basic types of marginalia can be distinguished:

- TYPE I, which comprises marginalia that are without any identifiable context;
- TYPE II, which comprises marginalia that exist within a context associated with that of the manuscript itself; and
- TYPE III, which comprises marginalia directly associated with the various texts that the manuscript contains.

A description of each classification and its sub-categories, most of which are briefly illustrated, follows. Where some confusion might arise (as with the complex series of Type III Narrative Reading Aids), more in-depth illustrations taken from *Piers Plowman* manuscripts HM 143 and Add. 35157 have been provided. In addition, each type of marginal comment is given its own unique abbreviation.

Type I Marginalia

The simplest type of marginalia, Type I marginalia, may be divided into four basic sub-types:

 i) OWNERSHIP MARKS (I-OM)
 ii) DOODLES (I-DO)
 iii) PEN TRIALS (I-PT)
 iv) SAMPLE TEXTS (I-ST)

 i) **Ownership Marks** (I-OM) usually take the form of genealogical details or names written on the flyleaves or on the main folios of a manuscript. Such marks were often arranged to show some respect for the contents of the manuscript, although it is not rare for owners' names or the records of family births and deaths to be written directly over the manuscript's texts, or on interior folios, rather than on its flyleaves. Ownership marks frequently obscure previous ownership marks. They include booksellers' marks, price codes and historical and contemporary shelf-marks.[17]

 ii) **Doodles** (I-DO) are defined as simple drawings which are clearly the work of non-professional artists who in turn were uninspired by any reading or supposed reading of a manuscript's text or texts. All professionally-created illustrations, even if they lack any conceivable textual relevance, may be considered to have a manuscript-oriented context, that is decoration for decoration's sake. Such works would qualify for membership in the Type II family of marginalia. All illustrations with direct textual relevance, whether professionally executed or not, are considered as Type III marginalia.

 iii) **Pen Trials** (I-PT) are perhaps the most common example of TYPE I marginalia, although it is important to differentiate between a pen test and an attempt to duplicate the manuscript's various scripts. While an Elizabethan late secretary hand appearing in a pen-trial in a fourteenth-century document written in *anglicana formata* is an example of Type I marginalia, an Elizabethan attempt at duplicating an *anglicana formata* alphabet may be seen as an example of TYPE II marginalia, since it obviously relates to the manuscript within which it appears.

 iv) **Sample Texts** (I-ST) are the most difficult sub-category of Type I marginalia to classify and require careful analysis before final demarca-

78

tion. Sample Texts are defined as being short works, in either poetry or prose, which were added in an unplanned if not haphazard manner to a non-related existing text.

For example, whereas medical receipts in a seventeenth-century hand found on the flyleaves of a fourteenth-century literary text might be considered Type I Sample Texts, the same receipts when found in a fifteenth-century medical text might be said to be examples of Type II Additional Text (II-AT) marginalia.

The same general context rule may hold true for more complex examples. In Hunterian MS 232, an ill-used copy of Lydgate's *Life of Our Lady*, several folios contain the same lines of doggerel verse.[18] On three occasions, the verse is limited to a single couplet. Since it is quite clear that the verse was copied, not to preserve it, but to aid in the teaching of a type of secretary script, it is not contextual with the manuscript itself, even though MS 232 is a collection of poetry. If, however, the verse had been systematically preserved, then it would be Type II Additional Text (II-AT). At the other end of the scale, if MS 232's doggerel verses somehow related either to Lydgate's religious vocation or to the text of the *Life of Our Lady*, and were systematically copied, they would be classified as examples of Type III Polemic Response (III-PR).

Type II Marginalia

Type II marginalia are much more sophisticated than Type I marginalia, and consist of a far more complex range of sub-types, eight in all:

   i) COPIED LETTERFORMS (II-CL)
  ii) COPIED ILLUMINATIONS (II-CI)
 iii) COPIED PASSAGES (II-CP)
  iv) ADDITIONAL TEXTS (II-AT)
   v) MARKS OF ATTRIBUTION (II-MA)
  vi) TABLES OF CONTENT (II-TC)
 vii) INTRODUCTORY MATERIALS (II-IM)
viii) CONSTRUCTION MARKS (II-CM)

i) **Copied Letterforms** (II-CL) or scripts are quite common. Hunterian MS 232, contains, for example, many sixteenth-century attempts at re-creating fifteenth-century lombardic capitals and other floriated initials. While these sometimes primitive efforts do not seem to have any textual basis, their creation would have been impossible without the models readily at hand. In many cases, much-damaged manuscripts (e.g. MS 232) not only contain re-creations of various decorated initials, but are missing the original patterns. It seems likely that some non-professional scribes learnt elements of their art from manuscripts which were used as combination copy and note books.

ii) **Copied Illuminations** (II-CI) are significantly more rare than copied letterforms or initials; they often take the form of pen outlines of existing illuminations, or, more frequently, added pen tracings made directly on existing illuminations. More common than full copied illuminations are details copied from decorations, such as small sections of copied acanthus leaf borders, or copies of the grotesques found in the floriation and vine-work of decorated initials.

iii) **Copied Passages** (II-CP) are quite common. In MS 232, for example, the bottom-most stanza on each folio was often duplicated in the manuscript's bottom margin, and, more often than not, was written in a script quite similar to the manuscript's own.

iv) **Additional Texts** (II-AT) must be distinguished from Type I Sample Texts (I-ST), as indicated above. To complicate matters, Additional Texts may go beyond offering thematic echoes of a text and may actually offer complex comment. For example, any prayer for salvation found at the end of a *Piers Plowman* manuscript has an obvious relationship with the general subject matter of the poem and must be considered as an example of Type II marginalia. On the other hand, it might be argued that a Wycliffite sermon added to a manuscript of *Piers Plowman* is a precise comment on the text, and therefore must be classified as a Type III Polemic Response (III-PR). Obviously a line must be drawn between the existence of a few Additional Texts in an otherwise unitary manuscript and the more complicated issues of *compilatio* regarding commonplace books and other collections.

v) **Marks of Attribution** (II-MA), whether seemingly correct or blatantly false, are very interesting and reveal an annotator's need not only to preserve his or her own understanding of a text's origins, but also to show some concern for future readers or for future owners. Some examples of attribution include those that are patently false, for example, colophons copied *ad literatim*.[19]

vi) **Tables of Contents** (II-TC) become common added features in late Tudor times. Many tables of contents make for interesting reading; some divide unitary works into numerous sub-sections, while others collect divergent works into a single section of text. MS 232 exemplifies the first process in a written note, now inserted into the manuscript's bindings, that divides *Life of Our Lady* into six distinct works.

vii) **Introductory Materials** (II-IM) constitute the most interesting and complex sub-group of Type II marginalia. Most commonly, they appear as suggested titles for an entire manuscript, or brief descriptive notes identifying the main theme or subject of a work.

viii) **Construction Marks** (II-CM) are those marks which persist from the manuscript's initial period of construction, such as limner's marks and the like. Although such marks do not offer any direct comment on a manuscript, they are useful tools in comparing the goals of the production of a manuscript to the work actually carried out by its scribes. Kathleen Scott's "Limning and Book-Producing Terms" offers a short guide to some of the marks associated with the manufacture of manuscripts, and provides excellent samples of the major types of limner's marks, many with accompanying illustrations.

Type III Marginalia

By definition, the presence of Type III manuscript marginalia implies a coherent reader response to a particular text, since all annotations and miscellaneous marks which lack conceivable textual context have already been accounted for in Type I and Type II. The proposed division of Type III marginalia, therefore, delineates the most common systems of reading texts, or in any event *Piers Plowman* texts,[20] and has been designed to help organize basic concepts and answer four simple questions: what was a particular reader interested in; how did a particular reader organize a text; what reactions did readers make to particular passages; and were the comments made along any general themes?

Although my classification of Type III marginalia was developed primarily with *Piers Plowman* C-Texts in mind, it is now quite clear that all the identified sub-types exist in other Middle English or Early Modern English annotations. Manuscripts of Chaucer, for example, seem prone to accumulating Source and Citation annotations.

This classification system does not imply that scribes or owners consciously planned how to annotate any given text, although a strong argument can be made that certain systems of marginalia were deliberate parts of a text's intended *ordinatio*. Clearly some scribes were aware that their annotations fell into broad categories; for example, the annotator of HM 143 used two different types of brackets, one type for identifying plot summaries, and one type for direct addresses to his intended readership. The question of "bespoke" annotations, that is texts added by request to aid a patron's reading of a difficult vernacular text, will have to remain unanswered, although the examination of a great many manuscripts suggests that the case for tailor-made reading aids is a strong one.[23] Additional research will undoubtedly illuminate this topic.

Although this study is confined to the period and type of manuscript discussed above, it should be noted that in the early days of printing, it was not unheard of for scribes to copy printed annotations.[24]

There are five sub-types of Type III marginalia:

i) NARRATIVE READING AIDS (III-NRA)

ii) ETHICAL POINTERS (III-EP)

iii) POLEMICAL REPONSES (III-PR)

iv) LITERARY RESPONSES (III-LR)

v) GRAPHICAL RESPONSES (III-GR)

i) **Narrative Reading Aids** (III-NRA) comprise most written elements of a manuscript's *ordinatio*, whether they be original features of the work or later additions to it. Later additions to a manuscript's *ordinatio* often arise when the original elements — for example embedded rubrics, running heads, foliation and the like — did not represent a fine enough division of a text to enable a cursory reader to navigate through its contents at will. In other cases, perhaps because of poor copying, a text loses its intended *ordinatio* or picks up a misleading or incorrect one. Scribes and their readers reacted to a need for further textual demarcation by creating more and more elaborate reading aids which were designed to enhance reading ease. Thus, Narrative Reading Aids not only comprise the most common sub-type of Type III marginalia, but contain a significant number of categories and sub-categories. In fact, there are presently eight categories and four sub-categories of Narrative Reading Aids:

a) TOPIC (III-NRA-T)

b) SOURCE (III-NRA-S)

c) CITATION (III-NRA-C)

d) DRAMATIS PERSONAE (III-NRA-DP)

e) RHETORICAL DEVICE (III-NRA-RD)

f) ADDITIONAL INFORMATION (III-NRA-AI)

g) TRANSLATION (III-NRA-TR)

h) SUMMATION

    1) TEXTUALLY-GLEANED MARGINAL RUBRICS (III-NRA-SM-TGMR)

    2) PARAPHRASED MARGINAL RUBRICS (III-NRA-SM-PMR)

    3) CONDENSED OVERVIEWS (III-NRA-SM-CO)

    4) TEXTUAL EXTRAPOLATIONS (III-NRA-SM-TE)

Narrative Reading Aids probably originated in the early Middle Ages. According to Irvine, the science of interpreting, *scientia interpretandi*, was divided into four distinct areas: the science of reading, *lectio*; the science of interpretation, *enarratio*; the science of correction, *emendatio*; and the science of criticism, *iudicium*. This model was in place during the early Middle Ages from approximately 350 to 1100 AD, but, as Irvine suggests, it influenced literature until the late Middle Ages:[26]

> The expectations for literacy and the basic principles of literary theory continued to be directed by grammatica in the twelfth through fourteenth centuries. In English literature, the works of Chaucer, Langland, and Gower continually reflect on the assumptions and values of grammatical culture.

Of the four branches of the *scientia interpretandi*, *enarratio* is most easily applied to the study of late medieval marginalia. *Enarratio* comprised sets of rules for interpretation. Irvine lists "tropes, topics of commentary, myth, syntactic and semantic classification," and includes with these, "marginal glosses; treatises on figures and tropes; running commentary."[27] As will become obvious, a certain number of Narrative Reading Aids clearly deal in these very areas of interest. Narrative Reading Aids are very common elements of any medieval manuscript's marginal supply. For example, out of the 208 non-graphical marginal notes in HM 143, over fifty per cent are Narrative Reading Aids. The term "narrative" used in the context of Narrative Reading Aids, does not presuppose that notes were necessarily created to identify only issues of actual narrative plot and the like; these notes instead were made to suggest discrete navigations of texts.

The first category is **Topic** annotation, which merely indicates the general theme or basic subject matter of a small block of text.[28] Consider the annotation in Add. 35157 at passus I:33 (fol. 11r):

Measure   Mesure is medecyne, though þe muche ȝerne

Here, hand G has identified "measure" as the topic of this section of the text.

The second category of Narrative Reading Aids annotations is **Source** annotation. Though generally uncommon in *Piers Plowman* manuscripts, one such annotation can be found in Add. 35157 at Prologue 111 (fol. 8v):

Samuel.1.Cap.4   Anoen as hit was told him þat þe childron of yrael
                 Wern disconnfit in bataile & araca Domini lorn
                 And his sones slaw þer he fel anoen fro his chaier
                    þer he sat
                 And braek his necke on tweyen

83

As Pearsall points out,[30] this book of the Old Testament is called the *Liber Regum* 1 in the Vulgate, so it can be assumed that Hand G, who wrote the note, had access to an English translation of the Bible.

The third kind of Narrative Reading Aids, **Citation** annotation, transcends simple source identification and provides direct quotations from authorities or other texts.[31] Though not appearing at all in HM 143 and only twice in Add. 35157,[32] Citation annotations are readily found in other vernacular and Latin texts, like Chaucer's *Canterbury Tales* and Peter Lombard's commentaries on the Scriptures.[33] Many of the annotations to the *Canterbury Tales* have been independently analyzed by Stephen Partridge, and pioneering work on the *Wife of Bath's Prologue* was carried out by Graham Caie.[34]

According to Susan Schibanoff, the annotations to Chaucer's *Wife of Bath's Prologue* take three basic forms: they cite the title of an analogue or source; quote the analogue or source without providing any indication of title; or provide both the title and text of an analogue or source.[35] Caie suggests that these annotations were designed to control and temper interpretation of the Wife's logic and use of language, while Pearsall argues that they were simply citations of well-known authorities.[36]

The fourth category of Narrative Reading Aids, **Dramatis Personae** annotations, identify the various characters within a work. This sort of annotation is very common in Middle English poetry, and, for example, comprises the majority of the annotations to Chaucer's *Troilus*.[37] As far as *Piers Plowman* is concerned, a typical example of this category of annotation can be found in HM 143 at passus VI:91 (fol. 24v):

|_ Repentance   þus redily qu<u>od</u> repentaunce / and thow be ryht sory
                       For thy synnes souereynly / and biseke god of m<u>erc</u>y

Although this annotation appears rather simple, it is ambiguous enough to pose a question: does scribe B's note indicate the topic of repentance, the allegorical character Repentance, or perhaps both? Scribe B used two framing devices: a combination bracket and underline (here shown as |_), and double virgules (shown below as //). Judging by annotations to II:9, II:30, VI:145, VI:164, VI:309, IX:106, IX:140, XI:96, and XI:86, it is possible to ascertain that the |_-device was used, for the most part, to identify the poem's characters, and that the //-device was used to indicate topics and summaries. Therefore, it is relatively safe to say that this example is indeed a Dramatis Personae annotation.

Rhetorical Device annotations, the fifth kind of Narrative Reading Aids, outline grammatical or logical processes. These annotations differ from the Literary Responses sub-type in that they merely show what rhetorical device is present, and refrain from entering into debate with the text. They are quite rare in HM 143, occurring only three times.[38] Like the Citation category, Rhetorical Device annotations bear some resemblance to Peter Lombard's marginal annotations to an early copy of the *Sentences*, as Parkes has shown:

> Rubrics at the beginning of each chapter define the topic under discussion, but in this early copy there are also other rubrics placed in the margin at certain points, sub-headings like "prima causa," "secunda," "tercia," "obiectio," "responsio," which serve to identify stages in the argument within the chapter.[39]

An example of this category of annotation can be found in HM 143 at passus XIII:193 (fol. 59v):

Responcio   And resoun aresonnede me / and sayde rethe þe neue<u>re</u>
               Why y soffre or nat soffre certes he sayde
               Vch a segge for hym sulue salamon vs techeth
               de re que te non molestat noli te certare

This annotation is clearly interpretive, and shows HM 143's scribe B making a deliberate attempt to delineate the process of argument from a scholarly perspective.

The scarcity of Rhetorical Device annotations in the *Piers Plowman* manuscripts and Hunterian Collection manuscripts that were examined for this study has left the sub-type relatively undeveloped. A study of a larger number of manuscripts would probably either identify a more complete array of annotations which would encompass the range of Rhetorical Devices open to a medieval audience, or it could, on the other hand provide significant clues regarding the transmission and general application of medieval rhetoric.[40]

The sixth category, **Additional Information** annotations, comprises any annotations which purport to provide additional information, not from recognised authorities, but from the scribes themselves.[41] In Add. 35157, for example, at passus III:241 (fol. 21v), hand I has misinterpreted Langland's allusion to the French campaigns of the mid-fourteenth century, and at the bottom of the folio has written: "kinge | henri the 6 was a simpell Religious man, w<u>hich</u> was the loose of his fathers heritage in Fraunce."

The seventh category of Narrative Reading Aids, **Summation** annotation, is itself divided into four sub-categories: Textually-Gleaned Marginal Rubrics, Paraphrased Marginal Rubrics, Condensed Overviews, and Textual Extrapolations.

Summation annotations differ from other Narrative Reading Aid annotations in their derivation and purpose. Other Narrative Reading

Aids hold some affinity to the scholarly world of Peter Lombard's scriptural commentaries, and treat their texts in very formal ways, dividing them into logical stages and providing citations of authorities. Conversely, whereas those categories delineated formal process, Summation annotations reveal purpose and content. They are less concerned with matters of academic formality and logical structure, and are more concerned with creating a narrative navigation of the text.

In general, Summation annotations function as extra-linear non-authorial rubrics. In this regard, they bear some resemblance to the rubrics Lucy Freeman Sandler identified with James le Palmer's work in the fourteenth-century compilation, the *Omne bonum*:

> The rubrics themselves vary in the quantity and kind of information they provide, as well as in their physical format. The most elaborate and detailed tend to be written across the full measure of the text column. They name the topic, give some hint of the range of contents, the method or conclusions, and refer to the main and subsidiary sources.[42]

While very few Summation annotations embody all of the qualities that Sandler observed in Palmer's compendium, two of the sub-categories of Summation annotation, the Textually-Gleaned and the Paraphrased Marginal Rubrics, usually display at least two of her descriptions' attributes, that of citing a passage's general topic and listing its contents in summarized form. The difference between these two forms is that a Textually-Gleaned Marginal Rubric quotes the text directly, while a Paraphrased Marginal Rubric paraphrases it.

A typical Textually-Gleaned Marginal Rubrication Summation annotation can be found in HM 143 at passus VI:350 (fol. 28r):

Now bygynneth gloton / for to go to shryfte	Glotonyȝe goþ
And kayres hym to kyrkeward / his coupte to shewe	to schryfte

HM 143's scribe B has taken this annotation almost directly from the poem's text, but has made one small change: he has shifted Langland's Glutton character to the sin of gluttony.

Paraphrased Marginal Rubrics usually take the form of inter- or intra-linear contractions. The annotation in HM 143 at passus VIII:205 (fol. 37r) is an excellent example:

Tho hadde \<Peres\> pitee vppon alle pore peple	hyer \<pers\> bad
And bade hung<u>er</u> in haste / hye hym out of contraye	hung<u>er</u> go aȝen
Hoem to his owene ȝerd / and halde hym þ<u>er</u>e eu<u>er</u>e	

Scribe B simply condensed the action across two lines, and in the process lost some of the sense of the passage. The marginal comment makes no mention that Hunger is to leave permanently, only that Hunger is to go away.

The third sub-category of Summation Narrative Reading Aid annotations is slightly harder to define and is, perhaps, simply a broader, more ambitious form of Paraphrased Marginal Rubrication. This sub-category is the Condensed Overview. To distinguish it from both species of Marginal Rubrication, arbitrary limits have been placed on its reach and scope. If an annotation condenses more than two lines of text and summarizes narrative, it is considered a Condensed Overview. For example, consider the annotation in HM 143 which accompanies passus II:217-21 (fol. 10r):

Drede stod at þe dore / and þe dene herde	
What was þe kynges wille / and wyghtliche wente	for drede
And bad falsnesse to fle / and his feres alle	falsnesse
Falsnesse for fere tho / fleyh to þe freres	fley3 to þe
and gyle doth hym to gone / agaste for to deye	frers

Here scribe B incorporated elements from several lines to create this annotation, thereby drawing attention to the cause and outcome of the action.

The final sub-category of Narrative Reading Aid Summation annotation is the Textual Extrapolation Summation annotation. One occurs in HM 143 at passus XIV:72 (fol. 60v):

Astronomy3e	Kynde wittede men han a clergie by hem sulue
	Of cloudes and of costumes / they contreude mony thynges
	And markede hit in here manere and mused þer on to knowe
	And of the selcouthes þat þei sye / here sones þer of þei tauhten
	For they helden hit for an hey science here soti tees to knowe
	Ac thorw here science sothly / was neuere soule ysaued
	Ne brouhte by here bokes / to blisse ne to ioye

Though it may seem a confusing, I define Extrapolated Summations as those Summations carried over two lines of text and which condense topics rather than narratives.

ii) **The Ethical Pointers** (III-EP) sub-type may be seen as direct demonstrations of ethical positions, as based on a medieval classification of literary modes, and may be divided into the following categories:

a) PRECEPTIVE POINTS (III-EP-PP)
b) EXEMPLIFICATIONS (III-EP-EXP)
c) EXHORTATIONS (III-EP-EXH)
d) REVELATORY ANNOTATIONS (III-EP-REV)
e) ORATIVE ANNOTATIONS (III-EP-OR)
f) DISPUTATIVE ANNOTATIONS (III-EP-DM)

The following examples of Ethical Pointer annotations have been adapted from Kerby-Fulton and Depres's work on Douce 104,[43] which, as previously noted, is a manuscript of Piers Plowman whose text is believed to be a genetic pair with Add. 35157.[44]

Starting from A. J. Minnis's work on the medieval theory of authorship,[45] Kerby-Fulton shows that the medieval reader not only gained an understanding of textual modes from the Bible, but applied the resulting knowledge to literary texts.[46] The classifications of biblical *modi*, for example, are "very helpful in making sense of the massive amount of didactic annotation in Douce 102 as well as in other [manuscripts]."[47] From Alexander of Hales, she identifies five basic categories: Preceptive Points, which are found in the Pentateuch (*modus praeceptivus*); Historical and Exemplificative Points, which are found in the Historical books (*modus historicus and exemplificativus*); Exhortations, which are found in the Sapiential books (*modus exhortivus*); Revelatory Modes, found in the Prophetic books (*modus revelativus*); and Orative material, which is found the Psalter (*modus orativus*). In addition to Hales's categories, Kerby-Fulton adds Disputative Mode (*modus disputativus*), which may be found in the Book of Job and in the work of the Apostle Paul.[48] She provides the following examples:

• A **Preceptive Point** may be seen in Douce 104 on fol. 88r at passus XIX:96, where the annotating scribe has written: "nota to low god abow al þynges & þi neghtbour."

• An **Exemplification** may be seen in Douce 104 on fol. 15v at passus III:323, where the annotating scribe has written: "houu god ȝaw Salamon grace & tok hit from hym ayayn."

• An **Exhortation** may be seen in Douce 104 on fol. 67v at passus XV:78, where the annotating scribe has written: "be war of fals freris."

• A **Revelatory Annotation** appears in HM 143 on fol. 17r at passus III:454, when the annotating scribe writes: "lo how iewe schull conuerte for ioye."

- An **Orative Annotation** appears in Douce 104 on fol. 70r at passus XV:245, when the annotating scribe writes: "nota de pater noster."
- A **Disputative Annotation** appears in HM 143 on fol. 52r at passus IX:249, when the annotating scribe writes: "Culorum."

iii) **Polemical Responses** are anchored to social or political issues raised in the text, may be directed to situations described in the text or applied to situations contemporary with the commentator, and are divided into the following three categories:

- SOCIAL COMMENT (III-PR-SC)
- ECCLESIASTICAL COMMENT (III-PR-EC)
- POLITICAL COMMENT (III-PR-PC)

These three sub-types are fairly common. As is shown in chapters 6 and 7 of my unpublished study of Add. 35157, they make up a large proportion of that manuscript's marginalia.[49] Polemical Responses comprise all marginal notes which identify some sort of social, ecclesiastical or political concern and offer comment.

An example of a **Social Comment** occurs in Add. 35157 at passus VIII:33 (fol. 48v), where hand I writes: "the poore I are gluttons I in harvest I tyme." Hand I's comment is somewhat misguided, since that at this point in the text Piers is promising the knight that he will work hard to produce food.

An **Ecclesiastical Comment** occurs in Add. 35157 at passus V:65 (fol. 30r), where hand I writes: "basterds fitt for slauerye." In this situation, hand I's comment is motivated by Langland's discussion of the proper attributes for members of the clergy.

An example of a **Political Comment** occurs in Add. 35157 at passus III:381 (fol. 23v), where hand I writes: "hipocreticall I pucritans I are/Indirecte."[50]

iv) **Literary Responses** may be divided into the following four categories:[51]

- READER PARTICIPATION (III-LR-RP)
- HUMOUR AND IRONY (III-LR-HI)
- ALLEGORY AND IMAGERY (III-LR-AI)
- LANGUAGE ISSUES (III-LR-LI)

In general, **Reader Participation** enter into dialogue with the text. One appears in Add. 35157 on fol. 91v at passus XVII:276, when hand G writes: "an Vnsownd I opynion." Another appears in Add. 35157 on fol. 75v at passus XIV:171, when hand G writes: "a pretye & right I seme-lye comparason I betwene the rich I man & ye peacok."

Humour and Irony annotations comment on, rather than merely identify (as in Rhetorical Device annotations), humorous or ironical passages. The annotator of Douce 104 often notes such material. At passus XXII:183 (fol. 109r), for example, he is clearly delighted by the play on receding hairlines and comments: "nota de helde yede ouer men <ys> hedys."[52] Such work, Kerby-Fulton asserts, reminds us that "medieval readers were not necessarily the stern moralists we have been told they were."[53]

Allegory and Imagery annotations comment on allegorical, metaphorical or other "poetic" elements of the text. For example, Add. 35157's hand G often comments on metaphors, as on fol. 99r at passus XIX:117, where he writes: "A symilitude of I y<u>e</u> trenytie & y<u>e</u> hande."

Research to date suggests that **Language** annotations are relatively rare in the thirteenth and fourteenth centuries but become more common in the fifteenth and sixteenth centuries.[54] Comparing the contents of Add. 35157, Douce 104 and HM 143, reveals that Language annotations appear with any regularity only in Add. 35157, and even then, only take the form of translations from Latin and Middle English into Early Modern English.[55] A good example of a bad translation occurs in Add. 35157, when at passus VII:104 (fol. 40r), hand I has written:

For thi y rede ʒou riche • reueles when ʒe make
Forto solace ʒour soules suche mynstrals to haue
foulbage ar   þe pore ⌋may⌊ for a [foulsage] ⌋piper⌊ • sittinge at þi
babpype   table

Here, Add. 35157's scribe B decided to "correct" the text, and transformed "foulsage" into "piper." Hand I, seeing the remnants of scribe A's sigma-shaped "s," probably thought it was a "b," and therefore quite confidently defined "foulbage" as "babpype."

v) My examinations of **Graphical Responses** (III-GR) is still preliminary, so this is the least developed of all types of marginal comment. Nevertheless, four categories can tentatively be suggested:

- ILLUMINATIONS (III-GR-ILM)[56]
- INITIALS (III-GR-INT)[57]
- PUNCTUATION (III-GR-PUN)
- ICONOGRAPHY (III-GR-ICON)

Of these four categories, only Punctuation and Iconography can, at this stage, be described with any confidence.

Punctuation as a Graphic Response usually refers to placement of paraph marks, caesura, virgules, double virgules and the like, but other marks are also important. In "The Life of a Book," I discuss the extra-textual motivations apparently behind the scribe's use of *commata* in Add.35157.

Here the term **Iconography** refers to any systemised form of graphic shorthand. In HM 143, for example, the manuscript's scribes used a simple crown to indicate prophecy.[58] Perhaps the most common form of Iconography are marginal pointing hands of any kind (i.e., whether attached to an arm or not).[59] They can take the form of an entire arm or merely the hand itself. Heads are also used for the same indicative function, but so far remain unnamed.[60]

Conclusions and Applications

The above system for the classification of insular annotations should be useful in achieving an overall reading of a manuscript's marginalia. Perhaps the best way to approach a given work is to reconstruct an over-all reading based on the whole range of marginalia, or to compare two manuscripts of the same text, in order to see how readings differed or agreed. One of the major objections that I have to my own system is that the act of classification seems to require some reconstruction of autho-rial intent. In Add.35157, for example, many of Hand I's marginal com-ments could be interpreted in a variety of ways. It is unclear, at times, whether a selected note is a Translation, a Summary or a Polemical Response. The issue of reconstructing intent, however, diminishes in importance if some consistency is applied to classification, and if the process of sorting annotations is used to produce a general under-standing of the basic types of comment made by early commentators. The relative densities of each type of marginal note should work in pro-viding clues to an annotator's motives and objectives.

As previously stated, this system is still under development, and more work is certainly required. It is hoped other researchers will refine it, and that new categories and sub-types will be added to accommodate newly discovered or newly defined types of annotation. What follows is a brief description of Add. 35157 and HM 143, and complete tran-scriptions of their respective marginalia.

The Marginalia of Add. 35157

There is good reason to believe that Add. 35157 is the earliest copy of the third version or C-Text of William Langland's fourteenth-century alliterative poem *Piers Plowman*.[61] Like many other manuscripts of the C-Text, Add. 35157 is very heavily annotated, and like Bodleian Library,

Digby 102, it contains marginalia contemporary with its creation as well as annotations from a variety of later readers and owners.

The manuscript probably dates to the period between the final composition of the C-Text and the turn of the fifteenth century. The main text was written in a light brown ink in a highly professional yet understated *bastard anglicana*, with Latin phrases in *textualis rotunda* with some *anglicana* influences. The scribe signs himself "Preston" on fol. 124r and is possibly the same Preston who wrote the Missal of Abbot Nicholas Litlyngton in 1386 (Westminster Abbey Library No. 37). Including scribe A, there are eight hands roughly contemporary to the manuscript's construction:

Scribe 1	illumination
Scribe 2	initials and pen decorations
Scribe A	main text
Scribe B1	red pen underlining fols. 7r-25v
Scribe B2	red pen underlining from fols. 26r-124r
Scribe B	interlinear corrections and annotations
Scribe C	interlinear corrections and annotations
Scribe D	annotations

The appearance of some of hand B's annotations in the rubrication ink suggests that hands B1, B2 and B were the work of same scribe. Scribe B was possibly the A-scribe of Trinity Cambridge MS R.3.2.

Add. 35157 suffered damage to its first quire (possible rodent damage) and was repaired s.XVI$^{2-3}$ by Thomas Thyrnbeke, who signs his name on fol. 124v. Two patches cover holes on fols. 10r to 11v, and the top part of fol. 9r has been completely replaced. The missing text was re-supplied from either the second or third of Robert Crowley's 1550 editions of *Piers Plowman*. Thyrnbeke has been assigned hand E for his repairs and F for his marginalia.

Although Add. 35157's origins are somewhat obscure, it was owned by the Surtees family of County Durham until the mid-sixteenth century, when it became the property of the Ayscough family of Cottam, Lincolnshire; after the mid-seventeenth century, it resided with the Johnson family of Spalding, Lincolnshire, until January 7, 1898 when it entered the British Museum.

Nearly a thousand marginal notes in eight non-contemporary marginal hands labeled E- L litter the folios of Add. 35157. Of these eight hands, E-J contributed the bulk of the manuscript's enormous marginal supply. The hands range from the mid-fifteenth to early twentieth centuries and are presumed to be the work of the following individuals:

Hands E and F	Thomas Thyrnbeke s.xvi$^{2-3}$
Hands G and H	Sir Edward Ayscough s.xvi$^{3-4}$
Hand I	Francis Ayscough s.xvi^{4}-xvii^{in}
Hand J	Maurice Johnson s.xviii^{in}
Hand K	Robert Machill s.xv
Hand L	British Museum Staff (?) s.xix^{ex}

Much data has been accumulated on Add. 35157 and its scribes, including dialectology and biographical analysis, but space concerns makes further discussion in this article impossible. Therefore, no transcriptions of the introductory texts, running heads, extant catchwords, illuminations, initials, or quire signatures have been provided. Texts from the flyleaves following folio 124r have been omitted.

The Marginalia of HM 143

The Huntington Library in San Marino, California, came into possession of MS HM 143 following a 1924 sale at Sotheby's.[62] The manuscript proved to contain a previously unknown copy of the C-Text of *Piers Plowman* and was the twenty-sixth such text to be found. Recently, the manuscript has moved to the forefront of C-Text studies, forming the copy-text of the recent Athlone Press critical edition by Kane and Russell. Previously, it served as the basis for Derek Pearsall's exemplary 1978 edition of the poem, which was the first modern edition of the C-Text since Skeat's.

Perhaps one of the more interesting features of HM 143 is its impressive number — over 200 — of contemporary annotations. With the rise in interest in *Piers Plowman* marginalia, and since these comments have never been completely published, it was decided to present them in a quick-reference form.[63] No interpretation of the data is presented, but a brief discussion of the manuscript, a description of the annotating scribe's work, and some brief notes on certain paleographical and codicological assumptions have been included.[64] No transcriptions of the catchwords, the running heads, the quire signatures, the corrector's marks, the fragmentary *Troilus*, or the fragmentary *Piers Plowman* have been provided. Neither have I given the locations of doodles, rubrications, initials or illuminations.

Like the majority of *Piers Plowman* C-Text manuscripts, HM 143 is relatively unassuming, but is by no means a cheap or unprofessional product.[65] Judging from the hands used in its construction and the basic pattern of its codicology, HM 143 probably dates no later than the end of the first quarter of the fifteenth century.[66]

Distinctive hands, use of different regional dialects, brevigraphical conventions, ink overlays and basic work methodologies indicate that HM 143 was created by more than one scribe, and was, most likely, the product of between three to five scribes working more or less sequentially. For the purposes of this article, these scribes have been identified as:

Scribe A	main text
Hand 1	lombardic capitals
Hand 2	initial illumination
Scribe R	rubrication and some correction
Scribe B	annotations and corrections

Their work on HM 143 probably comprised the following eight stages:

1. preparation of the bifolios
2. main text written by scribe A
3. primary correction by scribe A
4. construction of booklets and addition of lombardic capitals
5. rubrication, including other elements of *ordinatio*, some corrections by scribe R
6. secondary correction by scribe B
7. booklets sewn together
8. annotation by scribe B and final binding

Scribe B worked in a purple-brown ink, which contrasts with Scribe A's light brown ink. Scribe B's hand also differs considerably from Scribe A's and may be described as an *anglicana cursiva* with some *formata* and *semi-quadrata* features.[67] In particular, Scribe B used a cursive "w" with a left-leaning elongated central loop, while scribe A used a much less spacious, far more formal style. There are also major differences between the letters "h," "k," "s," and "3."[68] Scribe B's hand appears on the whole more rushed and less concerned with conventions than Scribe A's almost pure book hand.

Although the number of items found Scribe B's dialect survey is quite limited, his usage seems to indicate that he favoured a southwest Midlands dialect, and was perhaps from the Somerset area.[69] Given Samuels's general analysis of the rest of HM 143's dialect,[70] and its possible connection to Glastonbury Abbey,[71] it is not unlikely that Scribe B would also be a southwesterner. It may be supposed that when Scribe

94

B's interlinear corrections are studied in relation to his annotations, a clearer picture will emerge, but that data awaits more detailed analysis than can be afforded in this paper.

The HM 143 marginal text has been transcribed from the Chambers facsimile of the HM 143 and checked against both a microfilm and the manuscript itself.[72] Although the Chambers facsimile includes some ultra-violet readings, the manuscript, where permitted, was also examined under ultra-violet light. The folio numbering used is based on the Huntington Library's collation by Chambers.[73] The passus and line numbering used is that of Pearsall's 1978 edition of the C-Text.[74] No emendations have been made except where the manuscript has been damaged and there is little doubt as to the original content. Although none of the correcting/annotating scribes used punctuation in the marginalia, original brackets and underlinings have been preserved as closely as possible.

The Add. 35157 marginal text has been transcribed from microfilm and compared repeatedly against the manuscript itself, which (when permitted) was examined under ultra-violet light. Like the marginalia from HM 143, the Add. 35157 material is keyed to Pearsall's edition.

Transcription of Add. 35157's Marginalia

FOLIO/LINE	CLASSIFICATION	CONTENT	HAND
FR	MA	This book was written and daited the 10 of the ides ⌊of⌋ Marche ye Seconde yere of Kinge John of famous memorie by Peers Plowman Pensionare ⌊or rather Seruant⌋ to the said King as John Gowere Recordethe quoth Francis Aiscoughe	I
7R:P:10	?	Pers his <...> ‖ of all welth	I
7R:P:13	PR-EC	Hierulalem <....>	I
7R:P:14	PR-EC	Roma	I
7R:P:16	?	T<...>	I
7R:P:19	?	h<....>	I
7R:P:19	NRA-T	Middell earth	I
7R:P:22	?	<....>	I
7R:P:23	?	<....>	I
7R:P:24	?	<....>	I

7R:P:25	?	<....>	I
7R:P:27	NRA-T	cloyst<....> and frier<....>	I
7R:P:29	?	<....>	I
7R:P:32	NRA-TR	licame I ye epicurie	I
7V:P:33	NRA-SM-TE	Fidlers cannot I Ryghtwiss can	I
7V:P:36	NRA-SM-CO	Ayenst mynstrels & countrefetes	G
7V:P:40	NRA-T	bawdy pepill	I
7V:P:41	?	against <...> kings <...>	G
7V:P:44	PR-EC	begers main be in I by abbies and I nunries.	I
7V:P:49	NRA-T	pylgrymes	G
7V:P:49	NRA-T	& there I ancres	I
7V:P:54	NRA-T	hermytes	G
7V:P:54	NRA-T	& there I Hores	I
7V:P:60	NRA-T	& freares	G
7V:P:64	GR-ICON	(pointing hand)	G
7V:P:64	PR-EC	famous Kinge I Henry Viij I fulfillid in I his time	I
7V:P:64	PR-EC	ye light of ye truthe	I
8R:P:70	NRA-T	wicked men	I
8R:P:70	NRA-SM-CO	Ayenst pardoners	G
8R:P:70	EP-EXH	not<a>	I
8R:P:71	NRA-T	lewed pardoners	G
8R:P:76	EP-EXH	nota	B
8R:P:76	PR-SC	ye pore I bleed	I
8R:P:78	PR-EC	parsons I and parr<esh> I clarkes gitt I thereby profitt	I
8R:P:78	NRA-T	bysshops	G
8R:P:89	NRA-T	byshopps Tellers I and officors in I ye exchecare	I
8R:P:90	EP-EXH	<n>ot<a>	I
8R:P:93	NRA-T	all offices in I the Clergie	I
8R:P:95	EP-EXH	nota	I
8R:P:95	EP-EC	This conscience is now supposed I to be Kinge James ye Sixt I to punishe the couitousnes of the clergie I of Brittaine	I
8V:P:99	NRA-SM-CO	Ayenst prelates I & prestes	G

8V:P:111	NRA-S	Samuel.1.cap.4	G
8V:P:114	NRA-SM-CO	olde Helies punnishment	I
8V:P:119	EP-EXH	not<a>	I
8V:P:120	EP-EC	for Idolatrye | God will take | vengeaunce ou__er__ | prest__es__ chiefly	G
9R:P:139	EP-EXH	nota	I
9R:P:139	NRA-TR	who maid many | knightes | his strengh	I
9V:P:167	NRA-SM-CO	ye talle | of ye cat | & raton__es__	F
10R:P:204	NRA-C	omnium doctissimorum suffragio dicun tur hec de lassiuis, fa tuis, aut in eptis principi bus, non de etate tenellis quasi dicat, vbi rex puerilis est	F
10R:P:214	PR-PC	the insaysiablines | of y__e__ lawyers	I
10R:P:218	PR-PC	will the catt | y__e__ kinge and | the kittnes | distroye	I
10R:P:223	PR-PC	evne nowe | at hande	I
10V:I:7	NRA-SM-PMR	The most people | desyre Wo__r__ship.	G
10V:I:25	NRA-S	genicis	I
10V:I:25	NRA-AI	Loot first | planted | grappes	I
11R:I:33	NRA-SM-TE	Measure	G
11V:I:60	NRA-T	y__e__ Deuill	I
11V:I:62	NRA-T	Cayn	F
11V:I:63	NRA-T	Judas	F
11V:I:72	PR-EC	True = Religion & not y__e__ Popp	I
11V:I:81	NRA-SM-TE	Charytie.	G
12R:I:90	NRA-SM-TE	ordo__ur__ of knygtes	B
12V:I:118	NRA-T	<Lu>cyfers | Hall | in | Imo Celi	I
12V:I:126	NRA-T	lucyfers fall.	G
12V:I:136	NRA-SM-TGMR	Trewth is | ye greate<..> | treasur	F
12V:I:146	NRA-AI	or Carritas ying	I

12V:I:146	LR-AI	A Simmoly I as Treacle or Medridat, expulseth pouison in ye body I So loue, and godly charitie, expulseth sin in the soule.	I
12V:I:146	NRA-T	Love	G
13R:I:147	NRA-T	Love	G
13R:I:176	NRA-T	Almesse	G
13V:I:180	PR-EC	no muritt in I any worcks	I
13V:I:182	NRA-SM-TE	instifinige I faith only I work inge.	I
13V:I:187	EP-EXH	not<a>	I
13V:I:187	NRA-SM-CO	ye couuitous I of ye clergie	I
13V:I:192	NRA-T	vncharytable I chaplaynes	G
13V:I:197	NRA-SM-TE	Love & truth	G
14R:II:6	NRA-DP	false & favell I fyckell tonge & I Lyar	G
14R:II:10	PR-EC	ye Purpill whore I of Rome I Meed & Favill I Antichrist	I
14R:II:19 truth.	NRA-SM-TE G	Meede or Reward I enemye to	
14R:II:25	NRA-SM-PMR	Meede a Basterd is I doughter to favell	G
14R:II:28	NRA-S	christs parable in Mathewe	I
14V:II:51	NRA-SM-CO	Meede shalbe I maryed to I Falsehod./	G
14V:II:54	NRA-SM-CO	Theyr Names yat I wer bydden to ye I mariage./	G
14V:II:63	EP-EXH	nota	B
15R:II:78b	NRA-C	maritagium prauum cum feoffemento in malo feodo de peruersa tenura.	F
15R:II:96	?	Turne	I
15V:II:119	NRA-SM-CO	the kynred of I Meede./	G
16R:II:140	NRA-SM-CO	who is occaucoun yat ye church is broght lowe	F
16V:II:165	NRA-SM-CO	Meede rydeth to I Londan to be I ayvised by law I if she shall I marry falshod	G
16V:II:177	NRA-SM-CO	what ho I rses ya<t> I had yrode I with mede	F

17R:II:200	NRA-SM-CO	trewth maketh I hast to ye kyng	F
17R:II:216	NRA-SM-CO	dreyde maketh ye I gyleye fle	F
17R:II:220	NRA-SM-CO	falshod flyeth to the frers	H
17R:II:221	NRA-SM-CO	gyle is shut up in merchauntes I shops.	H
17V:II:231	NRA-SM-CO	lyar is puld I into pardoners house	H
17V:II:234	NRA-SM-CO	dwelled with I physycans I polycaryes I mystrelles I messengers I & is fetched into I the Freares.	H
18R:III:9	NRA-SM-CO	courtissaire I inbrasheth I Meed ye maid I and setteth I by hir	I
18V:III:42	NRA-SM-PMR	the freare I shryveth mede	H
18V:III:56*	EP-EXH	nota	B
18V:III:57	EP-EXH	Reade this syde	H
18V:III:59	NRA-SM-CO	hit is but I originall I sinne of I frailtie	I
18V:III:62	NRA-SM-CO	seuenne sinne<s> I drawne out of I Adams loines	I
18V:III:66	EP-EXH	nota	I
18V:III:66	NRA-SM-CO	sonne pardoned	I
18V:III:69	PR-EC	the deuosion I of Supersticion	I
19R:III:80	NRA-SM-CO	three Bees thatt stinge I the poore & nedy	I
19R:III:99	PR-EC	our lady a Mediator	I
19V:III:111	NRA-SM-CO	Against I vserers& I Regraders I yfrancheised	I
19V:III:118a	NRA-SM-CO	Meed corr I upteth I all estaits	I
20R:III:142	NRA-SM-CO	Meed shulde be I married to truth I and reason or I consience but I Refusseth them I all to take crafte	I
20R:III:149	EP-EXH	nota	C
20R:III:157	NRA-SM-CO	Meed is fauls of faith I and ficle of tonge	I

20V:III:164	NRA-SM-PMR	Meed a common | Strumpitt	I
20V:III:185	PR-EC	Meed y<u>e</u> Pops | Darlinge | and the | Prestes | Baude	I
20V:III:190	NRA-SM-PMR	wo to that | realme | where | Meed | Mastereth	I
21R:III:211	NRA-SM-PMR	y<u>e</u> clergie w<u>ith</u> Meed | are turned into | gyle	I
21R:III:215	NRA-T	Meeds fained Annswere to the Kinge	I
21V:III:241	NRA-AI	Peers liued | in Henri | the sixt | his daies | who lost | his heritage | in Fraunce | w<u>hich</u> his father | had wonne	I
21V:III:256	EP-EXH	nota	I
21V:III:260	NRA-AI	kinge | henri the 6 was a simpell Religious man, <u>which</u> was | the loose of his fathers heritage in Fraunce	I
22R:III:270	NRA-SM-TE	the Pope reneth by | corrupcion of Meed	I
22R:III:283	NRA-SM-CO	Meed pr<u>e</u>fared by y<u>e</u> | Kinge before consience	I
22V:III:310	NRA-SM-CO	Reward<u>es</u> of | masse pr<u>estes</u>	H
23R:III:328	NRA-SM-CO	Sallomons Sauluacion | dobtefull.	I
23V:III:381	PR-EC	hipocreticall | pueritans | are | Indirecte	I
24R:III:413	NRA-TR	Dauid caulled a knaue, becausse he was Sauls man | not that he was one butt by cause he was A | Shepperd	I
25R:III:449	EP-EXH	nota	B
25R:III:451	NRA-SM-PMR	Love & Conscyence | shall make Lawe a | Laborer.	H
25R:III:454	NRA-SM-CO	y<u>e</u> Jewes muste | be conuerted | to the faith | before thi<s> | tyme	I
25R:III:467	NRA-SM-CO	The reformed | clergie | schall rule | the Kinge	I

25R:III:472	NRA-SM-CO	siuill lawe I taken clene I away for I sellinge of I Sinne	I
25V:III:477	EP-REV	nota I a prophesi	B
25V:III:479	NRA-SM-CO	ye Jewes ye I Sophic and I the Turcke I shalbe con- I uertet to I ye faith.	I
26R:IV:36a	EP-EXH	nota	I
26R:IV:36a	LR-RP	Script i6o3 I Thus farr of prophises yet to come I all the reste followinge are past Isauing the fall of ye lawe and Bishopps I nowe at hande.	I
26V:IV:67	NRA-SM-PMR	laweyers I vse handy I Dandy	I
27V:IV:113	PR-EC	Nunc quam I in Anglia I but in the I lande of I conqueste	I
27V:IV:118	NRA-SM-PMR	bishopes I must be backers I bruers and I tailors	I
27V:IV:118	EP-EXH	nota	I
28R:IV:139	NRA-SM CO	Reson telleth wronge I and Meede yat lawe I for abush shalbe I come A laborour.	I
28R:IV:144	NRA-SM-CO	lawe shall not rul I but fauoure by med\<e\>	I
28R:IV:144	EP-EXH	nota	I
28R:IV:147	PR-PC	The abuse of lawe, shall cause it I to falle	I
28R:IV:158	EP-EXH	\<n\>ota	I
28R:IV:158	NRA-TR	who that is I marriede quoth con\<science\> I his goodes shalbe I Covuntted	I
28R:IV:161	NRA-SM-CO	Meed a durtie commo\<n\> I Strmpit both in I siuill lawe and I common	I
28V:IV:165	PR-PC	princes I Counsell I should be I ruled by I conshouns I & Resoun	I
28V:IV:174	NRA-SM-CO	loue and I good lyff I to be the I lawe	I
28V:IV:174	EP-EXH	nota	I

28V:IV:182	NRA-TR	warres= & sworde	I
28V:V:2	NRA-SM-CO	pers dwelled in I cornewell with I his frind christofor I or his wyf Catte I in there beds I had a vision	I
29R:V:4	PR-EC	peres became a I protestant and I loued his lyke.	I
29R:V:30	PR-EC	lowlars regarded I not fridaies I fast.	I
29V:V:35	EP-EXH	nota	I
29V:V:36	NRA-SM-CO	brought I in a I cloystere.	I
29V:V:44	EP-EXH	nota	I
29V:V:44	NRA-SM-CO	peres a I beginge I frier which I was an I easie lyfe	I
29V:V:55	NRA-SM-CO	pastors should I be of knowlege I reputed and I Mecke	I
29V:V:61	EP-EXH	nota	D
29V:V:63	NRA-SM-CO	pastors of I good paran- I tage and I chaystly I married.	I
29V:V:66	NRA-SM-CO	no I basterds	I
30R:V:65	PR-SC	basterds fitt for slauerye	I
30R:V:72	NRA-SM-CO	merchantes knightes I gentelmen I there printices	I
30V:V:111	NRA-T	ye worlde	I
30V:V:115	NRA-SM-CO	fained I hollynes I for pride	I
31R:V:128	NRA-SM-CO	pure hippocracy I reproued.	I
31R:V:138	NRA-SM-PMR	Spare the rood I and spill ye child.	I
31R:V:141	NRA-SM-CO	pastors muste I do as they teche	I
31R:V:145	NRA-SM-CO	, prelaitts loue I of decimes & I lords take th<er> I linamges.	I
31R:V:146	EP-EXH	nota	B
31R:V:151	NRA-SM-CO	againste non I residence I and pleasure I and purcas<e> I in prelaitts	I
31R:V:151	NRA-SM-CO	heaven & ease I on earth is in I cloyster.	H
31V:V:162	GR-ICON	(pointing hand)	B

31V:V:166	NRA-AI	A prophecye.trulye | fulfilled by Kinge | henrye.the.viij.th	G
31V:V:171	NRA-SM-TGMR	ad pristinum statum	B
32R:V:194	EP-EXH	nota	B
32V:V:197	NRA-SM-CO	Reason against pil- | grimage to Sanctus | butt to trueth	I
32R:VI:1	NRA-DP	Prowde harte	H
32V:VI:13	PR-EC	Repentaunce biddeth | Pride become lowly | meaninge ye clergie	I
32V:VI:35	NRA-SM-CO	A discription | of fained | hippocracy	I
32V:VI:43	EP-EXH	nota	I
33R:VI:62	NRA-DP	Envye	H
33R:VI:71	NRA-SM-CO	ye nature of | Envye.	I
33V:VI:103	NRA-DP	Wrath	H
33V:VI:118	NRA-SM-T	collerricke deuines | vnperfitt prechers	I
33V:VI:122	NRA-SM-CO	emulacou | in all degres	I
34R:VI:131	EP-EXH	nota	H
34R:VI:138	NRA-SM-CO	A descri | ption | of wrath | at large	I
34R:VI:147	EP-EXH	nota	I
34V:VI:159	NRA-SM-CO	causeth fluxes	I
34V:VI:160	LR-RP	fatt | fole	I
34V:VI:166	NRA-SM-CO	wine Inne | witt oute	I
34V:VI:171	NRA-DP	Lecherye.	H
34V:VI:171	PR-EC	in the | clergie | and others	I
34V:VI:180	NRA-T	places of lechery	I
34V:VI:181	PR-EC	ye fruites | of friday | fast and | steeuues	I
34V:VI:189	PR-SC	bawdy | songes | and bauds | mirces of | lecherye	I
35R:VI:191	NRA-SM-CO	lecherie had by sorcery | or ells by Rapine | lecherie de<..>ersching	I
35R:VI:196	NRA-DP	Covetyse	H
35R:VI:198	EP-EXP	William. | Aiscough	I
35R:VI:199	NRA-SM-CO	marks of covetise | folckes	I

35R:VI:203	NRA-TR	in a torne coote	I
35R:VI:207	NRA-TR	an vseror or marchant	I
35R:VI:215	PR-SC	Drapers drep	mens purses	I
35V:VI:226	PR-SC	decepte in	ailewines	I
35V:VI:234	NRA-SM-CO	She robbid	hir gestes	a slepe	I
35V:VI:241	NRA-T	lumbards	crafte	I
36R:VI:285a	NRA-SM-CO	filthy & bitinge	vsurie	I
36V:VI:299	EP-EXH	nota	B
36V:VI:304	PR-EC	vsure is	compared	to the Pops	stues rente	I
37R:VI:338a	EP-EXP	exemplata usque <...>	B
37R:VI:344	EP-EXH	nota	B
37R:VI:349	NRA-DP	Glotoun	B
37R:VI:350	NRA-DP	Glotonye	H
37R:VI:351	NRA-SM-CO	Glotonye wil	faste on all	Fridayes	I
37V:VI:357	NRA-SM-CO	the nature	of gluttony	I
37V:VI:366	LR-HI	the sabothes	in thos daies	well keppte	I
37V:VI:367	NRA-SM-CO	companions	of the ale	Rood.	I
38R:VI:400	NRA-SM-PMR	gluttonnys horne his	tale	I
38R:VII:3	NRA-DP	Slewthe.	H
39R:VII:30	EP-EXH	nota	C
39R:VII:30	PR-EC	Slewthe the badge	of the clergie	I
39R:VII:36	NRA-SM-CO	a forsworne	lyer.	I
39R:VII:42	NRA-SM-CO	ingratfull	I
39R:VII:45	NRA-SM-CO	bribery	I
39R:VII:49	NRA-SM-CO	wast gods	good brontie	I
39V:VII:59	PR-SC	wanhope	haith	deceaued	many a	foullyhe	youth.	I
39V:VII:70	NRA-SM-TE	the branches	of slewth	is to live with	oute gods fere	I
39V:VII:75	LR-LI	vsury	I
39V:VII:82	NRA-SM-CO	againste	bawdy	Jesters	I
39V:VII:82	EP-EXH	nota	B
40R:VII:97	NRA-SM-CO	the good poure	to be releued	before Minstrils	I
40R:VII:101a	NRA-S	dicit christus	I

40R:VII:102	NRA-SM-CO	feastes banckits	I
40R:VII:103	NRA-TR	may	I
40R:VII:103	NRA-TR	piper	I
40R:VII:104	NRA-TR	foulbage ar	bagpype	I
40R:VII:112	?	re	I
40V:VII:125	NRA-T	Adams	fall	I
40V:VII:138	NRA-T	blyshed	Mary	I
41R:VII:144	NRA-T	a secret of ye trinnitie	I
41R:VII:149	PR-EC	ye corruption of yat time	I
41R:VII:156	PR-EC	ye people were blindfolded	by superstission	I
41V:VII:172	NRA-TR	in Bethlem Jud<ea>	I
41V:VII:177	EP-EXH	nota	I
41V:VII:192	NRA-SM-TE	ye nature	of truth	I
41V:VII:200	LR-RP	ye Author	Tome tell	truth	I
42R:VII:206	NRA-SM-CO	The waye to truthe	H
42V:VII:241	PR-EC	preaer to such is not	ye way to truth	I
42V:VII:241	PR-EC	ye error of	yat time	I
42V:VII:243	EP-EXH	marke	I
42V:VII:250a	PR-EC	nay rather per christum	I
42V:VII:250a	EP-EXH	not<a>	I
43R:VII:270	NRA-SM-TGMR	vij systers that	serve Truthe	H
43R:VII:272	NRA-SM-TGMR	Abstenence.1	Humilitie.2	Charritic.3	Chastitie.4	Pacience.5	Pease.& 6	Largenesse.7	I
43R:VII:283	NRA-SM-CO	a Cutpurshe and	a Beartward haue	no truth at all	I
43R:VII:283	EP-EXH	nota	C
43R:VII:287	NRA-SM-TE	ye Author	commends truth	with mercye	I
43R:VII:291	LR-RP	duringe this pilgramace	I
43R:VII:298	NRA-S	ye parrable of ye bidd to ye marriag<e>	I
43V:VIII:2	EP-EXH	nota	C
43V:VIII:8	NRA-SM-CO	meane	and gentill	women	liue by ye	plowghe	I
44V:VIII:71	NRA-SM-TE	Idell	roges	shalle	wante	brede	I

44V:VIII:73	NRA-SM-TE	fryers & theire order<s> I wiped out of gods I booke	I
45R:VIII:90a	NRA-TR	we must not do as they do but I as they saye I the clergie I teachethe	I
45R:VIII:95	NRA-SM-TE	The will of I Pers plouthman	I
45V:VIII:143	NRA-SM-TE	Pers will I releue the I impotente I poore but I not Idell I vacabonnds	I
46R:VIII:152	EP-EXH	<n>ota	I
46R:VIII:152	NRA-SM-TE	England harboreth more I theues and beggers I then any countrie	I
46R:VIII:156	EP-EXP	exemplata usque h<...>	B
46R:VIII:158	NRA-SM-TGMR	wasters and I rioters make I things deare	I
46R:VIII:173	PR-PC	nota Brittaine shalbe bitten I with hungere when the I plouth shalbe I neclected by I inclosers	I
46R:VIII:173	EP-EXH	nota	I
46V:VIII:201	NRA-SM-TE	sir hunger I enimie to I Idelnes	I
47R:VIII:223	NRA-T	hungers counsell	I
47R:VIII:240	NRA-SM-CO	he that will I not laboure I ys not I worthy to I eate	I
47V:VIII:262	EP-EXH	nota	C
47V:VIII:274	NRA-T	Dyet	H
48R:VIII:285	NRA-T	Almesse	H
48R:VIII:291	NRA-SM-CO	Idelness I causeth I sicknes I mode I fat I labor I to I phisissians	I
48R:VIII:293	EP-EXH	bewaire of I dogge leches I pictpurses	I
48R:VIII:304	LR-RP	nota I peres I was a I pecke I man	I
48R:VIII:304	NRA-SM-CO	the ploughman I diet graue I chesses and I potage or I croudes I and milcke	I
48V:VIII:310	NRA-T	A poore I dyete	I
48V:VIII:333	NRA-SM-CO	the poore I are gluttons I in harvest I tyme	I

49R:VIII:344	GR-ICON	(pointing hand)	H
49R:VIII:344	NRA-SM-CO	famyn through I floodes.	H
49R:VIII:350	EP-REV	nota bene prophesi	B
49R:IX:1	EP-EXH	nota	C
49R:IX:1	EP-EXH	nota	I
49R:IX:1	PR-PC	the kinge I of skootes	I
49R:IX:13	LR-RP	butt not proud I pralaites	I
49R:IX:13	EP-EXH	nota	B
49R:IX:17	NRA-SM-PMR	lordes lecher<y> I abollyshede	I
49R:IX:8	EP-EXH	nota	I
49V:IX:24	NRA-T	Marchauntes	H
49V:IX:45	NRA-T	Lawyers.	H
50R:IX:51	NRA-SM-TE	A cauiat to Laweyers	I
50R:IX:51	EP-EXH	nota	C
50R:IX:61	NRA-T	Beggers	H
50R:IX:75	NRA-T	the true I nedye	H
50V:IX:91	NRA-T	the true nedye	H
50V:IX:97	NRA-SM-PMR	feede the I lame and I the blinde	I
50V:IX:107	NRA-T	madmenn & I lunatyk I beggers	H
51R:IX:114	NRA-SM-CO	thes kinde of men sometimes prouisie the truthe	I
51R:IX:120a	NRA-AI	huc	B
51R:IX:131	NRA-T	Lewde mynstrelles	H
51R:IX:136	NRA-SM-TGMR	godes mynstralles	H
51V:IX:159	NRA-T	the false nedye	H
51V:IX:162	EP-EXH	nota	C
51V:IX:162a	EP-EXH	nota	D
52R:IX:175	NRA-T	the true nedye.	H
52R:IX:187	NRA-T	lewde I hermyttes beggers	H
52R:IX:194	NRA-T	holy hermyttes	H
52V:IX:212	NRA-T	lollers hermyttes	H
53R:IX:242	NRA-T	lollers and I lewde hermyttes	H
53R:IX:245	NRA-AI	Sovenday I deriued of the I vij day I dominica I domini	I
53R:IX:246	EP-EXH	nota Bene	C
53R:IX:255	NRA-SM-PMR	bisshopes the I Cause of ignorunt I pasters at this I day	I
53R:IX:255	NRA-AI	(of ma) ⌋ny⌊ (bisshopes)	I

53R:IX:260	PR-EC	Bisshopes dare not barck | against the offences of | oure staite	I
53R:IX:266	EP-EXH	nota	I
53R:IX:266	NRA-SM-CO	skabbed hirelings | skabbed sheepe	I
53R:IX:266	NRA-TR	under a durtie Dauver	I
53R:IX:267	PR-EC	Interiectio | pastor | wantinge both | currage and | a barkinge | dogg	I
53R:IX:273	NRA-SM-CO	A bluddy curssed was | vppon careles pastors | when they shalbe | caulled to an | accompte	I
53V:IX:275	NRA-T	A hirelinge	I
53V:IX:280	NRA-TR	no pardon helpeth	H
53V:IX:282	PR-EC	A prittie | interogation | with a secret | discouerie | of the popes | game of all | bulles	I
53V:IX:290	NRA-SM-TGMR	but doo well | & | haue well	H
54R:IX:325	NRA-SM-CO	Doo well is better | then ye Popps | bulles	I
54R:IX:325	EP-EXH	nota	I
54R:IX:332	EP-EXH	nota	D
54R:IX:333	NRA-SM-CO	Dowell | ys better | then ye | Popes | trionalls	I
54V:IX:344	NRA-SM-CO	pardons nor | Indulgences | will helpe	H
55R:X:21	LR-RP	do well dwells | not amonste | friers allwaies	I
55R:X:28	EP-EXH	nota	I
55V:X:76	NRA-T	doowell	H
55V:X:82	NRA-T	DooBetter	H
56V:X:89a	NRA-SM-CO	A description | of witt	I
56R:X:90	EP-EXH	nota	D
56R:X:92	NRA-T	DooBest	H
56V:X:127	EP-EXH	nota	D
56V:X:133	NRA-TR	the soule | of Man= | kinde	I
56V:X:134	NRA-TR	The deuill	I
56V:X:143	NRA-SM-CO	inwitt | hath fiue | daughters	I
57R:X:151	NRA-AI	and Nature	I

57R:X:151	PR-EC	god I only	I
57R:X:156	NRA-SM-CO	of Animall reasson	I
57R:X:156	PR-EC	to Christ I in his I manhodd	I
57R:X:158	LR-AI	A parable	I
57V:X:180	EP-EXH	not(a)	I
57V:X:180	NRA-SM-PMR	wisdom & healthe I two greate blissinges	I
57V:X:191	NRA-SM-TE	bisshopes I should I haue no I more lands I then Christe I hadd	I
57V:X:208	NRA-T	Basterdes	H
58R:X:211a	NRA-SM-CO	an vnregenerat I father begitteth I a curssed sonne	I
58R:X:211a	EP-EXH	nota	I
58R:X:219	NRA-T	kaytiffe of kayn	H
58R:X:232	EP-EXH	nota	D
58R:X:238	EP-EXH	nota	H
59R:X:274	NRA-T	donmowe Bacon	H
59R:X:278	NRA-T	of maryages	H
59R:X:279	NRA-SM-CO	wedd I there licke	I
59R:X:283	NRA-SM-CO	Marriage I fittist on I young	I
59R:X:288	EP-EXH	nota	I
59R:X:289	NRA-SM-CO	a man maie offend with I his wyfe, brnge in I hir flowers	I
59V:XI:3	NRA-DP	wytte & I Stodye	H
59V:XI:4	NRA-AI	his wif	I
59V:XI:14	NRA-T	Covetyse	H
59V:XI:18	NRA-TR	Begyle truth	H
59V:XI:21	LR-RP	nicholas I Saunderson	I
59V:XI:21	EP-EXH	nota	I
59V:XI:23	PR-EC	all gripinge I parsons	I
59V:XI:27	EP-EXH	nota I the riche I are comonly I the enimies I to rigt and I truthe	I
60R:XI:27a	EP-EXH	nota	B
60R:XI:29	NRA-T	the religious I and godly I person	I
60R:XI:48	NRA-SM-CO	the rich gyveth I les almes then I meann menn	H
60R:XI:52	NRA-SM-CO	hipocrites of ye clergie I and laitie	I

60R:XI:52	EP-EXH	nota	I
60R:XI:55	EP-EXH	nota	I
60R:XI:56	PR-EC	conninge | of the | prela= | tes	I
60R:XI:58	NRA-SM-CO	sterringe the simple pepell to almes | for there owne proffitt	I
60V:XI:72	NRA-SM-CO	gyve to the nedy | in thy life tyme.	H
61R:XI:94	NRA-T	Stodye techeth	H
61R:XI:99	NRA-SM-PMR	The way to doo | well.is.. | to suffer woo | regard no riches | flee women | wyne Ire | & Slewth.	H
61V:XI:129	NRA-SM-TGMR	Theologye is no | Scyeunc but a | sothfast beleofe	H
61V:XI:132	EP-EXH	nota	B
61V:XI:133	NRA-SM-CO	and teacheth vs | to love.	H
61V:XI144	NRA-T	Doo Well.	H
62R:XI:161	NRA-T	Beleefe, Truth, | & Love.	H
62V:XI:186	NRA-T	Age	H
62V:XI:205	NRA-SM-CO	Nota yat the | Elect are | wrytten & | The Reprobate | vnwrytten.	H
63R:XI:216a	NRA-SM-CO	Salomon and | Aristotell in | wysdom & workes | both good yet | dyed evelly	H
63R:XI:228	NRA-SM-CO	Neyther wyt | no coninge but | godes grace	H
63R:XI:236	NRA-SM-PMR	The wysest menn | & lernedst do | seldom lyve as | they tech	H
63R:XI:239	EP-EXH	nota	C
63V:XI:254	GR-ICON	(pointing hand)	H
64R:XI:285	NRA-SM-CO	not Wytte but ye | grace of god.	H
64R:XI:291	NRA-TR	none ravisshed | soner from fayth | then coning Clerkes | and none soner | saved then commen | people.	H
64R:XI:302	EP-EXH	nota	D

65R:XII:28	EP-EXH	nota	H
65R:XII:37	NRA-SM-CO	Secrettes I to be kept.	H
65V:XII:58	NRA-T	nota of denyall I of fayth	H
65V:XII:71	NRA-SM-PMR	mercye above I all godes workes	H
65V:XII:73	NRA-DP	Troianes	H
66R:XII:84	GR-ICON	(pointing hand)	H
66R:XII:101	NRA-SM-CO	feastes ought I to be made to I the pore & not I to the Riche	H
66V:XII:114	EP-EXH	Lend to the nedy	H
66V:XII:127	NRA-SM-PMR	To be lowe true I & loving ech to othir	H
67R:XII:140	NRA-SM-PMR	patyent povertye I is greter blessing I then Rychesse.	G
67V:XII:174	NRA-SM-TGMR	patyent povertie I prynce of vertues	G
67V:XII:180	LR-AI	A Comparason of I Wheate.	G
68R:XII:222	EP-EXH	not<a>	I
68R:XII:222	NRA-SM-TGMR	sonne ripp sonn<e> I Rotten	I
68R:XII:225	EP-EXH	nota	D
68V:XII:240	NRA-T	The Mischeves that I much riches bringe	G
68V:XIII:8	NRA-T	Abraham.	G
69R:XIII:16	NRA-T	Job.	G
69R:XIII:20	NRA-SM-CO	patyence and I povertie springeth	G
69R:XIII:32	NRA-T	Marchunnte & I Messenger	G
69V:XIII:78	EP-EXH	nota	D
70R:XIII:92	NRA-SM-CO	the mede is as much I to the pore for a I Myte as to the I riche for all his I Money./	G
70R:XIII:98	EP-EXH	nota	D
70R:XIII:98	NRA-SM-TGMR	the pore & patient I life is perfectest./	G
70R:XIII:103	NRA-SM-CO	ayenst byshops I and prestes.	G
70V:XIII:110	EP-EXH	nota	C
70V:XIII:116	NRA-SM-TE	Ayenst prestes.	G
70V:XIII:125	NRA-SM-CO	Ayenst bishops.	G

70V:XIII:130	LR-AI	A Vysion of y<u>e</u> | Creatures in y<u>e</u> | Elememt. in the | seca. & on y<u>e</u> Earth	G
71R:XIII:140	EP-EXH	nota	D
71R:XIII:146	NRA-T	males to | males	G
71R:XIII:148	NRA-SM-TE	No beaste after | Conception doth | covet lust but | Man and his make | out of reason.	G
71V:XIII:178	EP-EXH	nota	D
71V:XIII:179	NRA-SM-CO	Reson always | ruleth in beast | but not in Man | for man surfeteth | in meate, drynke | in women, aparel | and in wordes.	G
71V:XIII:196*	EP-EXH	nota	B
71V:XIII:198	NRA-T	Suffra<u>u</u>nnce.	G
72R:XIII:216	NRA-SM-TGMR	Doowell seeth much | and suffreth.	G
72R:XIII:220	EP-EXH	nota	D
72V:XIII:241	NRA-T	Shame.	G
72V:XIV:6	NRA-SM-CO	The way to | Doo Well.	G
72V:XIV:17	EP-EXH	nota	D
72V:XIV:18	GR-ICON	(pointing hand)	G
73R:XIV:19	NRA-SM-CO	Covetos averice and | vnkynde Riches dryve | away doo well./	G
73R:XIV:31	NRA-T	Wytte of sterres.	G
73R:XIV:33	NRA-SM-PMR	Grace. Wytte | and lerninge./	G
73V:XIV:65	NRA-SM-CO	Lerninge to be | reverensed./	G
73V:XIV:75	NRA-SM-CO	Ayenst Astronom<u>er</u>s	G
74R:XIV:105	LR-AI	A Comparason | betwixt the lerned | et vnlerned.	G
74V:XIV:135	LR-RP	of the theefe y<u>at</u> | was saved on good | frydaye. a rare | opynyon./	G
75R:XIV:146a	EP-EXH	nota Bene	C
75R:XIV:152a	EP-EXH	nota	D
75R:XIV:155a	LR-RP	a litle taste of poprie	I
75R:XIV:157	LR-RP	the answer to | them that aske | why. and. how./	G
75V:XIV:171	LR-AI	A pretye & right | semelye comparason | betwene the rich | man & y<u>e</u> peacok.	G

75V:XIV:185	NRA-T	the pore man & I the larke	G
75V:XIV:198	EP-EXH	nota	D
76R:XIV:205	NRA-T	Troianes	G
76R:XIV:207	NRA-T	thre kyndes of I cristyninge.	G
76R:XIV:209	NRA-SM-PMR	the true truth I deserveth	G
76R:XIV:215	NRA-SM-CO	Love and gret I Rewarde with I a curtesie more I then Covenunte./	G
76R:XV:5	NRA-SM-TGMR	fortune at I most nede, & I bewtye in age I fayleth./	G
76R:XV:9	NRA-SM-CO	freares followe I after the riche I & regarde not I the pore.	G
76V:XV:13	NRA-SM-TGMR	Covetyse ouercometh I all sectes.	G
76V:XV:15	NRA-T	Lewd Curates	G
76V:XV:27	NRA-DP	Conseyence & I Clergie.	G
76V:XV:33	NRA-DP	pacyence.	G
76V:XV:40	NRA-DP	Reason.	G
76V:XV:43	NRA-DP	Scripture	G
77R:XV:51a	EP-EXH	nota	D
77R:XV:53	NRA-SM-PMR	Conscyence causeth I Scripture to give I bread to pacyence	G
77R:XV:66	PR-EC	Doctor Robinson I Doctor Barfout I of lincoln I with many mor	I
77V:XV:76	NRA-T	of the glotones I freare	G
77V:XV:78	PR-EC	Bonner bush= I hoppe of London	I
78R:XV:111	NRA-SM-TE	the freare is I apposed what I is Doo Well./	G
78R:XV:127a	EP-EXH	nota	D
78R:XV:128	NRA-SM-PMR	pers ploughman I all kynde conynge I & craftes inpugneth I except such as be I of Love Loyaltie I & humylitye./	G
78R:XV:135	NRA-SM-PMR	All thinges are I imperfyt. but true I love & truthe.//	G
78V:XV:141	NRA-T	Lessons how to I Doo Well./	G

78V:XV:155	NRA-SM-CO	true Love lytle | Coveteth./.	G
78V:XV:160	NRA-T	pacyence./	G
79R:XV:172	NRA-T	of the pope.	G
79R:XV:182	NRA-SM-TGMR	perfyt pacyence | fyndeth perfytnesse	G
79R:XV:190	PT	A	?
79R:XV:195	NRA-SM-CO	pers ploughmans | man a waferer	G
79V:XV:210	NRA-SM-CO	the pore | and rich | praethe | for pers | the plough | man	I
79V:XV:217	EP-EXH	nota	D
79V:XV:224	NRA-SM-CO	ayenst the pope	G
80R:XV:238	NRA-SM-TGMR	No life but | hath lyfelode.	G
80V:XV:265	NRA-SM-CO	men lyved 40 yers | & tylled not ye erth	G
80V:XV:270	NRA-SM-CO	men slept .60. yere | & | wont meate./.	G
80V:XV:274	NRA-T	Mekenesse and | Milde speche	G
80V:XV:278	NRA-SM-CO	patyent pouertye | better yen Riches.	G
80V:XV:281	EP-EXH	nota	D
80V:XV:287	NRA-SM-CO	Death is more | dredefull to the | riche, then to | the pore./.	G
81R:XV:303	GR-ICON	(pointing hand)	G
81R:XV:303	NRA-SM-PMR	Many haue ther | Joye in yis life./.	G
81R:XVI:8	NRA-SM-PMR	the riche haue | not two hevvens.	G
81V:XVI:19	NRA-SM-PMR	God might haue | made all men | of like welth & | witte./.	G
81V:XVI:36	NRA-TR	Contricioun | Confession & | Satissactioun./.	G
81V:XVI:46	NRA-SM-CO	riches | bringeth | reuerence | of ye poore	I
82R:XVI:48	NRA-SM-CO	the riche is reuerensed | the pore put bak | though he be wiser.	G
82R:XVI:58	NRA-SM-PMR	pryde regneth in | the riche rather | then in ye pore.	G

82R:XVI:64	NRA-SM-PMR	the pore is eu*er* | redye to please y*e* | Riche.	G
82R:XVI:64	LR-RP	but y*e* | rich hateth | y*e* poore	I
82R:XVI:75	LR-RP	y*e* dronken roge	I
82V:XVI:82	NRA-SM-TGMR	Covetyes hath long | hands and armes.	G
82V:XVI:91	NRA-SM-TGMR	Lecherye loveth | not the pore.	G
82V:XVI:100	NRA-SM-PMR	the patyent pore | may claime heven.	G
82V:XVI:103	NRA-SM-PMR	But it is hard for | him y*at* hath Londe | Lordship & lykinge | of bodye.	G
82V:XVI:106	LR-AI	A Comparasoun.	G
83R:XVI:115	NRA-T	A diffynico*un* of | povertye./.	G
83R:XVI:115	NRA-SM-TE	describid | in .9. pa*rt*es | & declared | by paciencs	I
83R:XVI:116d	LR-RP	A grett compfort | to y*e* pacient pore	I
83R:XVI:119	NRA-SM-TGMR	pryde hateth pou*er*tye	G
83R:XVI:119	NRA-SM-PMR	the firste | point 1 | pou*er*tye is seldom | put in auctoritie | the second | pointe .2. | wi*th*out consiens | stained .3. | pou*er*tie getts | his goods | w*ith* good | consience | y*e* .4. pointe | pouertie | addorneth | the soule | y*e* .5. pointe | pouertie | ys the | pathe of | pees y*e* | .6. pointe	I
83V:XVI:143	NRA-SM-PMR	pou*er*tie is A | well of | wisdome y*e* | .7. pointe	I
83V:XVI:146	NRA-SM-PMR	pou*er*tie is A | consience to | deserue well | y*e* .8. pointe.	I
83V:XVI:153	NRA-SM-PMR	pou*er*tye a blessed life.	G
83V:XVI:153	NRA-SM-PMR	swettere | then sugare | absqu*e* timore | sollicitudine | felicitas y*e* | .9. pointe	I
83V:XVI:154a	NRA-SM-CO	y*e* meane estait moste | blessed	I

83V:XVI:168	LR-RP	In medeo concistit virt\<us\>	I
84R:XVI:173	NRA-T	the propertyes of I Liberum arbitrium	G
84R:XVI:180	NRA-T	Liberum arbitrium	G
84R:XVI:182	NRA-T	Anima.	G
84R:XVI:183	NRA-T	Animus.	G
84R:XVI:184	NRA-T	Mens	I
84R:XVI:185	NRA-T	Memoria.	G
84R:XVI:187	NRA-T	Ratio.	G
84R:XVI:187	NRA-T	Sence	I
84R:XVI:191	NRA-SM-PMR	Consience I gods Notory	I
84R:XVI:193	NRA-T	Liberum Arbitrium	I
84R:XVI:195	NRA-T	Amor or leell I loue	G
84R:XVI:197	NRA-T	Spiritus.	G
84V:XVI:200f	NRA-AI	liberum Arbitrium qui declinat a malo ad bonum	I
84V:XVI:203	PR-EC	Metropolita= I nus Doctor I Sed pastor I Solus est	I
85R:XVI:225	NRA-SM-PMR	subtyle scyences I make men proude.	G
85R:XVI:229	PR-SC	propertie bredeth I singularitie & I pride.	I
85R:XVI:234	NRA-SM-CO	Ayenst freares.	G
85R:XVI:235	NRA-T	Skornefull I flatterers	I
85R:XVI:236	EP-EXH	nota	I
85R:XVI:240a	NRA-TR	to haue no respecte of persons	I
85R:XVI:241	EP-EXH	nota	D
85R:XVI:241	NRA-SM-PMR	perfect presthod bringeth I forth holynes.	G
85R:XVI:244	NRA-SM-TGMR	inperfect presthod all euell	G
85R:XVI:250	LR-AI	A Comparasoun.	G
85V:XVI:257	EP-EXH	nota	D
85V:XVI:264	NRA-SM-TGMR	to preach & prove I it not, is Ipocrisye.	G
85V:XVI:265	NRA-T	pride in ye I clergie	I
85V:XVI:271	NRA-S	Johannes I Cristotomus	I
85V:XVI:271b	NRA-SM-CO	aganste I three bad I pes	I
85V:XVI:274	NRA-SM-CO	Ayenst Inperfect I prestes & prechers	G
85V:XVI:277	NRA-SM-CO	Hirelings to I impropriaci= I ons	I

85V:XVI:280	NRA-SM-CO	whose goodes euel | gotten are as | euell spent./.	G
85V:XVI:282	EP-EXH	nota	D
85V:XVI:282	NRA-SM-CO	bothe Bushopps | and coutitous | patrones	I
86R:XVI:302	NRA-T	Charytie.	G
86R:XVI:308	EP-EXH	nota	I
86R:XVI:309	LR-RP	afflicions, persicutions, and Sorrowes, | compared truly to heuenelye mussick | to a regenerat man	I
86V:XVI:329	NRA-T	Charytie.	G
86V:XVI:337	EP-EXH	not(a)	I
86V:XVI:338	NRA-SM-PMR	pers ye Ploughman perfitly knowethe | Charitie	I
87R:XVI:339	NRA-SM-PMR	Charitie is known | by workes./.	G
87R:XVI:346	PT	Jesus Christ	I
87R:XVI:351	NRA-SM-CO	Charitie seldom | sene in ye freres	G
87R:XVI:357	NRA-SM-CO	nor in ye kinges | courte except | covetyse be | absent	G
87R:XVI:362	NRA-SM-CO	nor in Coustorye | Courte nor | with Bisshops.	G
88R:Top	PT	John	C
88R:XVII:30	PT	John	I
88R:XVII:35	NRA-SM-TGMR	freres & monkes | lyvelode of | lyther Wyinninges	G
88R:XVII:41	EP-EXH	nota	D
88R:XVII:42	NRA-SM-CO	If men of holye | Church wold do | nought but right | then Wold Lordes, | Lawyers, and | merchauntes, do lyke.	G
88R:XVII:53	NRA-SM-TE	Ayenst Monkes | and Chanons | freres prestes | pardoners.	G
88R:XVII:53	EP-EXH	nota	D
88V:XVII:58	NRA-SM-CO	Charitie is yat | furst we helpe | father & kynred | & then such as | haue most nede | before freres | & cetera	G

88V:XVII:68	EP-EXH	nota	D
88V:XVII:69	NRA-SM-PMR	the pore haue I right to a parte of I Christes treasure I in prestes handes	G
88V:XVII:73	LR-RP	a bad body dothe shewe w<>	I
88V:XVII:73	PR-EC	counterfett curartes	I
88V:XVII:77	LR-AI	A Comparason I betwixt a false I Christpian, & a bad I penye wyth a I good prynte./.	G
88V:XVII:78	NRA-SM-CO	all cristi I ans arte I not faithfull	I
89R:XVII:90	NRA-SM-TE	if we did our dutie as all I other creatures, then I shold we haue peace I & plentye./.	G
89R:XVII:108	NRA-SM-CO	Gyle & flatterye I Master & vssher I in all scyences & I degrees.	G
89R:XVII:117	NRA-T	of Masse prestes.	G
89V:XVII:127	NRA-SM-PMR	holy church chere I is Charytie.	G
89V:XVII:133	NRA-SM-CO	Jewes & Sarazins I do both beleue in I God the father	G
89V:XVII:136	NRA-SM-CO	No Loue vnlaufull I is to be allowed.	G
90R:XVII:159	EP-EXH	nota	D
90R:XVII:163	NRA-TR	bewtie without bountie I kynde without curtosye.	G
90R:XVII:165	NRA-SM-CO	Matometh was I crystened & wold I haue ben pope.	G
90R:XVII:175	NRA-T	the deceyte of I Matometh by I a Dove./.	G
90V:XVII:194	EP-EXH	nota Bene	D
90V:XVII:197	NRA-SM-TGMR	holyemen had no I boke but Conscyence	G
90V:XVII:205	NRA-SM-CO	Covetyse shall I ouertorne Clerkes.	G
90V:XVII:214	EP-EXH	nota bene	
91R:XVII:219	NRA-SM-PMR	Bisshops shall lose temperall I Landes & lyve of teuthes.	G

91R:XVII:220	EP-EXH	nota	C
91R:XVII:222	NRA-SM-PMR	An Angell cryed y<u>at</u> I y<u>e</u> church was poysoned	G
91R:XVII:227	NRA-SM-CO	A Counsayll for I Kyng<u>es</u>. to take I possessions from I the pope & all y<u>e</u> I clergie	G
91R:XVII:239	EP-EXH	nota	C
91R:XVII:239*	EP-EXH	nota	B
91R:XVII:240	NRA-SM-SM	Matometh I & the pope I compared.	G
91V:XVII:250	NRA-SM-TGMR	presthod inp<u>er</u>fyt	G
91V:XVII:276	PR-EC	an Vnsownd I opynion.	G
92R:XVII:283	NRA-T	A Bisshops office	G
92R:XVII:283	EP-EXH	nota	D
92V:XVIII:3	NRA-DP	liberum arbitrium	G
92V:XVIII:4	NRA-T	Cor hominis.	G
92V:XVIII:7	NRA-T	Imago.Dei.	G
92V:XVIII:14	NRA-T	Charitas.	G
93R:XVIII:30	NRA-T	the world.	G
93R:XVIII:36	NRA-T	the fleshe.	G
93R:XVIII:68	PT	m	?
93V:XVIII:85	NRA-T	Matrimonye.	G
93V:XVIII:86	NRA-T	Wydowhod.	G
93V:XVIII:89	NRA-T	Vyrginytie	G
94V:XVIII:127	NRA-AI	Jhesus A I carpenters I sonn y<u>e</u> sonn I of y<u>e</u> Judge of I all justices I in this worlde	I
94V:XVIII:134	PR-SC	A wench I ought to be I A virgine I butt hardly I in this wickitt I age	I
94V:XVIII:143	NRA-AI	Marie I Magdiline	I
94V:XVIII:151a	EP-EXH	nota	I
94V:XVIII:151a	NRA-T	The sinn aganst y<u>e</u> holly goste	I
95R:XVIII:175	NRA-DP	Judas.	G
95V:XVIII:188	LR-RP	Abrahams I Armes thre I proues y<u>e</u> I holy & blished I Trinitie	I
96R:XVIII:221	NRA-SM-CO	Matrimony of I the Bible wh<u>ich</u> y<u>e</u> I Pappistes and munks I do allowe is here I disconmended	I

96R:XVIII:221	NRA-SM-PMR	nota	Barrenes	of the	wome	I
96R:XVIII:228	LR-AI	A Symylitude	betwixt the	Trenytie &	Adam, Eve &	Abell.	G
96R:XVIII:241	EP-EXH	nota	I
96R:XVIII:242	NRA-SM-CO	Abraham	sawe thre	angells et	worshiped	before his	tente dore	which resemblid	tthe Trinitie	I
96V:XVIII:256	NRA-SM-CO	nota	ye faithfull	Seed of:-	Abraham	are not only	promissed all	temporall	pleshinges	butt also	eternaell	I
96V:XVIII:270	NRA-SM-CO	John Baptist	bore in	his bosham	christe in	the simillitid	of A layser	before his	commninge	in the flesh	which layser represented	all the faithfull Borne	before Christe	I
97R:XVIII:278	NRA-SM-CO	no pleges in oure times butt the <Re>atyes londe <.> Criste notin the faitful before his deathe & comminge	I
97R:XVIII:282	EP-EXH	nota	I
97R:XIX:3	NRA-TR	ye olde and the	newe testamente	I
97R:XIX:7	NRA-SM-PMR	nota Christe is ye	seale of the	testament	I
97R:XIX:12	EP-EXH	nota	I
97R:XIX:13a	NRA-TR	Moyes tabill whereni ye lawe was writt<en>	I
97V:XIX:19	NRA-SM-CO	fayth kepinge the	Comamdmenntes saveth	G
97V:XIX:27	NRA-SM-PMR	Abraham sawe ye .3.	persons of ye trenytie.	G
97V:XIX:44	NRA-SM-TGMR	the lawe lerned	& lytle vsed.	G
98R:XIX:51	NRA-T	the samarytan	G
99R:XIX:117	LR-AI	A symilitude of	ye trenytie & ye	hande./.	G

99V:XIX:162	LR-AI	A symylitude of | the synne ayenst | the holy gost./.	G
99V:XIX:162	LR-AI	to the palme | of the hande	I
99V:XIX:167	LR-AI	a symyle of | a torche./.	G
100R:XIX:176	NRA-T	peccatum contra Spiritus Sancti./.	G
100V:XIX:217	NRA-SM-PMR	No pardon can dispens | with vnkyndnes	G
100V:XIX:223	NRA-T	ayenst vnkyndnes | in riche men./.	G
100V:XIX:228	EP-EXH	nota	D
101R:XIX:236	NRA-SM-TE	of Diues ye | riche mann an | argument a | Maiore./.	G
101V:XIX:263	NRA-SM-CO	Murther ye worst | synne ayenst ye | holye gost./.	G
101V:XIX:266	EP-EXH	Qu<are>ere./.	G
102R:XIX:294	NRA-SM-TGMR	sorowe of herte | is satisfactoun | to yem yat connot | payc./.	G
102R:XIX:296	EP-EXH	nota	C
102R:XIX:298	NRA-SM-TE	A Wycked Wyfe | an house vncouercd | & the smoke. are | compared to. | the flesh.	G
102R:XIX:313	NRA-T	Syknesses.	G
102V:XIX:321	NRA-T	Covetyse and | vnkyndnes.	G
102V:XIX:325*	EP-EXH	nota	B
103R:XX:52	NRA-AI	A sponge of | vinniger.	I
103V:XX:65	LR-RP	the Authore | varieth some | what from | ye worde of | god.	I
103V:XX:67	LR-RP	nota A dombe speche of | deade bodies	I
103V:XX:78	EP-EXH	nota	I
103V:XX:78*	EP-EXH	nota	B
104V:XX:117	NRA-AI	heaune in | ye weste	I
104V:XX:117	EP-EXH	nota	I
104V:XX:119	NRA-DP	Mercye	G
104V:XX:122	NRA-DP	truthe.	G
104V:XX:132	NRA-T	Mary the | Virgine.	I
104V:XX:135	NRA-TR	Christe was | borne without | a medwyfe | in a manger	I
104V:XX:144	GR-ICON	(pointing hand)	G

105R:XX:150	EP-EXH	nota	I
105R:XX:150	PR-EC	truth is I directly I against I purgatory I and limbo I patrum	I
105R:XX:157	NRA-SM-PMR	the venym of Scorpions I styngeth till deth./.	G
105R:XX:166	NRA-T	Rightwysenes.	G
105R:XX:171	NRA-T	peace. patyence I and Love	G
105R:XX:176	EP-EXH	nota	I
105R:XX:176	NRA-SM-CO	pees bringeth I plentie & pride	I
105R:XX:178	NRA-AI	Spalme Dauid. I Mercy. and truth, are mett together. I Rightwsenes, & pees, haithe cished ech other	I
106R:XX:237	PR-PC	Englands I careles I Securitie	I
106R:XX:237	EP-EXH	nota	I
106R:XX:240	EP-EXH	nota	I
106R:XX:240	NRA-TR	The Bibil I Book.	I
106V:XX:258	NRA-T	Symonds sons	G
106V:XX:258	NRA-SM-CO	which were in Hell	H
107R:XX:278	LR-RP	nota a question where I Lazarus was when I Abraham was in Inferno.	G
107V:XX:309	NRA-AI	nota I vijm yere I was Adam I in Hell. I contrary I to Elias I computa= I cions.	I
108R:XX:354	NRA-SM-CO	ayenst lyers	G
108V:XX:380	NRA-SM-CO	ye serpinte I aleged god I <s> cripture I to Eue	I
109R:XX:397	LR-RP	by ye frute of a tree dampned I by ye death on tree Saued	I
109R:XX:410 resurrectoun	NRA-SM-TGMR G	the vayle of I Josephat	
109R:XX:418	EP-EXH	note this	G
109V:XX:439	NRA-SM-PMR	Justyce in hell I Mercye in heven.	G
109V:XX:448	NRA-SM-CO	not all ransomed	G
110R:XX:474	PR-EC	Idolatrye	G
110V:XXI:12	NRA-SM-CO	pers plough I man wereth I ye cote armor I of Christ	I

110V:XXI:34	NRA-SM-CO	Jewes vnder tribute	I
111R:XXI:61	NRA-SM-PMR	Christ betokneth I conqueror.	I
111R:XXI:61	EP-EXH	nota	I
111R:XXI:66	LR-RP	without the cros I no Crowne?	I
111R:XXI:70	LR-RP	Jhesus A I sumonre	I
111V:XXI:82	EP-EXH	nota	D
111V:XXI:85	NRA-T	A definition I of the I offerings I of the I three I wismen	I
111V:XXI:91	NRA-T	Reson I Righti= I onsnes I Truth	I
112V:XXI:135	LR-LI	ye Madens I or biriydes	I
112V:XXI:149	EP-EXH	nota	D
112V:XXI:161a	EP-EXH	nota	I
112V:XXI:161a	NRA-TR	women I can kepe I no counsell	I
113R:XXI:183	NRA-T	peter	I
113R:XXI:187	LR-RP	ye ploughman I sonnest pardoned I for his sinnes then I any other caullinge	I
113V:XXI:213	LR-RP	grace is more I aquanted with I the ploughman I then any oth<er> I trad<e.>	I
113V:XXI:213	EP-EXH	nota	I
113V:XXI:219	EP-EXH	nota	I
113V:XXI:221	NRA-T	Antichrist ye	I
113V:XXI:221	NRA-T	false prophetes I pope I Covetyse.	G
113V:XXI:222	NRA-SM-CO	nota shall I sitt in gods sett I and bost him selfe I as g<o>d	I
114R:XXI:229	NRA-SM-PMR	preachers prestes I and lawyers lyve by I labor of tonge	G
114R:XXI:259	NRA-SM-CO	The ploughman I the worlds I stuarde	I
114V:XXI:262	NRA-T	The Evangelistes	G
114V:XXI:266	?	nota peers the I deuins purit	I
114V:XXI:269	NRA-T	The Doctors.	G
114V:XXI:277	NRA-T	prudence	G
114V:XXI:284	NRA-T	Temporance	G
114V:XXI:291	NRA-T	fortytude.	G

115R:XXI:303	NRA-T	Justyce	G
115V:XXI:324	GR-ICON	(pointing hand)	G
115V:XXI:324	NRA-T	vnytie	G
115V:XXI:336	NRA-DP	pryde	G
116R:XXI:369	NRA-SM-CO	common hores & I Sumpners I enimies to the I the Churche	I
116R:XXI:370	EP-EXH	nota	I
116R:XXI:385	PR-EC	gods body vnder I ye elliment of I brede not I transsubstan- I tiacon	I
116R:XXI:385	EP-EXH	nota	I
116V:XXI:396	NRA-DP	A baudy I Bruer	I
116V:XXI:408	NRA-DP	A vile I vicare	I
116V:XXI:417	NRA-SM-PMR	Lecherye regneth I wher Cardynals I dwell./.	G
117R:XXI:428	NRA-SM-PMR	the pope shold I save	G
117R:XXI:444	NRA-SM-CO	the popes vyces	G
117V:XXI:455	EP-EXH	nota	I
117V:XXI:455	NRA-SM-PMR	prudence in I oure daies I ys but gyle	I
117V:XXI:469	NRA-SM-CO	the Kinge is I above his Lawe.	G
117V:XXI:469	PR-PC	yet ounder I ye rigore I of ye lawe I by reprehension I as Nathan I rebucked I Dauid.	I
118R:XXII:10	NRA-SM-TGMR	Need hath I no Lawe./.	G
118V:XXII:33	EP-EXH	nota	I
118V:XXII:33	LR-RP	Timor dei I is wisdome	I
118V:XXII:34	EP-EXH	nota	I
118V:XXII:36	NRA-SM-CO	Neede I meeketh I a prouod I minde	I
118V:XXII:37	NRA-AI	Diogines dissyre I all vaine gl<orie>	I
118V:XXII:41	NRA-SM-CO	Christ became I need for vs	I
118V:XXII:44	NRA-T	Needye.	G
118V:XXII:48	NRA-SM-CO	A greate compfort in necesyti<e>	I
118V:XXII:48	EP-EXH	nota	I
118V:XXII:55	NRA-SM-PMR	freares folowe I Antechriste.	G
118V:XXII:57	NRA-SM-PMR	Gile ye ground of I Antechrist	I
118V:XXII:57	EP-EXH	nota	I

118V:XXII:61	NRA-SM-CO	as mart I Christ I gods <....> this	I
118V:XXII:62	NRA-SM-PMR	but fooles will I rather dye./.	G
119R:XXII:70	NRA-T	Antechristes battayl I ayenst Conseyence.	G
119R:XXII:75	NRA-SM-CO	vnite ye castell I of christianite I of all gods I Fooles in the I churche	I
119R:XXII:86	NRA-SM-CO	a legion I of angels I attend I on I ante= I christe	I
119R:XXII:86	NRA-SM-CO	pestilences I and warres I are sent of I god to right I againste Antechrist I and his I angells	I
119V:XXII:95	NRA-SM-PMR	old age bereth I deathes standerd	G
119V:XXII:101	NRA-SM-CO	Death killeth I all estates.	G
119V:XXII:112	NRA-SM-CO	Lecheryes I battayll I ayenst Conscience	G
119V:XXII:115	NRA-SM-CO	lecherie liuerye is I continuall Idelnes I with flatterie I and decepte	I
119V:XXII:121	NRA-SM-PMR	Covetyse also I ayenst Consciens	G
119V:XXII:121	NRA-SM-CO	Covetysnes I liuerye is I in garlines I and wiles	I
120R:XXII:125	NRA-SM-CO	symonye causeth I ye pope to hold with I Antechryste I knocketh conseyence I dryveth away fayth I overthroweth Wisdom I of Westminster hall I overturneth truth I turneth syvile in I ye Arches./ & I parteth Matrimonye I by devorce./	G
120R:XXII:140	GR-ICON	(pointing hand)	G
120R:XXII:141	PR-EC	liuely loue I clad in rome I harlottry which I holdeth religion I a geste	I
120R:XXII:143	EP-EXH	nota	I
120R:XXII:147	NRA-SM-CO	Conscyence accompted I folye./	G

120R:XXII:148	EP-EXH	nota	I
120R:XXII:148	NRA-SM-CO	vaine | folly | of youtfull | lyfe.	I
120R:XXII:151	NRA-SM-CO	lyf health and pride | of harte regards | not consience | nor deathe	I
120R:XXII:153	EP-EXH	nota	I
120V:XXII:154	NRA-SM-CO	lyf and fortun\<e\> | begate in there | youth Sleuth | who marrid | in his boysage | a Post Knigtes | Daughter | in a vaine | hope of | youthe	I
120V:XXII:159	EP-EXH	nota	I
120V:XXII:176	PR-EC	ye vicare of | Bindbrocke.	I
120V:XXII:180	NRA-SM-CO	No surgerye nor | physik ayenst | old age./.	G
120V:XXII:182	NRA-SM-CO	age is | bald | before \<...\>	I
121R:XXII:190	EP-EXH	nota	I
121R:XXII:190	NRA-SM-CO	ye ere yelds to elde | ye teth and | grinders | decaeth | ye leges are | gouttie	I
121R:XXII:197	NRA-SM-CO	mariage and elde | killeth lust | of ye body.	I
121R:XXII:199	LR-RP	all men muste | paie there | debt to | Nature	I
121R:XXII:210	EP-EXH	nota	I
121R:XXII:210	NRA-SM-CO	ye godlie which loue god truly | shall never lacke in this | lyfe, nor in ye lyfe to come	I
121V:XXII:221	EP-EXH	nota	I
121V:XXII:222	NRA-SM-CO	litle or no | consience to | be found | in the | marches of | Ireland	I
121V:XXII:232	NRA-SM-CO	Ayenst prestes | & freres	G
122R:XXII:259	NRA-SM-CO	Conscyence will | not give ought | to ye freres. they | are so many & | out of Nombre	G
122V:XXII:294	NRA-SM-TGMR	Envye fyndeth | freres at Schole	G

122V:XXII:300	NRA-T	prechares	I
122V:XXII:300	NRA-SM-PMR	ypocrysie | woundeth many	G
123R:XXII:314	NRA-SM-CO	freare flatterye a | phisician & surgean	G
123V:XXII:346	NRA-SM-CO	hippocrieticall | women friers | with the salue | of loue	I
123V:XXII:347	EP-EXH	nota	I
123V:XXII:367	NRA-SM-CO	contrition | ys filled | with Ipocracy	I
123V:XXII:369	EP-EXH	nota	I
124R:XXII:371	LR-RP	daubers with | vntempered | morter	I
124R:XXII:371	EP-EXH	nota	I
124R:XXII:373	NRA-SM-PMR	sleuth | & prid<e> | enimies | to conscience	I
124R:XXII:382	NRA-SM-CO	consience | desiers ye | company | of ye plough | man who | is moste | voyde of | pride | of all occupacens	I
124R:XXII:382	EP-EXH	nota	I
124R:B	LR-RP	Concience ys a sleppe till he come in againe	I
124R:B	OM	William Aiscough	-
124R:B	OM	Arther Surteys	-
124R:B	OM	Cussin I hope ty you pray to kepe this boukc | bothe nyght & dai	I
124R:B	LR-RP	per me Fraun: Aiscoughe de Ccottam | Consnence will not come into this lande till the proude | Prelates and Couitous lawyeres be swepe awai | which will not be longe to Amen So be it	I

NOTE: * indicates red ink.

Transcription of Hm 143's Marginalia

FOLIO/LINE	CLASSIFICATION		CONTENT
1V:P:51	NRA-SM-TGMR	//	hermytis wente | to walsyngham

127

1V:P:56	NRA-SM-TGMR	//	hyer preched frerys
2R:P:81	NRA-SM-TGMR	//	hyer parsones & parische prestes I playned to þe bischop
2R:P:95 prelates	NRA-SM-PMR	//	Concyence I acusede
2V:P:139	NRA-SM-TE	//	þe commune & kynde I wit ordayned a plow
3R:P:164	NRA-T	//	notate men of lawe
3R:P:169	NRA-SM-CO	//	hyer made ratonys I a parlement
3V:P:196	NRA-SM-PMR	//	hyer spekyþ I a mous of renoun
4V:I:27	NRA-SM-PMR	//	lo how loot I lay be his douȝtres
5R:I:69	NRA-SM-CO	//	hyer askyd wille I who was þat woman I þat spak to hym
5V:I:112	NRA-SM-TE	//	lo fend is I fille for pride
6R:I:129	LR-RP		loke be neþe for I iii vers ben mys set
6R:I:132	LR-RP		war
6R:I:145	NRA-SM-TGMR	//	notate þat loue I is plante of pes
6V:I:175	PR-SC	//	notate ȝe ryche
6V:I:187	PR-EC	//	notate hic vn I kynde prestes
7R:II:5	NRA-SM-PMR	//	heyre prayde I will he moste I fals knawe
7R:II:9	GR-ICON		(pointing hand)
7R:II:9	NRA-DP	I_	Mede
7V:II:30	NRA-DP	I_	holicherche
7V:II:55	NRA-T	//	be hold þe I houshold of mede
8R:II:78	NRA-T	//	the feffement I a tuxe mede I & falsnesse
8V:II:109	NRA-T	//	witnessis of þe I feffement afayre I heþ
8V:II:116	NRA-SM-CO	//	hyer teologi chidde I eiuile & symonye
9V:II:178	LR-AI	//	Red hyer a blissed I companye per contrarium

10R:II:220	NRA-SM-CO	//	for drede falsnesse I fley3 to þe freris
10V:II:239	NRA-SM-CO	//	3it freris fette hom I lyere wyt hem to dwelle
10V:III:9	NRA-SM-CO	//	hyere was mede I conforted
11R:III:26	PR-EC	//	notate 3e lewed I auanced
11R:III:38	LR-AI	//	a comfessour as I a frere comforted I mede & sayde as I 3e may rede
11V:III:77	NRA-SM-CO	//	hyer prayde mede I for veteylers & I oþere mo to þe mair
12R:III:108	PR-SC		nota
12V:III:149	NRA-SM-CO	//	hyer was concience I cald to haue weddid I mede
13R:III:189	NRA-T	//I_	notate prestes gurles
13V:III:215	NRA-SM-CO	//	hycre muornede mede for concience acusede here
14V:III:283	NRA-SM-PMR	//	hyere holdeth þe kyng wyt mede
15R:III:311	NRA-T	I_	notate presbiteri
16V:III:409	NRA-C		Regum
16V:III:435	EP-PP	//	he þat sayth trewþe I schal be schent
17R:III:454	EP-REV	//	lo how iewe schull I conuerte for ioye
17R:III:476	EP-REV	I_	prophetia petri
18R:IV:19	NRA-SM-CO	//	hyer rayson bad sadele I his hors þat hy3te suffre
19R:IV:108	NRA-T	//	lo what resoun sayde
19V:IV:148	NRA-SM-CO	//	lo mede bad I men of lawe I stoppe resoun
20R:IV:160	NRA-SM-PMR	//	hyere murned mede I for sche was clepid hore
20V:V:8	NRA-SM-TE	//	hyer concience I & raysoun a ratyd I wille for his lol I lynge
21R:V:35	NRA-SM-CO	//	hyer wille answerid I to rayson

22R:V:104	NRA-SM-CO	//	hyer wente wille | to churche & ful al ȝen a sclepe
22R:V:115	NRA-SM-TGMR	//	· hyer raysoun | prechede
22V:V:146	NRA-T	|__	notate Religiosi
22V:V:165	EP-REV		prophetia petri
22V:V:168	GR-ICON		(crown)
23V:VI:14	NRA-SM-CO	//	pride scryueþ | hym hyere
24R:VI:61	NRA-SM-PMR	//	hyer goþ Envye | to scryfte
24V:VI:91	NRA-SM-CO	//	wrathe goth | to schryfte
24V:VI:105	NRA-DP	|_	Repentance
25R:VI:118	NRA-SM-CO	//	freris ben wrothe
25V:VI:145	NRA-SM-CO	//	hyer was letise | at stile y schent | for sche tok halibred | to rathe
25V:VI:145	NRA-T	|_	notate wyues
25V:VI:164	NRA-DP	|_	Repentance
25V:VI:170	NRA-SM-CO	//	hyer cam lecherye | to schrefte ward
26R:VI:196	GR-ICON		(male face)
26R:VI:196	NRA-SM-CO	//	hyere cam couetyse | to schrefte ward
26V:VI:233	NRA-T	<|_	r>ose þe regrater
27R:VI:254	PR-EC	//|_	notate diuites
27R:VI:284	NRA-T		leger
27V:VI:309	NRA-DP	|_	walsche man
27V:VI:316	NRA-DP	//	Robert | ryfflere
28R:VI:350	NRA-SM-PMR	//	Glotonyȝe goþ | to schryfte
29R:VI:412	NRA-SM-TGMR	//	Glotoun cowede a caudel | in clementis lappe
29R:VII:1	NRA-SM-PMR	//	schouthe cam | to schryfte
30R:VII:30	EP-EXH		nota
30R:VII:30	EP-EXH	|_	notate lewede prestes
32R:VII:157	NRA-SM-TE	//	hyer askyd þe puple | a palmere after treuþe
33V:VII:262	EP-EXH	|_	wrathe naȝt
34R:VIII:6	NRA-SM-TE	//	hyer bad <pyers> | ladies & oþer wymmen | worche
34V:VIII:25	NRA-SM-TE	//	hyer <pyers> ȝif | knyȝtes leue to | hunte & haueke | & kepe hym & hise

35R:VIII:79	LR-RP	//	loke hyer what I <pers> wyf hy3te & his I sone & his do3ter
35V:VIII:96	NRA-SM-PMR	//	hyer makyþ I <pers> his testa I ment
36R:VIII:136	NRA-SM-CO	//	hyere prayde faytours I for <pers>
36R:VIII:151	NRA-SM-PMR	//	hyer wastour chydde I <pers>
36R:VIII:157	NRA-SM-TGMR	//	hyer playned I <pers> to þe kny3t
36V:VIII:171	NRA-SM-PMR	//	hyer hunger fa3t I wyt þe wastour I & wyt þe bretoner
37R:VIII:206	NRA-SM-PMR	//	hyer <pers> bad I hunger go a 3en
39R:VIII:349	EP-REV		prophecia
40V:IX:92	NRA-T	I_	coterelis feste
40V:IX:106	NRA-T	I_	Lunatyk lollares
41R:IX:140	NRA-T	I_	propure lollares
41V:IX:169	NRA-T	//	byhold hyer I of lollaren children
42R:IX:203	EP-EXH	//	notate 3e lewede I ermytes
42V:IX:246	NRA-SM-CO	//	hyere mette I wille wyt lollarere I to þe mete ward
43R:IX:262	NRA-T	I_	notate episcopi
43R:IX:282	NRA-SM-PMR	//	hyer a prest askyd I persis bull to rede
43V:IX:305	LR-AI	//	a sample of I swenenys
44R:IX:335	NRA-T	//	notate de indulgennces I & pardones & trionales
44R:X:5	NRA-SM-CO	//	hyer wille I so3te dowel I & mete wyt I ii freris
44V:X:17	LR-RP	//	lo what a frere sayde I of dowel
44V:X:30	NRA-SM-CO	//	nota how þe ry3twise I falleþ vii syþis in I þe day & 3if standith I safly
45R:X:56	NRA-SM-CO	//	hyere departid will I & þe freris
45R:X:70	NRA-SM-CO	//I_	hyer wille wyt þo3t

131

46R:X:122	NRA-SM-CO	I_	hyere spekyþ wit
46V:X:164	EP-EXH	I_	notate hic aliqui
46V:X:175	EP-EXH		nota
48R:X:286	LR-AI		verso
48V:XI:1	NRA-SM-TE	//	wittes wyf chidde I wit for he sche I wed so muche I vn stodied
49R:XI:28	NRA-SM-PMR	//	harlottes are sonnest I holpe
49V:XI:52	NRA-SM-PMR	//	hyer he tellith I of prechinge at I paulis
49V:XI:71	NRA-SM-PMR	//	tobi ta3te I his sone I dele
50R:XI:86	NRA-SM-TGMR	//	Where clergie I dwellith
50R:XI:96	NRA-SM-PMR	//	lettygge to come I to clergie
50R:XI:105	NRA-DP	I_	studie
50R:XI:114	NRA-DP	I_	scrypture
50V:XI:122	NRA-C		sapience
50V:XI:150	NRA-C	I_	austyn
51R:XI:167	NRA-SM-CO	//	hyere fortune raueschid I will & schewed hym a myr I our þat hy3te myddyl3erd
52R:XI:239	EP-EXH	//	hyer hard sentence I for techeres 3if þay leue I no3t wel
52R:XI:249	EP-DA	I_	Culorum
53R:XI:312	NRA-SM-TE	//	hyer 3ougthe sette I at no3t al þis
53V:XII:18	EP-EXH	I_	notate hic freris
54V:XII:73	NRA-SM-TGMR	//	hyer cam a I trogian & sayde I baw for bokes
54V:XII:97	NRA-SM-CO	//	notate hyer how 3e schull I make festes
58V:XIII:99	NRA-SM-CO	//	where of seruen I tithes þat prestes han
58V:XIII:124	EP-EXH	I_	beth war bischoppus
59R:XIII:165	NRA-DP	I_	Raysoun
59R:XIII:182	NRA-DP		Raysoun
59V:XIII:182	NRA-RD	I_	Question
59V:XIII:193	NRA-RD	I_	Responcio

61R:XIII:212	EP-PP	//	Grace wyt oute grace | is noȝt
61R:XIII:217	NRA-SM-TE	l_	astronomyȝe
60R:XIV:28	NRA-T		Frer
60V:XIV:72	NRA-SM-PMR	//	hyer cawȝte | will colour
60V:XIV:89	NRA-DP	l_	ymaginatyf
62V:XIV:129	NRA-T	l_	notate theuis
63R:XIV:166	NRA-DP	l_	ymagenynge
63V:XIV:202	NRA-DP	l_	ymagytyf
63V:XV:3	LR-AI	//	hyer ȝe may | se schortly re | hersed þe visi | onis to fore | sayd
64R:XV:30	NRA-T	l_	notate fratres
65R:XV:77	NRA-T		frer
65R:XV:93	EP-EXH		nota
65R:XV:103	NRA-T		frer
66V:XV:183	NRA-SM-PMR	//	hyer wente | consience & pacience
66V:XV:194	NRA-SM-TGMR	//	actiua vita | pers plowmanis | prentys
68V:XVI:9	EP-EXH	//	notate ȝe ry | che men
69V:XVI:104	EP-EXH		nota
69V:XVI:107	EP EXH	l_	notate bene
70R:XVI:117	NRA-SM-CO	//	hyere ȝe may se | it is god to be | pouere
70V:XVI:156	NRA-T	//	what is liberum arbitrium
71V:XVI:229	NRA-SM-PMR	//	lo how frers | prechen fallas | & cetera
71V:XVI:233	EP-EXH	l_	nota bene
72R:XVI:242	NRA-T	//	notate de wikkyde | techeres
72R:XVI:253	LR-AI	l_	notate image
72V:XVI:273	EP-EXH	//	beth war of | þis lered & | lewed
72V:XVI:284	NRA-DP	l_	Charyte
73V:XVI:353	NRA-SM-CO	//	Charyte was | wyth freres
74V:XVII:35	NRA-T	l_	notate relegiosi
74V:XVII:41	NRA-C	l_	Thobi
74V:XVII:52	NRA-SM-TE	l_	Jop contra relegiosi
75R:XVII:58	NRA-SM-CO	//	takeþ kepe hyer | of lewed peple | tak clerkes to whom | ȝe schull first do

76R:XVII:142	NRA-T	//	notate bene de amor
76V:XVII:165	NRA-T	l_	notate de Macometh
76V:XVII:188	EP-EXH	//	be hold se lo l what prelates scholde do
77R:XVII:200	NRA-SM-PMR	//	þe croys l is coueytyd
77R:XVII:212	EP-EXH	l_	notate hic aliqui
77R:XVII:254	EP-EXP	//	i Credo in deum l patrem
78V:XVIII:1	NRA-DP	//	liberum l arbitrium
80V:XVIII:133	NRA-T	l_	Maria
80V:XVIII:152	NRA-DP		Ihesu crist
81R:XVIII:166	NRA-T	l_	Judas
81R:XVIII:183	NRA-DP	l_	Abraham
81V:XVIII:191	NRA-T	l_	Of the trinite
82V:XVIII:274	NRA-DP	l_	Fayth
82V:XIX:1	NRA-DP	l_	spes
83R:XIX:13	NRA-T	l_	mandata dei
83R:XIX:21	NRA-DP	l_	fayth
83V:XIX:44	EP-EXH		nota
83V:XIX:47	NRA-DP	l_	samaritanus
84R:XIX:81	NRA-DP	l_	samarita
84R:XIX:94	NRA-SM-CO	//	A question to l the samaritan
84V:XIX:109	NRA-T	l_	Of þe trinite
85V:XIX:175	NRA-T	l_	trinite
86R:XIX:226	EP-EXH	l_	notate
86V:XIX:269	NRA-T	l_	veniance
86V:XIX:274	EP-EXH		nota
87:XIX:294	EP-EXH	l_	notate hic bene
87V:XX:13	NRA-DP	l_	fayth
88R:XX:21	NRA-DP	l_	Ihesu crist
88R:XX:35	NRA-DP	l_	Pilatus
88V:XX:81	NRA-DP	l_	longys
89R:XX:96	NRA-SM-PMR	l_	fayth reproued iewes
89R:XX:107	EP-EXH		nota
89R:XX:112	NRA-DP	l_	Daniel
89R:XX:119	NRA-C	l_	mercy
89V:XX:123	NRA-DP	l_	truthe
89V:XX:132	NRA-SM-PMR	l_	Maria concepta
89V:XX:152	NRA-C	l_	Jop
90R:XX:168	NRA-DP	l_	Ryhtwisnesse
90R:XX:171	NRA-SM-TGMR	l_	pes clothed in patienc<e>

90R:XX:184	EP-EXH		nota
90V:XX:207	NRA-DP	|_	pees
91R:XX:240	NRA-DP	|_	boek
91R:XX:240	EP-EXH		nota
91V:XX:274	NRA-DP		nota Satan
91V:XX:295	NRA-DP	|_	lucefer
92R:XX:313	EP-EXH	|_	notate bene
93R:XX:370	NRA-DP	|_	lord
93R:XX:397	EP-EXH		nota
93V:XX:409	NRA-T	|_	Crist
94R:XX:441	EP-EXH	|_	nota hic bene
94V:XXI:4	NRA-SM-TE	//	hyer is a newe | metcl<u>es</u> how he | say p<u>er</u>s al blody
94V:XXI:19	NRA-T		Ihesu crist
95V:XXI:83	LR-RP		war
97V:XXI:219	NRA-T	|_	Ante c<u>ri</u>st
98R:XXI:261	NRA-SM-CO	//	hyer bygynn3 | <pers plow>
98R:XXI:265	NRA-DP		Ioha<u>nn</u>es
101V:XXII:4	NRA-SM-TGMR	//	hyer<u>e</u> he | mette wy<u>t</u> | nede
106R:XXII:340	PR-EC	//	a general name | for a frere

NOTES

[1] Carl James Grindley, 'From Creation to Desecration: The Marginal Annotations *of Piers Plowman* C Text HM 143," MA thesis, University of Victoria, 1992, p. 1. I should like to thank the Social Sciences and Humanities Research Council of Canada for generously funding this research project.

[2] A good working bibliography would now include: C. David Benson and Lynne S. Blanchfield, *The Manuscripts of "Piers Plowman": The B-version* (London, 1998); C. David Benson and Barry A. Windeatt, "The Manuscript Glosses to Chaucer's *Troilus and Criseyde*," *The Chaucer Review* 25.1 (1990), 33-53; Graham Caie, "The Significance of the Early Chaucer Manuscript Glosses (with Special Reference to the *Wife of Bath's Prologue*)," *Chaucer Review* 10 (1975-6), 350-60; Grindley, "From Creation"; Grindley, "The Life of a Book: British Library Additional Manuscript 35157 in Historical Context," PhD diss., University of Glasgow, 1997; Kathryn Kerby-Fulton and Denise Despres, *Iconography and the Professional Reader: The Politics of Book Production in the Douce "Piers Plowman"* (Minneapolis, 1998); George Russell, " 'As They Read It': Some Notes on Early Responses to the C-Version of *Piers Plowman*," *Leeds Studies in English* 20 (1989), 173-89; George Russell, "Some Early Responses to the C-Version of *Piers Plowman*," *Viator* 15

(1984), 275-303; Lucy Freeman Sandler, "*Omne bonum: Compilatio and Ordinatio in an English Illustrated Encyclopedia of the Fourteenth Century,*" in *Medieval Book Production: Assessing the Evidence,* ed. Linda Brownrigg (New York, 1990); Wendy Scase, "*Piers Plowman" and the New Anti-clericalism,* (Cambridge, 1989); Tanya Schaap, "From Scribe to Reader: A Study of the Marginal Annotations of *Piers Plowman C-Text* Oxford Bodleian Library Digby 102" (unpublished master's thesis, University of Victoria, 1996); Susan Schibanoff, "The New Reader and Female Textuality in Two Early Commentaries on Chaucer," *Studies in the Age of Chaucer* 10 (1988), 71-91; Kathleen Scott, "The Illustrations of *Piers Plowman* in Bodleian Library MS. Douce 104," *Yearbook of Langland Studies* 4 (1990), 1-86; Kathleen Scott, "Limning and Book-Producing Terms and Signs *in situ* in Late-Medieval English Manuscripts: A First Listing," in *New Science Out of Old Books: Studies in Manuscripts and Early Printed Books in Honour of A. I. Doyle,* ed. Richard Beadle and A. J. Piper (Aldershot, 1995), pp. 142-88; and, the ambitious and pioneering work of Marie-Claire Uhart, "The Early Reception of *Piers Plowman,*" PhD diss., University of Leicester, 1986.

[3] Benson and Blanchfield's work, while providing transcriptions of some of the *Piers Plowman* B-Text manuscripts, refrains from any coherent attempt at classifying its data.

[4] R. C. Alston, *Books with Manuscript* (London, 1994), pp. vi-vii.

[5] Benson, in his preface to his book with Blanchfield, excludes Robert Crowley's 1550 editions of *Piers Plowman* from their study on the grounds that they are "not themselves manuscripts; moreover, their annotations are both original and widely available" (Benson and Blanchfield, p. 1). This kind of attitude has caused considerable damage over the years to the study of marginalia: it is a well-known fact that, for a certain period at least, medieval libraries made no distinction between manuscripts and printed books; see N. F. Blake, "Manuscript to Print," in *Book Production and Publishing in Britain: 1375-1475,* ed. Jeremy Griffiths and Derek Pearsall (Cambridge, 1989), p. 404 . In addition, besides the few hundred copies of 1976 Paradine reprint of Pepys' first impression of Crowley, one would be hard pressed to find more than a few dozen copies, most of which reside in British Libraries; see Alfred W. Pollard and G. R. Redgrave, *A Short-Title Catalogue of Books Printed in England, Scotland & Ireland and of English Books Printed Abroad 1475-1640,* 2nd ed., ed. W. A. Jackson and F. S. Ferguson, completed by Katharine F. Pantzer, 3 vols. (London, 1986).

[6] One of the best contemporary bibliographers must be C. W. Dutschke, whose *Guide to Medieval and Renaissance Manuscripts in the Huntington Library* (San Marino, CA, 1989) is everything that a modern catalogue should be. For transcriptions of marginal texts see Benson and Blanchfield, Kerby-Fulton and Despres, Schaap, among others.

[7] All references to the *Piers Plowman* C-Text are taken from *Piers Plowman: An Edition of the C-Text,* ed. Derek Pearsall (Berkeley, 1979) (hereafter Pearsall, *C-Text*). I should like to thank the Trustees of the Huntington Library of San Marino, California, for permission to publish the marginalia from their MS HM 143 and for supplying me with a microfilm and access to the manuscript. I should like to thank the British Library for permission to publish the marginalia from their MS Additional 35157.

[8] M. B. Parkes, *English Cursive Book Hands: 1250-1500* (Oxford, 1969), pp. 28-30.

[9] Although this somewhat breaks with standard practice, I feel that brevigraphic practices were learned and perhaps localized behaviors. Say, for example, a scribe consistently uses a "pre-" form for "par-" and yet still writes "par-" out in full on occasion. It would be a shame to lose such an identifying idiosyncrasy. In an edition of a text, one might settle for documenting a scribe's brevigraphic practices and then standardizing his spelling.

[10] A full list follows: University of Glasgow, Hunterian Collection, MS 3, Queen Elizabeth I Warrants; MS 5, Lydgate's *Fall of Princes*; MS 7, Gower's *Confessio Amantis*; MS 61, Brut; MS 64, Medical Receipts; MS 74, *Brut*; MS 75, Clarendon Correspondence; MS 76, Selden's *Baronage*; MS 77, Love's *Mirror*; MS 82, Howard's *Abdication of Charles V*; MS 83, *Brut*; MS 84, Metrical Exposition of the Pater Noster; MS 93, Medical Receipts; MS 95, Medical Receipts; MS 97, Selden's *Privileges of Parliament*; MS 104, *Palladius*; MS 115, Catalogue of Minerals; MS 117, Medical Receipts; MS 136, Kemp's *Imitatio Christi*; MS 176, Wycliffe's *New Testament*; MS 185, Medical Receipts; MS 189, Wycliffe's *New Testament*; MS 191, Wycliffe's *New Testament*; MS 197, Chaucer's *Canterbury Tales*; MS 228, *Brut*; MS 230, *Brut*; MS 232, Lydgate's *Life of our Lady*; MS 239, Chaucer's *ABC*; MS 250, Love's *Mirror*; MS 270, Parker's *Dives et Pauper*; MS 303, W. H.'s *God's 2nd Maister-peece*; MS 307, Medical Receipts; MS 328, Medical Receipts; MS 329, Medical Receipts; MS 337, Wycliffe's *Gospel According to St Mark*; MS 359, Kellie's *Lord Boroscho*; MS 364, Banister's *Anatomy*; MS 367, Trevisa's translation of *Polychronicon*; MS 380, Queen Elizabeth I Proclamations; MS 388, Lydgate's *Troy Book*; MS 399, More's *Dialogue of Comfort*; MS 400, Hardyng's *Metrical Chronicle*; MS 409, Chaucer's *Romaunt of the Rose*; MS 410, Caxton's *Life of Jason*; MS 415, Robert of Gloucester's *Metrical Chronicle*; MS 443, Brut; MS 450, Appleyard's *Chronicle*; MS 466, Maister's translation of *Life of Scipio*; MS 472, Primer; MS 496, *Pore Caitif*; MS 497, Herbal; MS 509, Medical Receipts; MS 512, Calendar, Primer and Hours; MS 513, Medical Receipts; MS 520, *Pore Caitif*.

[11] It is hoped that Martin Irvine's promised follow-up volume to *The Making of a Textual Culture* will address many of these issues across the entire range of late medieval European culture. See Martin Irvine, *The Making of Textual Culture: "Grammatica" and Literary Theory 350-1100* (Cambridge, 1994), p. 466.

[12] Addressing similar issues in the early Middle Ages, Irvine suggests that the "special literacy" created at this time is still experienced in present-day Western societies; see pp. xiii-xiv.

[13] Irvine, p. 17.

[14] Alastair J. Minnis, *Medieval Theory of Authorship: Scholastic Literary Attitudes in the Later Middle Ages* (London, 1984), pp. 124-25.

[15] Regarding Kerby-Fulton's and Despres's *Iconography*, it must be noted that I have co-opted an entire sub-type of marginalia from their research (Type III: Ethical Pointers). In its most general aspects, Kerby-Fulton's and Despres's works comprise an in-depth examination of Douce 104, which, like Add. 35157, is a C-Text of *Piers Plowman*. Kerby-Fulton was constantly consulted during the refinement of this classification system for manuscript marginalia. Credit, as always, must go to her for suggesting that I look at manuscript marginalia in the first place.

[16] See Grindley, "From Creation" and "The Life of a Book." Aside from the two base texts used for the development of this system (Add. 35157 and HM 143), most first-hand manuscript examination was confined to books housed in the University of Glasgow's Hunterian collection (see n.10 above), to Oxford, Bodleian Library, MS Douce 104, and to San Marino, Huntington Library, MS HM 114, MS 128 and MS 137. The Hunterian collection proved adequate to the task of double-checking the classification scheme for marginalia. For a list of manuscripts in the Hunterian, see John Young and P. Henderson Aitken, *A Catalogue of the Manuscripts in the Library of the Hunterian Museum in the University of Glasgow* (Glasgow, 1908). The staff of the Hunterian collection, especially David Weston, were particularly accommodating. Ultra-violet light was utilized on most manuscripts which were then repeatedly examined. Although many manuscripts from outside the Hunterian collection were consulted in microfilm, in particular those from the British Library's microfilm series and the Cambridge University Library, in order to streamline this paper, no data have been reproduced from these sources. See *British Literary Manuscripts from Cambridge University Library* (Brighton: Harvester, 1984), and *British Literary Manuscripts from the British Library, London* (Brighton, 1984).

[17] For assistance with the preceding see David Pearson, *Provenance Research in Book History: A Handbook* (London, 1994), pp. 44-45.

[18] For a transcription, see Young and Aitken, p. 185.

[19] Hunterian MS 466, a scribal copy of William Maister's 1555 translation of Pseudo-Plutarch's *Life of Scipio*, claims in its introduction to have been copied out many years before it was.

[20] Stephen Partridge, in his dissertation and in various published and unpublished works, has identified the presence of many of the same types of marginalia in *Canterbury Tales* manuscripts.

[21] Grindley, "From Creation," pp. 22-40.

[22] See Kerby-Fulton and Despres, *Iconography*, Appendix I for evidence of pre-planned annotations in Douce 104.

[23] Particularly in the case of HM 143, which I believe was deliberately created for monastic use.

[24] Hand E/F of Add. 35157 did just this, reproducing several annotations from Crowley's second or third impression of the *Piers Plowman* B-Text.

[25] Detailed descriptions of each of these categories can be found in Grindley, "From Creation" and "The Life of a Book."

[26] Irvine, *The Making of Textual Culture*, pp. 69, 466.

[27] Irvine, p. 6.

[28] Topic annotations appear in Hunterian MS 5 (shelfmark S. 1. 5), a fine copy of Lydgate's *Fall of Princes*, and in many of the Hunterian's medical manuscripts including MS 328 (shelfmark U. 7. 22), a book on urines, and MS 513 (shelfmark V. 8. 16), a collection of medical recipes.

[29] Source annotations occur in two of the Hunterian's manuscripts of the *Pore Caitif*, MSS 496 and 520 (shelfmarks V. 7. 23 and V. 8. 23 respectively).

[30] Pearsall, *C-Text*, p. 34 n.

[31] Citation annotations appear in Hunterian MS 520 (shelfmark V. 8. 23), one of collection's two copies of the *Pore Caitif* (see note 10 above).

[32] For two annotations by hand F, see Grindley, "Life of a Book," chapter 5.

[33] Perhaps the strangest Citation annotations I have seen appear in MS W of the *Piers Plowman* C-Text (the now-lost Duke of Westminster's manuscript). The correcting/rubricating/annotating scribe (arguably the most common arrangement for these duties) padded out Langland's typically terse scriptural quotations with lines from the originals.

[34] Caie, "Early Manuscript Chaucer Glosses," 350-60. See Stephen Partridge's unpublished dissertation, "The Manuscript Glosses to the *Canterbury Tales*: A Reassessment."

[35] Schibanoff, "The New Reader," 73.

[36] Caie, 350-60; Derek Pearsall, "Gower's Latin in the *Confessio Amantis*," in *Latin and Vernacular: Studies in Late-Medieval Texts and Manuscripts*, ed. A. J. Minnis and D. S. Brewer, York Manuscripts Conferences, proceedings series, 1 (Cambridge, 1989), pp. 13-15.

[37] Benson and Windeatt, "Manuscript Glosses," 33-53.

[38] None of the Hunterian's Middle or Early Modern English manuscripts contained any Rhetorical Devices annotations. Interestingly, however, this subcategory is fairly well represented in Skeat's base C-Text, HM 137. Although the *ordinatio* of HM 137 has not been investigated, a cursory review of that manuscript suggests that a great many of its annotations easily fit into this category.

[39] M. B. Parkes, "The Influence of the Concepts of *Ordinatio* and *Compilatio* on the Development of the Book," in *Medieval Learning and Literature: Essays Presented to R. W. Hunt*, eds. J. J. G. Alexander and M. T. Gibson (Oxford, 1976), pp. 116-17.

[40] Tanya Schaap identified a large number of Rhetorical Device annotations in her study of Digby 102; see "From Scribe to Reader."

[41] Additional Information annotations appear in Hunterian MS 400 (shelfmark V. 2. 20), which is an early copy of Hardyng's metrical chronicle; they are clearly the work of the manuscript's main scribe and appear to be a planned part of the manuscript's *mise-en-page*.

[42] Sandler, "*Omne bonum,*" p. 184. Summation annotations appear in Hunterian MS 5 (shelfmark S. 1. 5), a fine copy of Lydgate's *Fall of Princes*.

[43] The intellectual debt that I owe to Kerby-Fulton is happily acknowledged. She identified the annotations and provided the examples, which I have taken from the early drafts of her book with Denise Despres, *Iconography*, pp. 179-230.

[44] Kane and Russell list it as being one of the more persistent pairings, with 129 aggreements. *Piers Plowman: The C-Version*, ed. George Russell and George Kane (London, 1997), pp. 30-31.

[45] Minnis, pp. 124-25.

[46] Kerby-Fulton and Despres, *Iconography*, pp. 192-94.

[47] Kerby-Fulton and Despres, *Iconography*, pp. 192-94.

[48] Kerby-Fulton and Despres, *Iconography*, p. 193.

[49] Grindley, "The Life of a Book."

[50] Hand I dates from the turn of the seventeenth century, but his remarks are in no way substantially different from any of Add. 35157's earlier annotators. Incidentally, I still see the same basic types of annotations being made today, although rubrication seems to have been displaced by the highlighting pen.

[51] The fourth category, that of Language Issues, is identified in Stephen Partridge's "Manuscript Glosses to the *Canterbury Tales*." Partridge distinguishes two types of glosses, one that explains the meanings of proper nouns (lexical glosses) and one that identifies the antecedents of pronouns (syntactical glosses), but I conflate these into Language Issues.

[52] Kerby-Fulton and Despres, *Iconography*, p. 197.

[53] Kerby-Fulton and Despres, *Iconography*, p. 197.

[54] With Partridge's work on the *Canterbury Tales* (see above), the classification of these types of annotations will have to be expanded and improved.

[55] Translation annotations appear in Hunterian MS 367 (shelfmark V. 1. 4), a copy of Trevisa's translation of Hidgen's *Polychronicon*, which also contains a contemporary table of contents, many pointing hands, a variety of other Narrative Reading Aids and a few sporadic Polemical Responses.

[56] Art historians may object that some illuminators obviously had not read their texts, so perhaps such context-free illuminations should constitute a new category of Type II marginal comment.

[57] At this stage, I think initials might be described and classified according to placement, frequency, size, colour, and, possibly, form. I am currently working on compiling a database of Lombardic initials in order to determine the regional nature of copy-book forms and the likelihood of identifying rubricators through their foliated initials.

[58] I have learned, rather belatedly, that the use of crowns as textual markers has some relation to Exchequer symbols. See Kathryn Kerby-Fulton and Steven Justice, "The *Modus tenendi parliamentum* and its Literary Relations," *Traditio* 53 (1998), 149-203.

[59] Pointing hands appear in the Hunterian collection's MS 117 (shelfmark T. 5. 19). MS 117 is an anonymous late-fourteenth-century collection of medical recipes.

[60] Heads as pointing hands appear in Hunterian MS 270 (shelfmark U. 5. 10), which is a fifteenth-century manuscript of Henry Parker's *Dives et Pauper*.

[61] Grindley, "The Life of a Book."

[62] Dutschke, *Guide to Medieval and Renaissance Manuscripts*, pp. 195-97.

[63] Russell published several of the annotations in "'As They Read It': Some Notes on Early Responses to the C-Version of *Piers Plowman*," and "Some Early Responses to the C-Version of *Piers Plowman*." An incomplete (and unfortunately inaccurate in places) transcription of the HM 143 marginalia appears in Uhart's pioneering study, *The Early Reception of Piers Plowman*. A complete transcription appears in Grindley's, "From Creation," pp. 22-40.

[64] For an interpretation of HM 143's marginalia see Grindley, "From Creation," pp. 41-81.

[65] Grindley, "From Creation," pp. 8-9.

[66] Dutschke, pp. 195-97.

[67] See M. B. Parkes, *English Cursive Book Hands,* and Michelle P. Brown, *A Guide to Western Historical Scripts from Antiquity to 1600* (London, 1993), for a discussion of similar hands.

[68] I find it odd that the more formal Scribe A should favour a cursive "s," whereas the generally more cursive Scribe B favours a semi-quadrata "s."

[69] Most forms in Scribe B's dialect survey localise to the general southwest area, and there are not many diagnostic spellings. More curious is his reluctance to tolerate Scribe A's forms for HE "a," 4. SHE "he," 5. HER "he," and his P/B voicing. For a discussion of the dialect of scribe A, see M. L. Samuels, "Langland's Dialect," in *The English of Chaucer and His Contemporaries, Essays by M. L. Samuels and Jeremy J. Smith,* ed. Jeremy J. Smith (Aberdeen, 1986), pp. 70-85. Sec also *A Linguistic Atlas of Late Mediaeval English,* ed. Angus McIntosh, M. L. Samuels and Michael Benskin (Aberdeen, 1986); and Michael Benskin, "The 'fit'-technique Explained," in *Regionalism in Late Medieval Manuscripts and Texts,* ed. Felicity Riddy (Cambridge, 1991), pp. 9-26.

[70] Samuels, "Langland's Dialects," p. 78.

[71] Unpublished work by Grindley.

[72] *Piers Plowman: The Huntington Manuscript (HM143) Master Negative Microfilm.* (Huntington Library, 1975).

[73] *Piers Plowman: The Huntington Manuscript (HM 123) Reproduced in Photostat, With an Introduction by R. W. Chambers and Technical Examination by R. B. Haselden and H. C. Schulz* (San Marino, CA, 1936), pp. 1-3 and *passim.*

[74] Pearsall, *C-Text,* p. 11. With my recent discovery of mistaken sigla in the Russell and Kane Athlone C-Text's apparatus, I can no longer confidently cite their work as a uniform critical text of Langland's poem.

[75] In the case of the periodic erasures of the various forms of the name "Piers Plowman," I am deeply indebted to the work of R. B. Haselden and H. C. Schulz in recovering readings for the defaced sections.

The Red Ink Annotator of
The Book of Margery Kempe
and His Lay Audience

Kelly Parsons

Surprisingly, the question of early audience readings of *The Book of Margery Kempe* seldom receives the scholarly attention it deserves. As Karma Lochrie has pointed out, studies of Margery Kempe "tend to view her work in isolation from its readership and the culture which read it in the fifteenth and sixteenth centuries."[1] This is regrettable; inquiry into early readings of this text cannot help but lead to a more meaningful context in which to read, respond to, and judge both Margery and her *Book* today.

How did medieval people actually read and respond to *The Book of Margery Kempe*? We can turn first of all to manuscript evidence — arguably one of our most reliable avenues to the past — in this case London, British Library MS Additional 61823, the single surviving copy of the work. Written by a scribe named Salthows between 1440 and 1450, probably in Norfolk, MS Add. 61823 is considered to be an early copy of the original written by Margery's second amanuensis; it was owned and extensively annotated by the Carthusians at Mount Grace Priory in Yorkshire.[2] The most prolific of these annotators, using red ink and a late fifteenth- or early sixteenth-century hand, has inscribed both in the margins and between the lines, a lively, fascinating and fully-engaged reading of the *Book*.

The Carthusian dedication to the contemplative life and interest in texts of mysticism and affective devotion are evident in the many such books which survive from their libraries.[3] This early monastic audience for *The Book of Margery Kempe* should therefore come as no surprise. But could it be that Margery and her *Book* reached an early lay audience as well? After all, as Lochrie points out, Kempe "seemed to pitch her treatise at a lay audience, since it is meant as an instructive example of a manner of living after the life of Christ."[4] Sue Ellen Holbrook summarizes the attitude of the Mount Grace annotator as follows:

> the [red ink] annotator responds not only to love, thinking, compassion, charity, mourning, detraction, reward, the acceptance of tribulation,

patience, the right way to heaven and so forth, but also to the problem of being a mystic when one is also a wife, the passionate quality and the marital form of her spiritual relationship to the Lord, and, notably, the visions, the cries, the feelings of weakness and of fire burning — i.e., the sensory manifestations of communion with God, and the similarity between Kempe's experiences and those of Methley, Norton and Rolle.[5]

As we shall see, much of the red ink annotator's *corpus*, especially when viewed as a whole and in the context of known Carthusian pastoral activities, is difficult, if not impossible to reconcile with an exclusively monastic audience. This essay will explore some of the ways in which the annotations in red ink, along with other codicological features of the manuscript, support a strong argument in favour of a lay audience for the *Book*. Indeed, there is compelling evidence not only that the text was prepared for use outside the walls of Mount Grace, but that the red ink annotator actually customized *The Book of Margery Kempe* for the devotional use of an audience of lay women.

The red ink annotations in MS Add. 61823 are addressed in Meech and Allen's Early English Text Society edition of the *Book*, but in a format that is not convenient for study and does not allow for a clear sense of the annotations as a body of work.[6] As well, Meech's edition has been found to contain some mistranscriptions and omissions.[7] In order to remedy these shortcomings and at the same time encourage further study of the annotations by providing a usable resource for scholars interested in the early reception of *The Book of Margery Kempe*, I provide below complete listings of all red ink annotations (appendix A), corrections (appendix B), and rubrications (appendix C).[8]

Although the Carthusians themselves were not often authors of anything in the vernacular specifically addressed to a lay audience,[9] the Carthusian order in England is well known for its transmission, translation, and preservation of both Latin and vernacular spiritual writings.[10] Indeed, as we have seen, it is the Carthusians of Mount Grace who are at least partially responsible for the survival of the unique copy of *The Book of Margery Kempe*. In addition to MS Add. 61823, only two other surviving vernacular manuscripts are known to have come from Mount Grace: Cambridge, University Library MS 6578, a copy of *Nicholas Love's Myrrour of the Blessed Lyf of Jesu Christ*; and London, British Library MS Harley 2373, which contains *The Cloud of Unknowing*.[11] The Carthusians were also owners, producers, and annotators of books of pastoral care, and from "early in its history [the order] . . . recognised that withdrawal from the temptations of the world did not eliminate the need for pastoral care of those in its communities."[12] The charterhouses were, in fact, responsible for the pastoral care of wealthy patrons, both men and women. According to Vincent Gillespie, "These kinds of contacts with the laity, and indeed with the secular clergy and clergy of other orders, must have increased the order's awareness of pastoral needs and of developments in pastoral techniques, in addition to their internal exercise of most aspects of the *cura animarum*."[13] The Carthusians also assumed responsibility for the pastoral care of their servants, many of whom were married.[14]

The red ink annotator appears to have been working within a long-standing pastoral tradition at Mount Grace, and we know that for most purposes pastoral duties in Carthusian houses were the responsibility of the prior.[15] Mount Grace — or the priory of the Assumption of the Virgin Mary, and St. Nicholas — was founded in 1398, and very early in its history we find two lay bequests to the prior: one in 1401 by Dame Isabella Fauconbergh of Cleveland of "her best furred mantle,"[16] and the other in 1402 by a knight, Sir John Depeden, which included a "picture of the crucifixion."[17] These gifts suggest some sort of meaningful contact between the prior of Mount Grace and the neighbouring lay community.

Perhaps even more interesting for our purposes, there is testamentary evidence from the mid-fifteenth century of books changing hands between Mount Grace and the outside world. William Banks of York bequeathed to Mount Grace twenty shillings in 1458, "on condition that they made no claim to a book called *Florarium Bartholomei*, which may have been a volume strayed from their possession which they desired to get back."[18] In 1433, the rector of Dighton, William de Anthorp, left "to the prior and convent of Mountgrace . . . besides a silver cup gilt and twelve silver spoons, a book called *Pupilla oculi* (probably the medieval manual for priests so called)."[19]

Two of the more well known Mount Grace Carthusians, Richard Methley and John Norton, as their Latin writings reveal, were both "extreme exponent[s] of 'sensory devotion.' "[20] Methley was vicar of Mount Grace at the time of his death c. 1527-28, and Norton was prior there from 1509 to 1522, the year of his death.[21] Both are referred to by the red ink annotator, as is Richard Rolle, in such a way as to compare and align Margery with their affective mysticism. For example, in chapter 73 where Margery has a vision of the parting of Mary and Christ, and thus falls down in a field among people, crying, weeping and roaring, we find written in the margin of folio 85r, "father M. was wont so to doo" (Meech, 174). In the outer margin of chapter 44, where Margery "wyth þe crying wrestyd hir body turnyng from þe o syde

145

in-to þe oþer," the words "so dyd prior Nort in hys excesse" are written in red (fol. 51v; Meech, 105). Where Margery felt the fire of love burning in her heart in chapter 35, Richard Rolle is noted in the margin of folio 43v (see fig. 1) as "so s. R. hampall." (Meech, 88). By drawing attention to "excesses" similar to Margery's in the mystical experience of Richard Methley, John Norton, and Richard Rolle, these red ink annotations serve to endorse or authorize Margery's affective mystical experiences.

As vicar at Mount Grace, Methley would have assumed some of the duties of the prior in his absence, particularly if the prior were a visitor,[22] duties which would likely have put him in close contact with the laity. According to James Hogg, "it is more than possible that [Methley's] reputation as a spiritual counsellor radiated beyond the confines of the remote charterhouse, lying away on the edge of the rolling Yorkshire moors, for his glossed translations of *The Cloud of Unknowing* shows him, even more than do his original writings, as a skilled spiritual director, wise in the ways of God towards souls seeking perfection."[23] Indeed, there is convincing evidence that Methley, probably in carrying out his pastoral duties as vicar, did have close dealings with Mount Grace's lay community, as can be seen in some of the money and goods bequeathed to him by the local gentry. In 1509, for example, the rich widow of a York merchant, Alison Clark, bequeathed "one of her three best altarcloths to 'Sir Richard mownk of Mowntgraice.' "[24]

A more direct example of Methley engaging in the pastoral care of non-Carthusians can be found in his authorship of the Middle English *To Hew Heremyte A Pystyl of Solytary Lyfe Nowadayes*, in which he responds to a request from a hermit, presumably one living somewhere in the vicinity of Mount Grace, for spiritual guidance. One of the activities recommended to Hew by Methley is the "redying of holy englysshe bokes."[25] As Nicholas Watson has pointed out, though it is unclear where these "holy englysshe bokes" are to come from, one option is Mount Grace, which would bear out the argument that the charterhouse was more than likely involved in loaning books to those outside its walls.[26]

As spiritual overseer responsible for the "gostly" guidance of a secular woman, a Carthusian advisor might well turn to a text such as *The Book of Margery Kempe* as an aid to this duty. A woman could particularly identify with the spiritual struggles and devotional practices of a married woman such as Margery, learning to emulate her successes and avoid her failures, all under the careful and conservative tutelage and control of a respected Carthusian advisor.

As mentioned above, many of the red ink annotations seem to have been tailored for female consumption. In chapter 57, Margery speaks to God:

> I haue gret mer-
> ueyl in myn hert Lord þat I whech haue ben so synful
> a woman & þe most vnworthy creatur þat euyr þu schewedist
> þi mercy on to, in alle þis werlde þat I haue so gret charite
> to myn euyn cristen sowlys þat me thynkyth, þou þei had
> ordeynd for me þe most schamful deth þat euyr myth |
> any man <or woman> suffyr in erde ȝet wolde I forȝeuyn it hem for
> þi lofe Lord.   (fols. 68v-69r; Meech, 141-42)

The red ink annotator has inserted with a red caret, the words "or woman" between "man" and "suffyr" (see fig. 2). Although in the context of the entire passage, this emendation could be just a correction based on the annotator's reading of Margery's intent, one must still ask of what relevance or interest would the inclusion of "woman" in this phrase be to a Carthusian brother? It would likely be of greater importance to a woman, and that woman might have been a pious lay patron or married servant in the annotator's pastoral care.

Other annotations involving women include an uncharacteristically lengthy marginal admonition in chapter 74, where Margery is trying to help a greatly troubled woman. This woman's many temptations, torments by the devil, and fears she would be killed by him, have made her afraid to bless herself or worship God. The pastoral tone of the annotation is clear: "nota A sotel & a sore temptacion. In siche a case we shold be more stronge & bold a-ga[n]ste our gostly enmy" (fol. 86v; Meech, 177). In another example, the Mount Grace annotator has flagged, as noted by Holbrook,[27] a passage in chapter 21 that would potentially be of great comfort and spiritual solace to a married woman, either chaste or widowed. The Lord reassures Margery,

> ȝa dowtyr trow þow rygth wel þat I
> lofe wyfes also. And specyal þo wyfys whech woldyn levyn
> chast, ȝyf þei mygtyn haue her wyl & don her besynes
> to plesyn me as þow dost For þow þe state of maydenhode be   n[ota]
> mor parfyte mor holy þan þe state of wedewhode & þe state . . . .
>   (fol. 24r; Meech, 49)

That the annotator has called attention to this passage with a red *nota* sign lends support to the likelihood that the manuscript's readership was intended to include women.

A great many of the red ink annotations in the *Book* seem to encourage an autobiographical reading of the text, a devotional style of reading important in monasteries.[28] There is no reason to think that the laity would not be interested in an autobiographical reading of the text as well, and many of the annotations could have been of interest to married women, particularly those interested in pursuing a mixed life. There are, for example, at least three marginal annotations emphasizing the presence of Margery's husband in her treatise. One, ".h. husband" (fol. 51r; Meech, 104), occurs in chapter 44 where Margery receives communion in her white clothes, and afterwards her husband comes to Norwich to accompany her home to Lynn, just before she becomes very ill. The second occurs in chapter 55 where Margery sends for her husband upon returning to Lynn from her visit to the Archbishop of York, after which she is arrested as a Lollard and eventually released; again, "husband" appears in the outer margin (fol. 66r; Meech, 136). Thirdly, Margery's husband is noted by the Mount Grace annotator in chapter 76:

> It happyd on a tyme þat þe husbonde of þe sayd creatur
> a man in gret age passyng thre scor 3er, as he   ⌊**her husband**⌉
> wold a comyn down of hys chambyr bar-foot & bar
> legge he slederyd er ellys faylyd of hys fotyng & fel . . . .
>   (fol. 87r; Meech, 179)

The pastoral care of women can be inferred from these annotations; a married woman's identification with the married (and child-bearing) Margery would enhance the effectiveness of the *Book* as a tool of pastoral care. Another marginal annotation likely to be of more concern to a married lay woman than to a celibate cleric occurs in chapter 48 where Margery has to answer to questions on the Articles of Faith, when she is called before the abbot, the Mayor of Leicester, and others:

>   þat I neuyr
> had part of mannys body in þis worlde in actual dede be wey
> of synne but of myn husbondys body whom I am bowndyn to
> be þe lawe of matrimony & be whom I haue born xiiij childeryn. ⌊**xiiij child**⌉
>   (fol. 56r; Meech, 115)

The outer margin bears a red annotation signaling to the reader "xiiij child." This point regarding the number of children borne by Margery, particularly of interest to women, perhaps signals that a large number of offspring need not be a deterrent to the pursuit of pious devotional life.

An annotation that would seem of particular interest to a lay reader-ship or audience, both male and female, occurs near a passage in chapter 51 in which some people of York speak up for Margery when she is being sent to jail to await an audience with the Archbishop of York:

Than   n*ota*⌊**seculer .p.**
þe seculer pepil answeryd for hir & seyde sche xulde not
comyn in p*ri*son for þei woldyn hem-self vndirtakyn for hir.
& gon to þe Erchebischop wy*th* hir . . . .
(fol. 59r; Meech, 122)

A red ink marginal notation of "seculer .p." is preceded by a red *nota* sign, perhaps meant to stimulate the lay reader's identification with Margery, who is being held up as a role model for living in imitation of the life of Christ.

Although they encouraged lay meditation, the Carthusians were also active in censoring or "watering down" many of the mystical texts they circulated, particularly among women, as can be seen in their translations and devotional allegorization of the texts of the female continental mystics such as Bridget of Sweden and Catherine of Siena, for the use of women connected with the Bridgettine Syon Abbey. According to Denise Despres, the Carthusians "were discriminating in selecting works for dissemination to a select lay audience, taking care . . . to modify or adapt the text for devotional, as opposed to contemplative purposes."[29] Censoring red ink emendations of Margery's *Book* occur in MS Add. 61823 in the form of excisions. An example can be found in chapter 84, where God is thanking Margery because

as sche in co*n*templacyon & in meditacyon had ben hys
modyrs maydyn {~~& holpyn to kepyn hym in hys childhod~~
~~& so forth in to þe tyme of hys deth~~} & seyd vn to hir . . . .
(fol. 98v; Meech, 203)

The passage "& holpyn to kepyn hym in hys childhod & so forth in-to þe tyme of hys deth" is repeatedly crossed through in red. The annotator seems to object to Margery's language and to be uncomfortable with her familiarity, albeit ghostly familiarity, with the humanity and physicality of Christ. He apparently believes others will also be offended, though exactly why he is offended is not entirely clear, since he seems to support and approve of Margery's affectivism elsewhere in the text.[30]

In the introduction to their edition of *The Chastising of God's Children*, Joyce Bazire and Eric Colledge state, "Constantly we shall find Margery

Kempe and her like claiming that they have been 'ravished into heaven': and their critics regard their thought and their language as dangerous."[31] Although these editors may be over-reading here,[32] the point is well taken; Margery Kempe had her fair share of critics. Several censoring emendations made by the red ink annotator seem at least partially to reflect this attitude. Note, for example, the red ink insertion in the chapter 86 passage where God, in discussing his spiritual marriage with Margery, praises her:

> And also dowt*yr* I thank
> þe for alle þe tymys þat þu has herberwyd me & my blissyd
> modyr in þi bed <**gostly**> for þes & for all oþer good thowtys. . . .
> (fol. 103v; Meech, 214)

In a similar fashion, "gostly" is inserted in red ink to precede "dawnsyn" in chapter 22 in the phrase "& so xalt þu dawnsyn in Hevyn" (fol. 26r; Meech, 52). While apparently approving of Margery's affective behavior elsewhere, in these instances the annotator censors her "bodily" references, upgrading them to a more conservative and therefore safer "gostly" status.

The red ink annotator seems to have taken great care to customize the manuscript for devotional use. In the numerous marginal and interlinear recordings of what appear to be his personal ecstatic response to the text, the Mount Grace annotator can be seen using the manuscript devotionally himself, in effect modeling affective piety for a readership that included women. One example of this occurs at the end of chapter 60, where the good priest who had read to Margery for seven years is gravely ill. Margery prays for him, and God answers that he "xulde leuyn & faryn ryth wel" (Meech, 147). After traveling about and much weeping and crying, Margery returns home to find the good priest has miraculously recovered:

> [He] recuryd & went
> a bowte wher hym lykyde þa*n*kyd be al mythy God for hys
> goodnes.   <**Amen Amen Amen**>
> (fol. 72r; Meech, 148)

The annotator has echoed his own thanks with "Amen Amen Amen." Another example of what Meech calls the annotator's "pious ejaculations" (p. xlii) occurs on folio 92v:

> þ*er*for
> dowt*yr* þu hast gret cawse to louyn me ryght wel for I haue
> bowt þi lofe ful der.   <**trew it is blyssyd lord**>
> (Meech, 191)

150

A blank space has given the annotator room to write "trew it is blyssyd lord." This personal response seems spontaneous and genuinely emotional, and as such is particularly uncommon in the marginalia genre, especially when compared, for instance, to *Piers Plowman* marginalia. John Cok, a *Piers* annotator, has a "strong tendency to highlight emotional passages," but with a *nota* sign only, not with his own personal ecstatic response.[33] In contrast, the many ecstatic responses of the red ink annotator are highly personal, perhaps akin to the personalized and somewhat emotional annotations of Irish scribes, as translated and described by Charles Plummer.[34] When further study is done on Carthusian marginalia we may be in a better position to know just how unusual these red ink annotations are. If they register episodes of rapture in the annotator's own devotional life, this would not have been unusual for a Carthusian, as witnessed by the affective mysticism of Nicholas Love, Richard Methley, and John Norton, all of whom were from Mount Grace. Moreover, it would appear that the red ink annotator also expected his audience to be familiar with this culture of "devotional rapture," presenting himself as he does, as an affective exemplar of the same.

Several marginal line drawings in red ink seem to indicate that our Mount Grace annotator understood and approved of the devotional use of images. We find drawings of hearts, hands, a pillar and, of particular interest, a graphic depiction of "flames of divine love" (fol. 43v; see fig. 1), bearing the inscription "ignis divini amoris" (Meech, 88). Contemplation of these marginal images, as unsophisticated as they may be, would have provided readers with an emblematic focus for their meditations, aiding in their ability to feel and experience personally what is being described in the text. As John Friedman has argued, affective piety in the form of intense interest in the Passion was particularly evident in Northern England, where the red ink annotations were made. The devotional use of images in the service of this affective piety was extremely common, especially images of the Sacred Heart (including the five wounds of Christ), the Holy Face, and the Holy Name (or sacred monogram). Pious readers were counseled to focus their attention on images in their books, enabling them to "imagine themselves bystanders at or even participants in the events they contemplate."[35] Such devotional practice was made popular in late medieval England by the Franciscans, in such Latin works as Bonaventure's *Lignum Vitae*, or the Pseudo-Bonaventuran *Meditationes Vitae Christi*, and later in Nicholas Love's Middle English translation of the *Meditationes*, the *Myrrour of the Blesed Lyf of Jesu Christ*.[36]

151

The red ink annotator has drawn an image (see fig. 3), apparently unnoticed by Meech, of one of the most common emblems of the Passion, Christ's wounded heart, inside a large rubric "T" at folio 31r, the beginning of chapter 27. One of several large rubricated "T"s, this one is like no other in the manuscript. It has been closed in to look rather like a shield, and appears to bear the five wounds of Christ, namely the two hands, two feet and the larger slit-like side wound. According to John Friedman, "Christ's torment was often expressed by various metaphors in which the body was likened to a parchment book, a scroll, a deed, or even a shield bearing a 'coat of arms' that could be read by the pious meditator."[37] Apparently Richard Rolle likened the five wounds of Christ to "a book with red ink."[38] Could the Mount Grace annotator have had this in the back of his mind when he chose to use red ink to annotate the Kempe manuscript? The side wound, says Friedman, "is imagined as a physical refuge in which the devout seek shelter and into which they actually enter and become one with the figure of the crucified Christ."[39] The employment of this image by the red ink annotator for his readers suggests that women were included in a community in Northern England conversant in the devotional use of images of the Sacred Heart and the side wound. Examples of this devotional practice, especially in connection with women, can be found in Mechtild of Hackeborn's Latin *Liber specialis gratiae* or in its Middle English translation *The Booke of Gostlye Grace*, as well as in Julian of Norwich's *A Book of Showings*, and Catherine of Siena's *Vita*.[40] An iconographically similar image, although more sophisticated than the "five wounds shield" in the rubric "T" of MS Add. 61823, appears in a late fifteenth-century Carthusian manuscript, London, British Library MS Additional 37049, at folio 46v (see fig. 4). A devotional miscellany written in the vernacular, it is believed to have been a Mount Grace manuscript,[41] and contemporaneous with MS Add. 61823, so it is quite possible that the red ink annotator had access to it and perhaps was influenced by it in his line drawings and annotations for the Kempe manuscript. Interestingly, like the Kempe manuscript, MS Add. 37049 seems to have been intended "for outreach to the laity."[42]

MS Add. 37049 also contains images emphasizing the Holy Name. Similarly, the sacred monogram "IHC" occurs often in the red ink annotations of Margery's *Book*, in the margins and frequently inside large rubric "O"s. This seems to be evidence of both the annotator's devotional use of images and his personal ecstatic response to the text, as well as what Hope Emily Allen describes as an indication of a "special devotion to the Holy Name" at Mount Grace.[43] Several northern manuscripts contain these Holy Name monograms, demonstrating widespread "interest in this motif for decorative and meditational purposes."[44] Again, we find here a likely example of the annotator modelling affective piety for his lay readers.

Another contribution by the red ink annotator to the *Book*'s marginal supply supports the suggestion that MS Add. 61823 was customized for female use. There is a drawing of the Blessed Virgin's smock (fol. 115r; fig. 5), which was witnessed by Margery when it was displayed at Aachen on St. Margaret's Day (Meech, 237). The dress, possibly a "houpeland," is very high-necked and conservative, an example of appropriately modest dress for a pious woman, surely of little or no interest to an audience of male monastics, unless we have here a male cleric wanting to encourage modesty in female dress. One does, however, see great interest in clothing styles in visions written by women, such as Mechtild of Hackeborn's *Booke of Gostlye Grace*,[45] or in Christine de Pizan's *Treasury of the City of Ladies*, which contains exhortations on "How women of property and city women should be suitably dressed."[46] It would appear, therefore, that such an image would more likely have been of keen interest to a person engaged in the pastoral care of women, and to the women themselves.

A number of codicological details seem to support the argument for the *Book* having been loaned out by its Mount Grace owners. Most surviving manuscripts connected to Mount Grace are in Latin and have Latin ownership inscriptions; for example London, British Library MS Harley 237 has the *ex libris, liber domus Montis Gracie ordinis carthusiensis*, and MS Harley 2373 is marked with *In vetero libro hujus domus viz. Montis Gracie, De quattuor gradibus humilitatis nulla fit mentio*.[47] The *Book* (MS Add. 61823), however, besides being a vernacular text has a bilingual *ex libris*, which reads "liber Montis Gracie. this boke is of Mountegrace."[48] As Nicholas Watson has suggested, the *Book*'s vernacular *ex libris* is unusual and suggests that it was loaned for use outside the walls of the monastery.[49] Furthermore, the manuscript, privately owned by Colonel William Butler-Bowdon when it was discovered in 1934, contains two bookplates of Henry Bowdon (b. 1754). It appears to have passed through the hands of many generations of Bowdons, an old Catholic Yorkshire family; perhaps, as Colonel Butler-Bowdon suggested, it was put into the hands of a family member some time before the suppression of Mount Grace in 1539.[50]

Further codicological examination of the manuscript may lead to new information about the provenance and early readership of the *Book*. Noteworthy in this regard is a five-line recipe written in Middle

English in a late-fifteenth- or early-sixteenth-century hand, on the verso of the last folio of the codex (fol. 124r; Meech, xliv). The recipe is almost impossible to read with the unaided eye; however, there is mention of cinnamon and sugar to be ground in a mortar. The question that comes to mind is, what would a recipe be doing in a book belonging to a Carthusian house, especially a recipe that includes such rich and exotic ingredients as cinnamon and sugar? The life of a Carthusian monk at Mount Grace was one of extreme asceticism and hardship:

> their meals were brought from the conventual kitchen and placed in an L-shaped hatch in the front wall of their "cell" . . . They never touched meat, poultry, or game, and took fish when it was given them in charity. Their food consisted mainly of eggs, pulses, and bread and water, but on one day in the week they fasted.[51]

In this rather austere context the recipe might suggest a provenance for the codex that could have included lay ownership, or at the very least prolonged lay use, around the same time the red ink annotations were made.

As Kathryn Kerby-Fulton has been able to determine through careful examination of the red ink hand, colour, tone, and functional range in MS Add. 61823, the red ink annotator was also the rubricator and the corrector of the mansucript.[52] In short, the *Book* appears to have arrived at Mount Grace unrubricated, and all marks in red ink seem to have been made by one man alone. Who was the red ink annotator? It seems likely that he was either a prior or a vicar of Mount Grace, in office in the early sixteenth century, perhaps just before the time of the dissolution. If the annotations refering to Methley and Norton in the past tense imply they were both dead at the time the annotations were written, then the red ink would have been added between c.1528 and the suppression of Mount Grace in 1539. John Wilson was prior of Mount Grace at the time of the dissolution in 1539, and had occupied that office for at least the preceding ten years and perhaps as many as twenty years.[53] It could be, therefore, that Wilson was the prior immediately following John Norton, making Wilson a promising candidate for the red ink annotator. It is much too soon to speculate any further, however, and much more research needs to be done on this subject.

This essay has considered but a small sampling of the multitude of questions raised by study of the red ink annotator's *corpus*; it is clear that much work remains to be done on the red ink annotations, and indeed the entire marginal supply of *The Book of Margery Kempe*. Vernacular texts with religious content circulated widely in Britain during the late

Middle Ages, and these books were altered and adapted to meet the individual needs and abilities of their readers.[54] We may never be in a position to determine whether or not *The Book of Margery Kempe*, as a manuscript and in its entirety, circulated to any significant degree among the laity or indeed, in monastic communities.[55] Nevertheless, the evidence suggests that this sole surviving copy of the *Book*, MS Add. 61823, did entertain both monastic and lay audiences, and was altered by its red ink annotator, apparently to meet the devotional needs of a lay female audience. Through emphasis, commentary, summary and emendation, the Mount Grace annotator greatly influenced readings of the *Book* subsequent to his own. Holbrook suggests that, had the red ink annotator "been selecting extracts, he might have produced a version of *The Book of Margery Kempe* dramatising the enthusiastic devotion of a particular woman."[56] Indeed, the evidence suggests that women were the red ink annotator's primary audience and consequently an early audience for *The Book of Margery Kempe* and for Margery's own enthusiastic devotional style. One would like to think Margery would have been pleased.

NOTES

I would like to thank Kathryn Kerby Fulton for her guidance, her patience and her exemplary scholarship. Special appreciation is also due to Maidie Hilmo for her many careful readings and insightful comments on early drafts, and to Nicholas Watson, who has been a most energetic and helpful reader; I have benefited tremendously from his insights in many more ways than I can document. Finally, my thanks also to Linda Olson, Catherine Parsons, Barbara Colebrook Peace, and Robin Woodworth, all of whom very kindly read and commented helpfully upon early drafts.

1. Karma Lochrie, *Margery Kempe and Translations of the Flesh* (Philadelphia, 1991), p. 204.

2. Sanford B. Meech and Hope Emily Allen, eds., *The Book of Margery Kempe*, EETS, o.s. 212 (1940; repr. London, 1961), p. xxxvi, hereafter cited as Meech. All quotations of the text will be from the manuscript, followed by page references to Meech. See the notes on transcription and apparatus preceding appendices A, B, and C.

3. See Michael G. Sargent, "The Transmission by the English Carthusians of Some Late Medieval Spiritual Writings," *Journal of Ecclesiastical History* 27 (1976); see also E. Margaret Thompson, *The Carthusian Order in England* (London, 1930); and N. R. Ker, *Medieval Libraries of Great Britain: A List of Surviving Books*, 2nd ed. (London, 1964).

4. Lochrie, *Translations of the Flesh*, pp. 206-07.

5 Sue Ellen Holbrook, "Margery Kempe and Wynkyn de Worde," in *The Medieval Mystical Tradition in England: Exeter Symposium IV*, ed. Marion Glasscoe (Cambridge, 1987), p. 37.

6 Meech discusses the annotations in the Introduction and cites most of them in footnotes to the text.

7 John Hirsh has noticed some of these omissions and accordingly provided listings of red ink marginal "n-signs" and "a-signs" omitted by Meech (although Hirsch's lists have omissions also). See John C. Hirsh, "Margery Kempe," in *Middle English Prose: A Critical Guide to Major Authors and Genres*, ed. A. S. G. Edwards (New Brunswick, NJ, 1984), pp. 109-19. These missing "n-signs" and "a-signs" have been included in appendix A and appendix B, respectively.

8 I would like to thank Kathryn Kerby-Fulton for her help with checking the manuscript.

9 Rev. Robert A. Horsfield, "*The Pomander of Prayer*: Aspects of Late Medieval English Carthusian Spirituality and Its Lay Audience," in *De Cella in Seculum: Religious and Secular Life and Devotion in Late Medieval England*, ed. Michael G. Sargent (Cambridge, 1989), p. 208.

10 See Sargent, "Transmission," pp. 225-40.

11 See Ker, *Medieval Libraries of Great Britain*, p. 132.

12 Vincent Gillespie, "*Cura Pastoralis in Deserto*," in *De Cella in Seculum: Religious and Secular Life and Devotion in Late Medieval England*, ed. Michael G. Sargent (Cambridge, 1989), p. 162.

13 Gillespie, "*Cura Pastoralis*," p. 171.

14 Gillespie, "*Cura Pastoralis*," pp. 167, 170.

15 Gillespie, "*Cura Pastoralis*," p. 161.

16 Thompson, *Carthusian Order in England*, p. 236, citing *Testamenta Eboracensia*, I, Surtees Society, p. 282.

17 Thompson, *Carthusian Order in England*, p. 236, citing *Testamenta Eboracensia* I: p. 294.

18 Thompson, *Carthusian Order in England*, pp. 330-31.

19 Thompson, *Carthusian Order in England*, p. 330.

20 Hope Emily Allen, "Notes," *The Book of Margery Kempe*, p. 330. Methley's surviving works are contained in three manuscripts: Trinity College Cambridge, MS O.2.56 (1160), containing *Scola Amoris Languidi, Dormitorium Dilecti Dilecti* and *Refectorium Salutis*; London, Public Record Office, SP I/239 preserves half of *Experimentum Veritatis* and contains his Middle English *To Hew Heremyte: A Pystyl of Solytary Lyfe Nowadayes*; Pembroke College Cambridge MS 221 contains *Diuina Caligo Ignorancie* (Latin translation of *The Cloud of Unknowing*), and *Speculum Animarum Simplicium*, a Latin translation of Margeurite of Porete's *Mirror of Simple Souls*; see James Hogg, "Mount Grace Charterhouse and Late Medieval English Spirituality," *Analecta Cartusiana* 3 (Salzburg, 1980), 29-30. Norton's main works, all in Latin, are found in Lincoln Cathedral Library, MS 57 (A.6.8), which contains *Musica Monachorum, Thesaurus Cordium vere Amancium*, and *Devota Lamentacio*; see James Hogg, "Mount Grace Charterhouse," 40-41.

[21] Hogg, "Mount Grace Charterhouse," 27-28, 40.

[22] James Hogg, ed., "Richard Methley: *To Hew Heremyte A Pystyl of Solytary Lyfe Nowadayes,*" *Analecta Cartusiana* 31 (Salzburg, 1977), 100.

[23] Hogg, "Richard Methley: *To Hew Heremyte,*" 101.

[24] Hogg, "Richard Methley: *To Hew Heremyte,*" 101, n. 28, citing *Testamenta Eboracensia* V, Surtees Society 79 (1884), p. 5.

[25] Hogg, "Richard Methley: *To Hew Heremyte,*" 118.

[26] Nicholas Watson, in correspondence, August, 1998.

[27] Holbrook, "Wynkyn de Worde," pp. 36-37.

[28] See Linda Olson's article, "Untangling the Thread of Internal Progress in a Benedictine Community: An Abridgement of Augustine's *Confessions* from Medieval Norwich," forthcoming 2001, in *Studies in Medieval and Renaissance History,* 3rd Series, vol. 1.

[29] See Denise L. Despres, "Ecstatic Reading and Missionary Mysticism," in *Prophets Abroad: The Reception of Continental Holy Women in Late-Medieval England,* ed. Rosalynn Voaden (Cambridge, 1996), pp. 141-60; quotation at 148.

[30] For discussion of medieval attitudes towards the body in relation to Margery Kempe, see Lochrie, *Translations of the Flesh.* For more generalized discussion, see *Medieval Theology and the Natural Body,* York Studies in Medieval Theology I, eds. Peter Biller and A. J. Minnis (Woodbridge, 1997); and *Framing Medieval Bodies,* eds. Sarah Kay and Miri Rubin (Manchester, 1994).

[31] Joyce Bazire and Eric Colledge, eds., *The Chastising of God's Children and The Treatise of Perfection of the Sons of God* (Oxford, 1957), p. 55.

[32] For some cautionary notes regarding Colledge's tendency to "fixate" more than is useful on the issue of heresy, see Nicholas Watson's "Melting into God the English Way: Deification in the Middle English Version of Marguerite Porete's *Mirouer des simples âmes anienties,*" in *Prophets Abroad,* pp. 24-25.

[33] See Kathryn Kerby-Fulton and Denise L. Despres, *Iconography and the Professional Reader: The Politics of Book Production in the Douce "Piers Plowman"* (Minneapolis, 1999), chapter 3 and especially p. 75.

[34] See Charles Plummer, "On the Colophons and Marginalia of Irish Scribes," *Proceedings of the British Academy* 12 (1926), 11-42.

[35] John B. Friedman, *Northern English Books, Owners, and Makers in the Late Middle Ages* (Syracuse, NY, 1995), p. 149.

[36] Denise Despres, "Franciscan Spirituality: Margery Kempe and Visual Meditation," *Mystics Quarterly* 11:1 (1985), 14-15.

[37] Friedman, *Northern English Books,* p. 164. Friedman refers his readers to Hope Emily Allen, ed., *The English Writings of Richard Rolle* (Oxford, 1931; repr. St. Clair Shores, Mich., 1971), p. 36, and more recently, Vincent Gillespie, "Mystic's Foot: Rolle and Affectivity," in *The Medieval Mystical Tradition in England,* ed. Marion Glasscoe (Exeter, 1982), pp. 199-230.

[38] Richard Kieckhefer, *Unquiet Souls: Fourteenth-Century Saints and Their Religious Milieu* (Chicago, 1984), p. 104.

[39] Friedman, *Northern English Books,* p. 165.

40 See Friedman, *Northern English Books*, p. 164; and Rosalynn Voaden's "Articulating Ecstasy: 'The Booke of Gostlye Grace of Mechtild of Hackeborn,' " unpublished MA thesis, University of Victoria, 1990, especially chapter 2, pp. 30-31 and 42. On Julian, see Friedman, *Northern English Books*, p. 165, and Voaden "Articulating Ecstacy," p. 43. And for Catherine of Siena, see Kieckhefer, *Unquiet Souls*, p. 92.

41 Friedman, *Northern English Books*, p. 191.

42 Kerby-Fulton and Despres, *Iconography and the Professional Reader*, p. 63.

43 Allen, "Notes," *The Book of Margery Kempe*, pp. 255-56.

44 Friedman, *Northern English Books*, p. 190.

45 See Voaden, "Articulating Ecstacy," especially chapter 5, pp. 87-103.

46 Christine de Pizan, *A Medieval Woman's Mirror of Honor: The Treasury of the City of Ladies*, trans. Charity Cannon Willard, ed. Madelein Pelner Cosman (New York, 1989), pp. 189-91.

47 Thompson, *Carthusian Order in England*, p. 331.

48 *Ex libris* inscription, in a late fifteenth-century hand on the verso of the binding leaf preceding fol. 1r of MS Add. 61823; see Meech, pp. xxxii and 1.

49 Nicholas Watson, in correspondence, August, 1998.

50 "It may be remembered that we are a Catholic family and believe that when the monasteries were destroyed, the monks sometimes gave valuable books, vestments, etc., to such families in the hope of preserving them . . . [T]his may have been the case with Margery Kempe's manuscript, and the Carthusians of Mount Grace may have given it to one of my family." Clarissa W. Atkinson, *Mystic and Pilgrim: The Book and the World of Margery Kempe* (Ithaca, NY, 1983), citing a notice of publication of Butler-Bowdon's translation of the *Book* appearing in *The Times* (London), September 30, 1936, p. 13.

51 David Knowles and R. Neville Hadock, *Medieval Religious Houses: England and Wales* (London, 1971), pp. 205-06.

52 See Kathryn Kerby-Fulton's introduction to this volume.

53 Hogg, "Mount Grace Charterhouse," 8.

54 Vincent Gillespie, "Vernacular Books of Religion," in *Book Production and Publishing in Britain 1375-1475*, eds. Jeremy Griffiths and Derek Pearsall (Cambridge, 1989), p. 335.

55 I.e., not the Wynkyn de Worde printed excerpts. Wynkyn de Worde published short and highly selective excerpts from the *Book* in 1501 and it is thought that this edition, entitled *A Shorte Treatyse of Contemplacyon*, did circulate among the laity. See Holbrook, "Margery Kempe and Wynkyn de Worde," pp. 27-46.

56 Holbrook, "Wynkyn de Worde," p. 38.

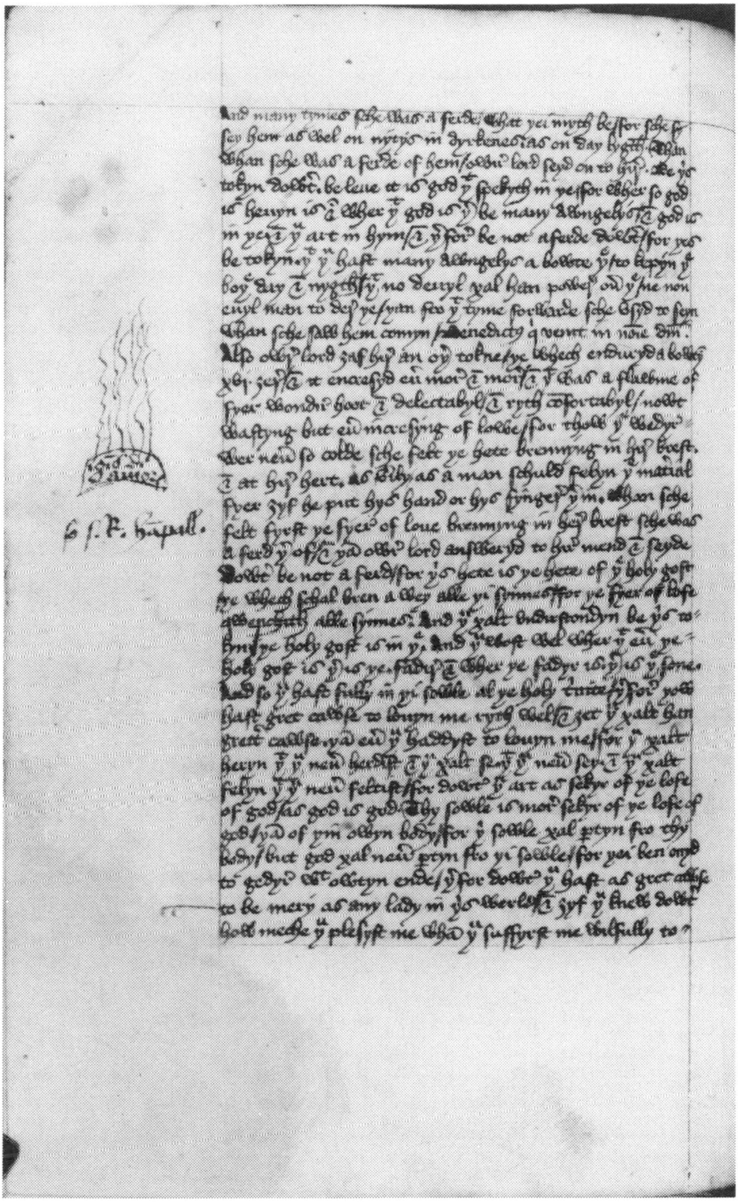

FIG. 1 The Flames of Divine Love and annotation: "so s. R. hampall.," *The Book of Margery Kempe*, British Library MS Additional 61823, fol. 43v (by permission of The British Library).

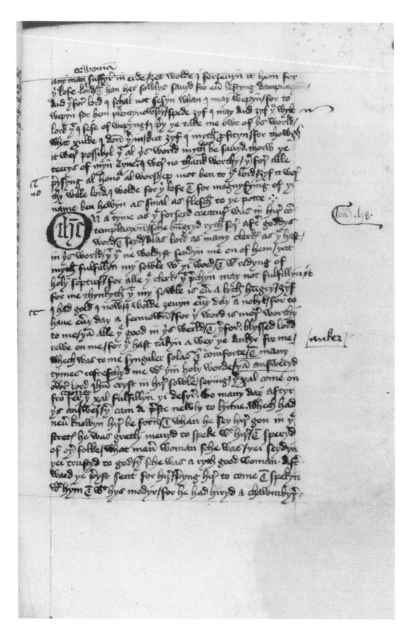

FIG. 2 Annotation: "or woman," *The Book of Margery Kempe*, British Library MS Additional 61823, fol. 69r (by permission of The British Library).

160

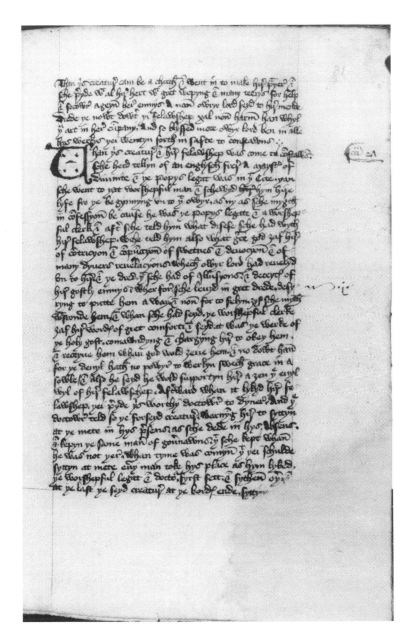

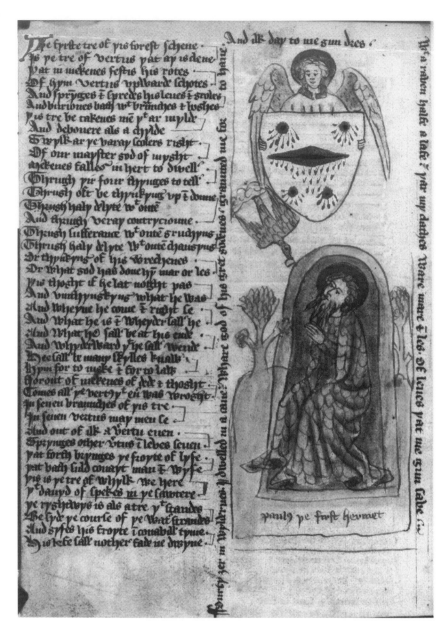

FIG. 4 The Five Wounds Shield, *Devotional Miscellany*, British Library MS Additional 37049, fol. 46v (by permission of The British Library).

162

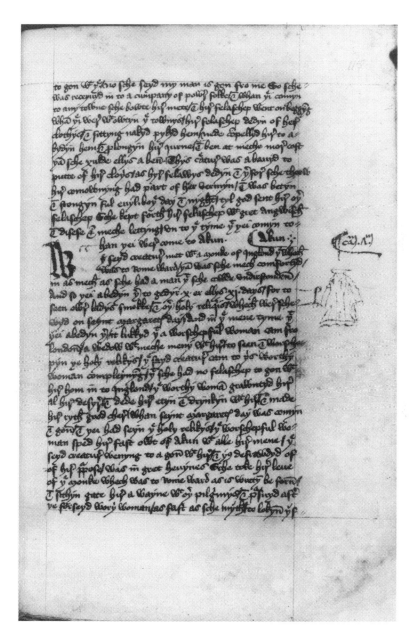

FIG. 5   The Blessed Virgin's Smock, *The Book of Margery Kempe*, British Library MS Additional 61823, fol. 115r (by permission of The British Library).

163

Editorial Procedures and Notes to
Appendices A, B & C
British Library MS Add. 61823

Appendix A — Red Ink Annotations
Appendix B — Red Ink Corrections
Appendix C — Red Ink Rubrications

- Meech's transcriptions have been checked against the manuscript and, where they are in error, have been corrected.

- Original punctuation & capitalization have been retained.

- Line endings, of both the text and the marginal supply, have been indicated with a vertical stroke |.

- The þ and ȝ have been preserved, as has the distinction between u & v and i & j.

- Expanded abbreviations are underlined. The exception is when the text is underlined in red, in which case I have used italics for the expansions.

- All red ink annotations, line drawings, and corrections are depicted in bold face type. Red ink line-drawn images are indicated by upper-case labels, e.g., **FACE**.

- I have recorded all words, diagrams, and "paraphs" (or "a-signs"); but not splashes, slashes, etc., or scribal marks in red, punctuation, etc., or "scribal" or "nota" signs consisting of 3 triangulated dots and a comma.

- Red ink "paraphs" or "a-signs" are indicated by ¶.

- A question mark "?" indicates an image, word, or letter that cannot be identified with certainty.

- Red ink insertions into the text, usually interlinear with a caret, are shown bold-face between angle brackets: < >. Preceding and following textual words are provided for context.

- Text underlined in red is shown as double-underscored.

- Letters, words, or phrases crossed out or "daubed" in red ink are shown as single strike-through.

- Letters, words, or phrases repeatedly crossed out in red ink are shown as {strike-through}.

164

- Annotations within a partial "cartouche"-like line-drawn box are shown as ⌞ if they are on the left of the annotation, or ⌐ if they are on the right. Annotations within a complete "cartouche"-like line-drawn box are shown between both this ⌞ and this ⌐.

- Lines drawn in red ink for the purpose of drawing attention to particular sections of the text, are referred to in the appendices as "attention-drawing lines." They are depicted as → for single line, and →→ for multiple lines.

- Historiated initials and rubric capitals are included in both appendix A (annotations) and appendix C (rubrications), because they belong in both categories.

- The distinction is sometimes blurred in the red ink annotator's roles; some items listed in Appendix B (corrections) could be considered as annotations. Therefore, both Appendix A (annotations) and Appendix B (corrections) should be referred to for a complete reading of the red ink annotations.

- "Decorated" indicates somewhat crude geometric "strapwork" lines, large dots, and sometimes circles.

- "Solid red" means the letters are filled in solidly with red ink.

- Decorative "line filler" is included in appendix C.

APPENDIX A — Red Ink ANNOTATIONS — British Library MS Add. 61823

Capitulum (Chapter)	EETS page/line	MS folio/line	Location on MS folio	CONTENT	Description
PROEM					
Proem	1/1	1r/1	upper margin	**ihc**	
Proem	2/33	1v/26	outer margin	**dalyid**⌉	
Proem	3/3	2r/2	outer margin	**ihc** in red **HEART** symbol	line drawing
Proem	3/8	2r/7	outer margin	**no̲ta**	
Proem	3/30	2r/30-31	inner margin	**no̲ta.	xx ȝere**⌉	
Proem	3/31	2v/1	upper margin	**ihc**	
Proem	5/23	3r/28	outer margin	**hale**	
Proem	5/26	3r/31	outer margin	**no̲ta**	
BOOK ONE					
1	6/26	3v/28	inner margin	**of lyn**	
1	7/9	4r/9	outer margin	**no̲ta**	
1	8/11	4v/13	outer margin	**ihc→**	with attention-drawing line
1	8/25	4v/26	inner margin	**no̲ta**	
2	9/32	5v/3	outer margin	**no̲ta**	
2	10/6	5v/12	inner margin	**no̲ta**	
2	11/7	6r/15	outer margin	⌊**merce**⌉	
3	11/12	6r/20-22	interlinear	**ihc** inside rubric capital **O**	historiated initial

3	11/15	6r/23	outer margin	nota	
3	11/34	6v/6	inner margin	nota	
4	14/2	7v/14	outer margin	nota	
4	14/32	8r/7	outer margin	nota	
4	16/4	8v/9	outer margin	dyspare⌉	
5	16/33	9r/1	outer margin	<¶> nota	red-paraphed previous (brown ink) annotation
5	17/6	9r/10	outer margin	nota	
5	17/14	9r/19	inner margin	nota	
5	17/33	9v/3	outer margin	M of P /	
5	18/8	9v/13	interlinear	.visio.	
8	20/20	10v/22	inner margin	nota	
8	20/36	11r/4	inner margin	C	?pen trial
8	21/2	11r/7	inner margin	C	?pen trial
9	21/12	11r/15-16	outer margin	⌊the flesshely l lust in ≠	attention-drawing mark, partial red box around previous (black ink) annotation
9	21/16	11r/18-19	inner margin	ihc helpe l me	
9	21/25	11r/25	outer margin	nota	
10	22/35	11v/31	inner margin	⌊vane.g.⌋	
10	23/3	11v/34	lower margin	HAND, MIDDLE FINGER POINTING	line drawing - "manicule"

Capitulum (Chapter)	EETS page/line	MS folio/line	Location on MS folio	CONTENT	Description
11	23/36	12r/29	inner margin	vow]	
11	25/11	13r/6	outer margin	nota	
11	25/12	13r/7	inner margin	⌊grace]	
11	25/24	13r/16	outer margin	⌊nota dyscrescion] →	with attention-drawing line
12	25/31	13r/23	inner margin	monke]	
13	27/18	14r/1-3	interlinear	ihc in rubric capital **O**	historiated initial
13	28/2	14r/16	outer margin	nota	
13	29/17	14v/32	inner margin	**loue**	
13	29/17	14v/32	lower margin	⌊**R Medlay. v.**icar	was wont so to say] →	with attention-drawing line
13	29/23	15r/4-6	inner margin	**PILLAR** symbol	line drawing - pillar with trefoil on top
14	30/15	15r/27	inner margin	**loue**]	
14	30/24	15v/1	upper margin	?**SOULS IN DIAPER** or **FONT** symbol	line drawing
14	31/1	15v/8-9	outer margin	⌊**meykly &**	**paciently**]	
14	31/7	15v/12-13	inner margin	⌊**heyn**	nota l	nota	
15	32/5	16r/10	outer margin	nota **pylg.**	
15	33/25	16v/22	outer margin	**By of Lyncone**	Bysshop of Lyncone
15	34/12	17r/9	outer margin	**.vol**	remaining letters trimmed

15	34/29	17r/22	outer margin	nota .xiij.	
16	36/30	18r/28	outer margin	dyscresion	
16	38/5	19r/7	outer margin	nota	
16	38/5	19r/8-9	interlinear/ outer margin	it begynnes thus in þe tyme / þe vj lefe efter	
17	38/6	19r/8	outer margin	?TEARS or WEEPING symbol	line drawing - sideways 2-pronged symbol with central circle
17	38/6	19r/9-11	interlinear	FACE in rubric capital O	historiated initial
17	38/12	19r/15	outer margin	⌊vyker⌉	
17	39/5	19v/9	outer margin	Pass<yon.>	modifying previous (faded brown ink) annotation
17	39/20	19v/25	outer margin	⌊ ⌉	empty red line drawn box
17	39/24	19v/27	outer margin	⌊brigytts.	partial box & period in red – emphasizing previous (black ink) annotation
17	40/6	20r/7	outer margin	nota ⌊feruent loue	
17	40/11	20r/12	outer margin	fader	?
17	40/30	20r/29-30	outer margin	nota / vij 3ere	last part damaged
18	41/2	20v/3-4	outer margin	⌊goyd whyte / frere⌉	
18	41/10	20v/9	inner margin	nota	

Capitulum (Chapter)	EETS page/line	MS folio/line	Location on MS folio	CONTENT	Description
18	42/1	21r/1	outer margin	⌊goyd con͟sel.⌉	
18	42/9	21r/8	outer margin	⌊dame Ielia͟n	
18	43/3	21v/6	outer margin	?WEEPING symbol	line drawing - pie-shaped with 3 red dots
18	44/3	22r/5	outer margin	no͟ta	
18	44/15	22r/15-16	outer margin	brokyn | bak ma͟n	
18	45/2	22v/3	outer margin	¢	large "slashed" C
18	45/17	22v/16	outer margin	letter⌉	red box around ?drypoint or faded brown ink annotation
19	46/19	23r/17	outer margin	no͟ta	
19	46/29	23r/26-27	inner margin	⌊ters wᵗ | loue.⌉	
20	47/15	23v/13-15	interlinear	ihc in rubric capital O	historiated initial
20	47/34	23v/30	outer margin	B	
21	48/25	24r/18-19	inner margin	?TEARS symbol	line drawing - sideways 2 pronged symbol with central circle
21	49/4	24r/31	outer margin	no͟ta	
21	49/9	24v/3-5	outer margin	⌊loue⌉	red box around ?dry point or faded brown ink annotation

21	49/21	outer margin	⌊nota⌋→	red-boxed previous annotation with attention-drawing line
21	50/9	lower margin	?WEEPING or TEARS symbol	line drawing - 3-pronged foliate image
22	50/18	inner margin	nota | totaliter	
22	50/29	outer margin	nota	
22	51/14	lower margin	?WEEPING or TEARS symbol	line drawing - 2-pronged foliate image with 3 circles in centre
22	51/30	inner margin	HAND - FOREFINGER POINTING	line drawing - "manicule"
22	52/11	outer margin	⌊no[a]	partially red-boxed previous (brown ink) annotation
22	52/15	outer margin	shal ben⌉	partially red-boxed previous (black ink) annotation
22	52/18	lower margin	for	
22	52/20	outer margin	nota	
22	52/25	outer margin	⌊singularis. Cristi. | amatrix⌉	
22	53/4	interlinear	nota	
22	53/7	interlinear	deo gracias in eternum	

Capitulum (Chapter)	EETS page/line	MS folio/line	Location on MS folio	CONTENT	Description
23	53/13	26r/23-29	outer margin	nota →	with attention-drawing line
23	54/4	26v/12	outer margin	jhc	
23	54/20	26v/26	inner margin	nota	
23	54/32	27r/4	outer margin	nota	
24	57/6	28r/11	outer margin	nota	
26	60/18	29v/19-21	interlinear	?TEARS symbol in rubric capital W	historiated initial
26	61/9	30r/13-14	outer margin	⌊iiij ȝere	
27	63/1	31r/7-9	interlinear	FIVE WOUNDS in rubric capital T	historiated initial
27	63/12	31r/18	outer margin	nota	
28	67/17	33r/17-18	outer margin	⌈she þen⌉ →	red-boxed previous (black ink) annotation with red line joining to text
28	67/21	33r/20	outer margin	nota	
28	68/22	33v/18	outer margin	⌊nota de c̄lamore	partially red-boxed previous (brown ink) annotation
28	68/31	33v/26-29	outer margin	⌊so fa RM ∣ & f Norton ∣ of Wakenes &l of þe passyon⌉ →	

28	69/19	34r/10	outer margin	nota	
28	71/7	35r/1	outer margin	**nota**	
29	73/7	36r/1	outer margin	nota	
30	74/16	36v/14	outer margin	⌊by & by	partial red line around previous (black ink) annotation
30	75/24	37r/18	outer margin	nota	
30	76/8	37v/2	outer margin	⌊nota de vestura	partially red-boxed previous (brown ink) annotation
30	76/31	37v/25	outer margin	anker⌉	
31	78/15	38v/7	outer margin	**Ihc est amor.** t[u]us	
31	78/18	38v/10	inner margin	nota	
31	79/30	39r/22	outer margin	⌊**florentyne**	
32	81/5	40r/2-3	outer margin	⌊nota de confessione	partially red-boxed previous (brown ink) annotation
32	81/4	40r/3	inner margin	I[hon] **E.**[vangelist]	
32	81/22	40r/19	outer margin	**nota bene**	
32	81/27	40r/23	inner margin	nota	
32	81/33	40r/29	inner margin	**loue**	
33	82/20	40v/12-13	outer margin	⌊nota mirabile l quod sequitur⌉	red-boxed previous (brown ink) annotation

Capitulum (Chapter)	EETS page/line	MS folio/line	Location on MS folio	CONTENT	Description
33	83/4	40v/29	outer margin	no<u>ta</u>	
33	83/31	41r/18	outer margin	no<u>ta</u>	
34	85/11	42r/1	outer margin	⌊A proud prist →	with attention-drawing line
34	85/15	42r/4	inner margin	no<u>ta</u>	
34	85/18	42r/6-7	inner margin	A meke | hanswer	
35	86/15	42v/3	outer margin	C	
35	87/18	43r/4-5	outer margin	⌊de desponsa[cio]ne | eius ad deum patrem⌉	red-boxed previous (brown ink) annotation
35	88/28	43v/10-16	outer margin	ig<u>n</u>is di<u>vi</u>ni | amoris enclosed in FLAMES OF DIVINE LOVE symbol	line drawing
35	88/33	43v/17-18	outer margin	so s. R. ha<u>m</u>pall.	
36	90/14	44r/30	outer margin	no<u>ta</u>	
36	90/30	44v/8-9	outer margin	HEART symbol	line drawing - with stems and 3 dots at top
37	91/14	44v/25-27	interlinear	ihc in rubric capital D →→	historiated initial - with attention-drawing lines
39	95/11	46v/16	outer margin	S. brid<u>is</u> mady<u>n</u> /	
40	96/35	47v/1	upper margin	?WEEPING or TEARS symbol	line drawing - 3-pronged foliate image
40	97/36	48r/2	outer margin	no<u>ta</u> vanytee	

174

41	98/29		outer margin	⌊ebrietas sancta⌋	
41	99/18	48r/31	outer margin	a→a→	attention-drawing lines "bracketing" lines of text
43	102/1	48v/19-33	outer margin	FACE in rubric capital **O**	historiated initial
44	104/27	49v/29-31	interlinear	**.h. husband**	
44	105/15	51r/13	outer margin	**ihc**	
44	105/17	51v/1	upper margin	⌊no**ta** de colore⌋	
44	105/20	51v/3	outer margin	⌊**so dyd prior Norton** | **in hys excess**⌋	
44	106/5	51v/5-7	outer margin	?**WEEPING** or **TEARS** symbol	line drawing - 3 lines with small "o" 3 dots
44	106/27	51v/21-28	outer margin	no**ta**	
45	107/25	52r/6	outer margin	**ihc** in rubric capital **O**	historiated initial
45	107/35	52v/1-3	interlinear	amor | im**paciens** /	
45	108/15	52v/10-11	outer margin	⌊**goyd merchand**⌋	
45	109/7	52v/25-26	outer margin	⌊**dalyd**⌋ →	with attention-drawing line
45	110/26	53r/9-12	outer margin	⌊**vij. day. fro** | **Brusto**⌋	
45	110/33	53v/24-25	outer margin	**v. days**⌋	
46	111/10	53v/30	inner margin	**fire of** | **loue.**	
46	111/29	54r/9-10	outer margin	⌊**v. tymes. mare**⌋	
46	112/2	54r/24	outer margin	no**ta**	
47	113/17	54r/29	outer margin	no**ta**	
		55r/2	outer margin		

Capitulum (Chapter)	EETS page/line	MS folio/line	Location on MS folio	CONTENT	Description
47	114/4	55r/22	outer margin	nota	
48	114/29	55v/9-11	interlinear	ihc in rubric capital **O**	historiated initial
48	114/37	55v/16-18	outer margin	**a deuoute. ⌋⌊prayer⌉**	red box & addition to previous (brown ink) annotation
48	115/15	55v/25-26	outer margin	**⌊examinacio | dura⌉** →	with attention-drawing line
48	115/32	56r/7	outer margin	**⌊xiiij child**	
48	115/32	56r/8	inner margin	nota	
50	120/1	58r/1	upper margin	**?WEEPING** or **TEARS** symbol	line drawing - 2 lines and 3 dots between beginning at circle point
50	120/5	58r/4	outer margin	nota	
51	121/2	58r/32	outer margin	**⌊questio⌉**	
51	122/34	59r/23	outer margin	nota⌊**seculer. p.**	
52	125/12	60r/32	outer margin	**⌊O ceci clerici**	
52	126/14	60v/31	outer margin	nota	
52	126/24	61r/4	outer margin	**⌊narracio⌉**	red-boxed previous (brown ink) annotation
52	126/24	61r/6-7	outer margin	**of þe preyst | & þe pertre**	
53	129/19	62r/28-29	outer margin	**⌊duke of B**	

53	130/15	62v/28	outer margin	⌊saint⌉	
53	130/32	63r/10	outer margin	notạ	
54	131/19	63r/30-32	inner margin	notạ ǀ iij tymes ǀ of þe da	
54	131/24	63v/5	outer margin	⌊home	
54	132/6	63v/22	outer margin	frere⌉	
54	134/16	65r/1	upper margin	?WEEPING or TEARS symbol	line drawing - 3-pronged foliate image
54	134/16	65r/1	outer margin	notạ	
55	135/26	65v/11	outer margin	⌊men of law⌉	
55	136/13	66r/1	upper margin	?WEEPING or TEARS symbol	line drawing - 3-pronged foliate image
55	136/14	66r/1	outer margin	husband	
56	137/20	66v/15	outer margin	⌊seyknes.⌉	
56	137/28	66v/26-36	outer margin	→→	attention-drawing lines "bracketing" lines of text
56	138/21	67r/15-16	outer margin	viij. ӡer⌉	
56	138/33	67r/27-28	outer margin	⌊Abundance ǀ of loue⌉	
56	139/1	67r/32	inner margin	notạ	
57	140/23	68r/19	outer margin	⌊langor amoris⌉	
57	140/24	68r/21-22	inner margin	x ӡere⌉	
57	140/36	68r/32	inner margin	purgᵗ	
57	141/7	68v/7-8	outer margin	petite et ǀ accipietis⌉	

Capitulum (Chapter)	EETS page/line	MS folio/line	Location on MS folio	CONTENT	Description
57	141/13	68v/12-13	outer margin	nota ⌊charitatem eius⌉	
57	141/20	68v/20-21	outer margin	wel of ǀ ters.⌉	
57	142/6	69r/4	outer margin	nota	
57	142/10	69r/10	inner margin	nota	
58	142/14	69r/12-14	interlinear	ihc in rubric capital O	historiated initial
58	142/25	69r/22	outer margin	⌊anker⌉	
58	143/15	69v/15	outer margin	good preyst⌉	
59	144/7	70r/7	outer margin	nota ⌊de revelacionibus⌉	
59	144/25	70r/25-26	outer margin	⌊nota eius ǀ dubitacionem⌉	
59	144/25	70r/28-30	outer margin	⌊o res mirabile ǀ O mutacio ǀ dextri excelci⌉	
59	145/24	70v/24	inner margin	⌊fantyses⌉	
59	145/34	70v/31-33	outer margin	⌊Angelus ǀ bonus⌉	
59	146/2	71r/1	outer margin	nota	
59	146/6	71r/4	outer margin	⌊xij days⌉	
59	146/19	71r/15-16	outer margin	⌊.payne. ǀ laudes deo⌉	
59	146/34	71r/30-31	interlinear/ lower margin	loquere Domine quia audit seruus tuus⌉ Audiam quid loquatur in me Dominus Deus	

60	147/18	71v/17-18	outer margin	⌊fyre of loue⌉	
60	147/22	71v/23	outer margin	vyker⌉	
60	148/15	72r/14	inner margin	nota	
60	148/27	72r/25	interlinear	**Amen Amen Amen**	
61	149/11	72v/10	outer margin	**good freyre**⌉	
61	149/33	72v/30	outer margin	⌊**Amor impaciens**⌉	
61	149/35	73r/33	lower margin	Non est in hominis potestate prohibere spiritum s[anctum] →	with red line joining annotation to text at line 32, folio 72v
62	152/32	74v/1	upper margin	?WEEPING or TEARS symbol	line drawing - 3-pronged foliate image
62	153/1	74v/6-9	outer margin	⌊**Maria de ⏐ oegines**⌉⏐ /liber/	
62	153/38	75r/6	outer margin	⌊**pryk of loue**⌉	
62	154/13	75r/18	outer margin	nota	
63	155/18	75v/23-24	outer margin	⌊nota contra ⏐ Melton⌉	red-boxed previous (brown ink) annotation
63	155/22	75v/27	outer margin	⌊**dispectus**⌉	
63	156/5	76r/8-9	outer margin	nota ⏐⌊**detraccion**	
63	156/9	76r/13	outer margin	nota	
63	156/37	76v/4	outer margin	nota	
64	157/26	76v/26-27	outer margin	⌊nota ⏐ loue⌉	
64	158/13	77r/15	outer margin	nota	

Capitulum (Chapter)	EETS page/line	MS folio/line	Location on MS folio	CONTENT	Description
64	158/21	77r/21	outer margin	no_ta	
64	158/27	77r/26	outer margin	⌊mody?r⌉	
64	158/34	77r/33	lower margin	?WEEPING or TEARS symbol	line drawing - 3-pronged foliate image
64	159/15	77v/15	outer margin	→→	attention-drawing lines ending in large red blots
65	159/21	77v/20-22	interlinear	ihc in rubric capital O	historiated initial
65	160/10	78r/5	outer margin	no_ta	
65	160/17	78r/11	outer margin	⌊no_ta bene⌉	
65	160/28	78r/22	outer margin	⌊S. poule⌉	
65	160/37	78r/29-30	outer margin	⌊sic in libro te°⌉	last trimed away ?tercio
65	161/1	78r/31	inner margin	SMALL CUP symbol with →	line drawing - cup symbol with line joining to text
65	161/2	78r/31	outer margin	no_ta	
65	161/5	78v/1	upper margin	?WEEPING or TEARS symbol	
65	161/6	78v/2	outer margin	no_ta semper.	
65	161/14	78v/9-10	outer margin	HEART symbol	line drawing
66	161/24	78v/21	outer margin	⌊fleysse⌉	
66	162/16	79r/8	outer margin	⌊gostly labore_s⌉	

66	162/21	79r/12	outer margin	nota	
66	162/28	79r/18	interlinear	deo gracias/	
67	162/29	79r/19-21	interlinear	FACE in rubric capital O	historiated initial
67	162/35	79r/24	outer margin	nota nota	
67	163/31	79v/21	outer margin	iij.	
67	164/6	80r/1	upper margin	SNOW CLOUD	line drawing - 3 arched wavy lines
67	165/10	80v/7-8	outer margin	nota materiam | istam	
68	166/7	81r/6	outer margin	.wystly.	
68	166/32	81r/30	outer margin	nota⌊deuout doctor	
69	167/37	82r/1-2	outer margin	⌊goyd clarkes⌉	
70	169/18	82v/20-22	interlinear	FACE in rubric capital O	historiated initial
70	169/30	82v/32	outer margin	to our lade.	
70	170/26	83r/25	interlinear	laudes deo in eternum Amen	
71	170/27	83r/26-28	interlinear	ihc in rubric capital O	historiated initial
72	172/13	84r/12-13	outer margin	nota bene. | eius perfeccionem	
72	173/27	84v/24	inner margin	nota	
73	174/12	85r/7-9	interlinear	ihc in rubric capital O	historiated initial
73	174/19	85r/13-16	outer margin	_father M. | was wont | so to doo⌉	
73	175/2	85r/25	outer margin	nota	

Capitulum (Chapter)	EETS page/line	MS folio/line	Location on MS folio	CONTENT	Description
74	176/11	85v/29-30	outer margin	nota ⎜⌊langyng loue⌉	
74	176/20	86r/4	outer margin	nota	
74	177/17	86v/1-8	outer margin	nota ⎜⌊A sotel & a ⎜ sore temptacion ⎜ In siche a case ⎜ we shold be ⎜ more stronge & ⎜ bold a·ga[n]ste ⎜ our gostly enmy	
75	177/33	86v/15	outer margin	Notabile q^d	
75	178/8	86v/24-25	outer margin	⌊d. R. fow ⎜ dyd so⌉	dan Richard [?"sometimes"] dyd s⊃
75	178/30	87r/8	outer margin	nota	
75	179/5	87r/20	interlinear	deo gracias	
76	179/6	87r/22-23	outer margin	⌊her husband⌉	
76	179/20	87v/1	upper margin	ihc	
76	179/28	87v/7	outer margin	⌊vow.⌉	
76	180/30	88r/4	outer margin	nota	
76	180/32	88r/5	outer margin	⌊caritas diuina.	
77	181/18	88r/26-30	outer margin	nota ⎜⌊dyscretion⌉	
77	181/28	88v/3	outer margin	wyl.	
77	182/4	88v/13	outer margin	⌊Responcio.⌉	

77	182/11	88v/20	outer margin	**planetes**	
77	182/20	88v/26	outer margin	⌊**potestas diuina**⌉	
77	182/24	88v/29	outer margin	**notandum**	
77	183/1	89r/4-5	outer margin	⌊**perfecta caritas | foras mittit ti**[**morem**]⌉	
77	183/9	89r/12	outer margin	⌊**teres**⌉ & **?WEEPING** or **TEARS** symbol	end of red box contains foliate drawing
77	183/28	89r/28-29	outer margin	⌊**manheyd of | cryst**⌉	
77	183/30	89r/31	inner margin	**nota**	
78	184/9	89v/5-14	outer margin	→→	attention-drawing lines "bracketing" text
78	184/9	89v/9	outer margin	⌊.**nota bene**.⌉	red-boxed previous (brown ink) annotation
78	185/6	90r/3	outer margin	**nota**	
78	185/33	90r/26	outer margin	**nota**	
78	186/1	90r/33	lower margin	⌊**dede**⌉	
78	186/15	90v/12	outer margin	⌊**in exemplum**⌉	
78	186/20	90v/18-19	outer margin	**nota** | ⌊**bonam voluntatem**⌉	
78	186/24	90v/22	outer margin	⌊**praer**⌉	
79	190/28	92v/24-26	outer margin	⌊.**racio hic | ponitur quare | sic plorans clamauit**⌉	
79	191/3	92v/33	interlinear	**trew it is blyssyd lord**	
81	197/38	96r/18	outer margin	**langyng loue**	

Capitulum (Chapter)	EETS page/line	MS folio/line	Location on MS folio	CONTENT	Description
82	198/1	96r/19-21	interlinear	FACE in rubric capital **O**	historiated initial
82	198/18	96v/1-2	outer margin	no.ta	**feruor of loue**⌐	
82	199/17	96v/32-33	outer margin	**3 DOTS**	tears?
82	199/20	97r/1	upper margin	?**LEAF** or **HEART** symbol	line drawing
82	199/25	97r/5	outer margin	nota	
83	200/20	97r/31	interlinear/ outer margin	**merveld**	
83	200/30	97v/6	outer margin	¢	large "slashed" C
83	200/30	97v/21	outer margin	O→	circle with attention-drawing line
83	201/33	98r/3	outer margin	nota	
84	203/16	98v/19	outer margin	<¶> nota bene	red-paraphed previous (brown ink) annotation
84	204/8	99r/9	outer margin	nota	
84	204/24	99r/23	outer margin	nota	
84	204/28	99r/27	inner margin	**mark**	
84	204/34	99r/32	outer margin	nota bene	
84	205/1	99v/1-2	outer margin	<¶> nota bene	red-paraphed previous (brown ink) annotation
84	205/12	99v/11	outer margin	**nota**	

84	205/36	99v/32-35	outer margin	→	wavy attention-drawing line "bracketing" text
84	206/19	100r/12	outer margin	nota	
84	206/26	100r/18	interlinear	deo gracias	
85	206/27	100r/19-21	interlinear	FACE in rubric capital O	historiated initial
85	207/29	100v/18	outer margin	⌊nota bene⌉	red-boxed previous (brown ink) annotation
85	207/29	100v/19-21	outer margin	FACE IN PROFILE	line drawing - reinforcing previous (brown ink) drawing "bracketing" text
85	208/16	101r/3	outer margin	nota	
85	209/5	101r/24	outer margin	nota	
85	209/15	101r/34	outer margin	nota	
86	209/27	101v/12-14	interlinear	FACE in rubric capital O	historiated initial
86	210/5	101v/24	inner margin	nota	
86	211/28	102r/9	outer margin	HEART symbol	line drawing - heart with dot in centre
86	212/2	102r/19	outer margin	→→	attention-drawing lines - "pointing" to text
86	213/8	103r/23-27	inner margin	→→	attention-drawing lines - "bracketing" text
86	213/8	103r/24-27	outer margin	→→	attention-drawing lines - "bracketing" text

Capitulum (Chapter)	EETS page/line	MS folio/line	Location on MS folio	CONTENT	Description
86	214/13	103v/28	interlinear	Amen	
87	214/35	104r/14	outer margin	⌊nota bene⌉	red-boxed previous (brown ink) annotation
87	215/10	104r/25	outer margin	nota our lade	
88	216/19	104v/34	lower margin	?WEEPING or TEARS symbol	line drawing - 3-pronged foliate image with 3 dots
88	216/20	105r/1	upper margin	FACE IN PROFILE	line drawing
88	216/22	105r/1-2	outer margin	⌊nota bene⌉	red-boxed previous (brown ink) annotation
88	216/23	105r/3	outer margin	mentall praer.	
88	216/31	105r/10	outer margin	nota	
88	217/6	105r/18-19	outer margin	→	attention-drawing line "bracketing" text
88	218/31	106r/3-4	outer margin	HEART symbol	line drawing - heart with dot in centre
89	219/3	106r/10	outer margin	A tokyn of grace	
89	219/30	106v/1	upper margin	ihc	
89	219/34	106v/4	outer margin	⌊nota bene & cave	tibi	partially red-boxed previous (brown ink) annotation

89	220/11	106v/16	outer margin	⌊drede⌉	
89	220/24	106v/28	outer margin	⌊copy.⌉	

BOOK TWO

1	221/1	107r/1	upper margin	⌊Secundus liber⌉	red box around chapter title
2	227/14	110r/4	outer margin	ihc	
2	227/25	110r/14	outer margin	⌊si deus pro nobis q[u]is	
2	229/10	110v/32	interlinear	Amen	
3	229/21	111r/10	outer margin	nota	
3	230/1	111r/25	outer margin	nota	
3	230/9	111r/33	outer margin	nota	
3	230/16	111v/4-5	outer margin	nota ǀ ⌊pacyence⌉	
3	230/33	111v/20	outer margin	h	
4	232/10	112r/28-29	outer margin	.Wylsnak. ǀ & THREE HOSTS symbol	line drawing - three circles with dots in centres
5	233/31	113r/12-13	outer margin	nota bene	
6	235/37	114r/20	outer margin	nota	
7	237/36	115r/16-19	outer margin	GARMENT – Virgin's smock with →→	line drawing - with attention-drawing lines "bracketing" text
10	245/31	119r/10	outer margin	syon⌉	
10	246/3	119r/18	outer margin	nota	

187

Capitulum (Chapter)	EETS page/line	MS folio/line	Location on MS folio	CONTENT	Description
10	247/17	119v/30-31	outer margin	⌊nota bene quod apud Deum ǀ non est transmutacio⌉	red-boxed previous (brown ink) annotation
10	247/29	120r/9	interlinear	A M E N	
PRAYERS OF THE CREATURE					
Prayers	249/13	121r/8	outer margin	nota	
Prayers	249/21	121r/16-30	outer margin	→→	attention-drawing lines "bracketing" text
Prayers	249/35	121r/29	outer margin	.wyll.	
Prayers	250/4	121v/1	upper margin	.oracio.	
Prayers	251/15	122r/8	outer margin	nota	
Prayers	251/32	122r/23	outer margin	nota	
Prayers	253/10	123r/1	outer margin	nota	
Prayers	254/3	123r/26	interlinear	A[men]	

188

APPENDIX B — Red Ink CORRECTIONS — British Library MS Add. 61823

Capitulum (Chapter)	EETS page/line	MS folio/line	Location on MS folio	CONTENT	Description
PROEM					
Proem	1/17	1r/17	interlinear	folwyn <oure> Savyowr	inserted with caret
Proem	5/22	3r/27	interlinear	peyr <of> spectacles	insertion
BOOK ONE					
1	7/16	4r/17	interlinear	& <be>gan scharply	insertion
2	9/31	5v/2	interlinear	sche <be>gan to	insertion
2	10/3	5v/10	interlinear	had pun<ne>ched hir	insertion
2	11/1	6r/10	interlinear	whos mend<e> was	"e" added
3	12/1	6v/9	interlinear	thowt <haue> etyn	inserted with caret
3	12/9	6v/17	interlinear	creature | ~~hewyd chast~~ cownseld	crossed out in red
3	12/25	6v/32	interlinear	had <hid> conselyd	inserted with caret
3	12/25	6v/33	interlinear	þe <be> gynnyng	inserted with caret
3	13/3	7r/13	interlinear/inner margin	or <mokyd.> japyd for	inserted with caret
4	15/9	8r/17	interlinear	& <be>gan	superscript insertion
4	15/12	8r/19	interlinear	went ~~to~~ þe	"daubed" in red
5	17/16	9r/20	interlinear	& <g>↑nawyn of	"g" written on top of "k"
5	17/17	9r/21	interlinear	raton <g>↑nawyth þe	"g" written on top of "k"

Capitulum (Chapter)	EETS page/line	MS folio/line	Location on MS folio	CONTENT	Description
8	20/25	10v/27	interlinear	askyst \<thow> mor	inserted with caret
9	22/21	11v/17	interlinear	it \<to> mech	superscripted insertion
12	26/4	13r/27	interlinear	to heryn\<g> I what	"g" added
12	26/5	13r/28	interlinear	affeccyon \<be>gan	superscripted insertion
13	29/7	14v/24	interlinear/ outer margin	þer \<than.> fond	inserted with caret
13	29/10	14v/26	interlinear	a do\<n> whyl	red nasal bar written above "o"
13	29/19	15r/1	interlinear/ outer margin	owyr lord \<Ihu> I whan	"Ihu" added to line
14	30/2	15r/16	interlinear	but \<for> dred	inserted with caret
14	30/8	15r/20	interlinear/ outer margin	woldist \<suffer deth> for →	red attention-drawing lines adding to previcus (black ink) insertion
14	30/23	15r/34	interlinear	watyr I fro & wasch	"fro" expuncted in red
14	30/31	15v/7	interlinear	hem \<to> whom	superscripted insertion
14	31/24	15v/28	interlinear	wher owyr Lord seyth to hys dyscyples	crossed out in red
14	32/1	16r/6	interlinear	Lord \<jhc> had	inserted with caret
15	32/2	16r/7	interlinear	is wrete\<n> be form	red nasal bar written above 2nd "e"

15	33/21	16v/20	outer margin	*	?corrector's mark - red reinforcing previous (brown ink) mark
15	33/22	16v/20	interlinear	al<l>wey	"l" inserted
15	34/5	17r/3	outer margin	*	?corrector's mark - red reinforcing previous (brown ink) mark
15	35/19	17v/16	interlinear	hir mend <soull> in	insertion
15	35/29	17v/25	interlinear	þe Archsh Archbusshop	crossed out by original scribe and in red
15	35/34	17v/30	interlinear	go t<o> my	"o" written on top of "y"
16	37/1	18v/2	interlinear	but <he pres>aprevyd hir	"he" written on top of "a"; original scribe's superscript "re" strengthened in red; "s" written on top of "v"
16	37/19	18v/19	interlinear	wepyn ry<ht> sadly	"ht" written on top of "t"
17	39/24	19v/27	interlinear	ne pride boke	crossed out in red
17	39/25	19v/28	interlinear/ outer margin	amoris <of. R. hampall> ne	inserted with caret
17	40/6	20r/8	interlinear	not <be>leuying	inserted with caret
18	43/7	21r/8	interlinear	for <S> Ierom	inserted with caret
18	43/12	21v/13	interlinear	þe sete of	"daubed" in red

Capitulum (Chapter)	EETS page/line	MS folio/line	Location on MS folio	CONTENT	Description
18	44/21	22r/20	interlinear	not \<**be**\> Ꟑ levyn	"be" added to line
21	49/34	24v/25	interlinear	not for\<g\>~~be~~\<t~~ryn~~ þi	"g" written on top of "ȝ"; "t" written on top of "ı"
22	50/31	25r/20	interlinear	to gedyr \<**i<u>n</u> loue**\> wyt<u>h</u> owtyn	inserted with caret
22	51/6	25r/27	interlinear	þe \<**thy**\> God	inserted with caret
22	52/8	25v/23	interlinear/ inner margin	hath \<**dere**\> Ꟑ bowte	added to line
22	52/14	25v/29	interlinear	<u>þerfor</u> ~~&~~ þei	"&" crossed out in red
22	52/29	26r/9	interlinear	dawnsyn \<**gostly**\> in	inserted with caret
23	53/9	26r/19	interlinear	& \<**to**\> wetyn	inserted with caret
27	63/4	31r/10	interlinear	schewyd ~~hir~~ hym	crossed out by origiral scribe and in red ink
27	64/2	31v/9	interlinear	don \<**byd**\> hir	insertion
27	64/11	31v/18	interlinear	The \<**her**\> company	insertion
27	64/25	31v/31	outer margin	a Ꟑ⌊anoone → swythe	partially red-boxed (black ink) insertion, and red attention-drawing lines
28	66/31	32v/32	interlinear/ inner margin	þis \<**to**\> Ꟑ su<u>m</u>me	added to line
28	70/23	34v/16	interlinear	nowt \<**not**\> to	inserted with caret

28	71/15	35r/10	interlinear	as ~~þ~~<w>e~~ł~~ may	"i" expuncted in red and "w" written on top of "þ"
29	71/34	35r/28	interlinear	wondyr <then> to	inserted with caret
29	73/32	36r/24	interlinear	þat <she> wer	inserted with caret
29	73/37	36r/30	interlinear	& worshepyn<g> me	"g" added
30	76/30	37v/23	interlinear	sche <of> hir	inserted with caret
30	78/6	38r/32	interlinear	women sey~~n~~	þis	"n" crossed out
31	78/14	38v/6	interlinear	dede <byd> hir	insertion
32	81/34	40r/30	interlinear	þan <to> beleuyn	superscripted insertion
32	82/3	40r/32	outer margin	whan <þu>	xalt	added to line
33	82/11	40v/4	interlinear/ inner margin	cherch in **Ro**[me]	lateranens	added to line
33	83/19	41r/7	interlinear	not <be> leuyng	inserted with caret
34	84/37	41v/22	interlinear/ inner margin	sire <**sade she**>	I	added to line
34	85/19	42r/7	interlinear	wetyth <ye> wel	superscripted insertion
35	87/8	42v/31	interlinear	wept <**sylente**> wondir	insertion
35	87/14	43r/1	interlinear/ upper margin	hand <**gostle**> in	inserted with caret
35	87/25	43r/10	interlinear	present ~~in hir sowle~~ preyde	crossed out in red
36	90/23	44v/2	interlinear	good <**wife**> owyth	inserted with caret

Capitulum (Chapter)	EETS page/line	MS folio/line	Location on MS folio	CONTENT	Description
36	90/30	44v/8	interlinear	louyn <me> þat	insertion
37	91/23	44v/33	interlinear	xuldest lye<g> in helle	"g" written on top of "e"
40	97/5	47v/9	interlinear	þat <s>he xulde	"s" added
41	98/24	48r/26	interlinear	sovereyn <lord> Crist Ihesu	insertion
42	100/14	49r/11	interlinear	haue no powr	crossed out in red
42	101/14	49v/5	interlinear/ outer margin	to sportyn <refresse> →> hir	crossed out in red & "refresse" added in margin with attention-drawing line
43	102/35	50r/23	interlinear/ outer margin	and <to> |joyn	added to line
43	103/13	50v/5	interlinear	& <he> wolde he not	marks in red to transpose "he" and "wold"
44	103/30	50v/19	interlinear/ outer margin	as <wostly> |grawnt	added to line
44	104/4	50v/28	interlinear	hir fullyeth to	"ch" crossed out
44	104/20	51r/8	interlinear	good | nes <he> dede	superscripted insertion
44	104/35	51r/21	interlinear	xuld <not> dey	insertion
44	105/8	51r/30	interlinear/ inner margin	þei <at lyn→> had	inserted with attention-drawing line
44	106/23	52r/2	inner margin	redy | <the> broke-bakkyd	added to line

46	111/6	54r/4	outer margin	crucyfyx <þat> was	inserted with caret
46	111/8	54r/6	interlinear	mend whe<r>thorw | sche	insertion
46	111/8	54r/7	interlinear	sche <be>gan <to> meltyn	"be" and "to" superscripted insertions with carets
46	111/31	54r/26	interlinear	town <of> Lynne	superscripted insertion
46	112/12	54v/4	interlinear	sche <was> meuyd	inserted with caret
46	112/12	54v/4	interlinear	of <þe> man	superscripted insertion
46	112/27	54v/16	interlinear	& ~~dede~~ <lete> hir	"lete" written on top of "dede"
47	112/30	54v/19	interlinear	þe st~~y~~<u>ward of	"u" written above "y"
47	112/32	54v/23	interlinear	þe st~~y~~<u>warde þe	"u" written above "y"
47	113/22	55r/6	interlinear/outer margin	beste <therein> | the	added to line
47	113/24	55r/8	interlinear	stro<g>beiyd	inserted with caret
47	113/37	55r/18	interlinear	for <þ>her distres	insertion
47	113/37	55r/19	interlinear	for <þ>her delyuerawns	insertion
48	115/6	55v/22	interlinear/outer margin	wheche | <made> ~~dedyn~~	"dedyn" expuncted in red and "made" added to line
49	117/18	56v/26	interlinear	myth <not> stondyn	insertion
49	117/33	57r/2	interlinear/outer margin	sone <T Marcyall> | purpposyng	inserted with caret
49	118/9	57r/13	interlinear	had sche ~~sche~~ for | ȝetyn	2nd "sche" crossed out
50	120/9	58r/8	interlinear	Mynster ~~at~~ <of> ȝorke	"of" written on top of "at"

Capitulum (Chapter)	EETS page/line	MS folio/line	Location on MS folio	CONTENT	Description
50	120/10	58r/8	interlinear	ȝorke ~~forseyd~~ a	crossed out
50	120/23	58r/21	interlinear	& <be>gan to	superscripted insertion
50	120/27	58r/24	interlinear	hir ~~h~~<w>oo l kept	"w" written on top of "h"
51	121/3	58r/33	interlinear	Sche answeryng<e> seyd	insertion
51	122/19	59r/10	interlinear	Syr <t>hem ȝe	insertion
51	123/3	59r/28	interlinear	worschip <be> to	superscripted insertion
52	125/22	60v/6	interlinear	þow <wreeche> what	insertion
52	126/10	60v/28	interlinear/ outer margin	& þe <pappys> tetys	inserted with caret
53	129/16	62r/26	interlinear	for ~~se~~he durst	"sc" crossed out
54	132/27	64r/7	interlinear	wil ha~~n~~<ue>hir	"ue" written on top of "n"
54	133/36	64v/15	interlinear	it ~~ky~~ lyke	"ky" expuncted by original scribe and crossed out in red
54	134/14	64v/32	interlinear	Erchebischop <my> Lord	inserted with caret
56	137/14	66v/6	interlinear	not he<o>ldyn a	"o" written on top of "e"
57	139/6	67v/4	interlinear	in <t>her chapel	insertion
57	139/10	67v/8	interlinear	excusyd þe~~t~~ sche	"daubed" in red
57	139/10	67v/8	interlinear	no mo<r> howselyd	insertion
57	140/29	68r/25	interlinear	bodily my<g>tys	inserted with caret

57	141/18	68v/17	interlinear	as ~~þei~~ <thow> I	"thow" written on top of "þei"
57	142/1	69r/1	interlinear	man <or woman> suffyr	inserted with caret
57	142/8	69r/6	interlinear	for thow<gh> I it	insertion
58	142/20	69r/17	interlinear/outer margin	fulfillyn <it> I for	added to line
58	142/28	69r/26	interlinear	fer <contre> þat	inserted with caret
58	143/29	69v/25	interlinear	Incendium Amoris <hampall> &	insertion
58	143/32	69v/29	interlinear/outer margin	fer <contre> þat	inserted with caret
59	144/11	70r/12	interlinear	& <it> was	inserted with caret
59	144/24	70r/24	interlinear/outer margin	God <in þat> but	inserted with caret
59	145/22	70v/21-22	interlinear	mendys ~~eledyn~~ I ~~wyth hir~~ wer	crossed out by original scribe and in red
59	146/18	71r/16	interlinear	þe ~~þei~~ <thu> he	"thu" written on top of "þei"
59	146/26	71r/22	interlinear	was wone<t> I to	"t" written on top of "e"
60	147/14	71v/13	interlinear	& <to> þankyn	insertion
60	148/16	72r/15	interlinear	euyr <to> thynkyn	insertion
61	149/19	72v/17	interlinear	& ~~he~~ I beheldyng	crossed out by original scribe and in red
61	151/33	73v/31	interlinear	was <sertan> ȝerys	insertion

Capitulum (Chapter)	EETS page/line	MS folio/line	Location on MS folio	CONTENT	Description
62	152/34	74v/3	interlinear/ outer margin	a l \<**be**\>leuyd	added to line
63	156/36	76v/3	interlinear	my wyl\<**l**\> þe	"l" added
67	164/28	80r/21	interlinear	diuinite \<**& sade**\> l	inserted with caret
68	166/2	81r/2	interlinear	onto ȝow\<**e**\> in	superscripted insertion
68	166/33	81r/31	interlinear	ȝow \<**th**\>þow ȝe	"th" written on top of "þ"
70	170/10	83r/11	interlinear	in \<**þe**\> towne	superscripted insertion
72	173/6	84v/5	interlinear	owr \<**lord**\> God	inserted with caret
72	173/34	84v/30	interlinear	a man to\<**no**\> sa l uowryn	insertion
72	174/1	84v/32	interlinear	wepist \<**thow**\> so	inserted with caret
73	174/15	85r/10	interlinear/ outer margin	how owr \<**lady**\> toke	black ink inserted with red caret
73	174/27	85r/20	interlinear	neuyr \<**tell**\> aftyr	inserted with caret
73	174/28	85r/20	outer margin	*	?corrector's mark - red reinforcing previous (black ink) mark
73	174/30	85r/23	interlinear/ outer margin	heuyn l \<**ther**\>for sche	added to line
73	175/7	85r/28	interlinear	was \<**as**\> hir	superscripted and inserted with red caret

74	177/18	86v/1	interlinear	þe oo<n> woman	red nasal bar written over "oo"
76	179/17	87r/31	interlinear	hys he<u↗>rd vndir	"u" reinforced in red and "y" "daubed" in red
76	179/26	87v/6	interlinear	as <it> is	superscripted and inserted with red caret
76	180/3	87v/15	interlinear	owyn <hurt> faylyng	inserted with caret
77	182/22	88v/28	interlinear	wher <me> likyth	inserted with caret
77	183/4	89r/8	interlinear	al tyme<s>	Also	"s" added
78	186/31	90v/27	interlinear	ryth wikke<d> þat	"d" added
79	190/18	92v/15	interlinear	as it <had> ben	inserted with caret
79	190/19	92v/16	interlinear	& <he> went	inserted with caret
79	190/35	92v/29	interlinear	seyd to <in>	hir	"in" written on top of "to"
81	196/18	95v/6	interlinear	go by in onyment	"in" crossed out
81	196/21	95v/9	interlinear	was <wyth> owr	superscripted insertion
81	197/16	96r/1	interlinear	hast <takyn> a wey	inserted with caret
82	198/34	96v/15	interlinear	a <mok> jape &	"mok" inserted with caret; "jape" crossed out
82	199/1	96v/17	interlinear	to <holy> Ioseph	inserted with caret
82	199/5	96v/21	interlinear	louyn <hym> &	inserted with caret
84	203/11	98v/13	outer margin	d	corrector's mark - ?deleatur

Capitulum (Chapter)	EETS page/line	MS folio/line	Location on MS folio	CONTENT	Description
84	203/11	98v/13-14	interlinear	maydyn {& holpyn to kepyn hym in hys childhod & so forth in to þe tyme of hys deth} &	repeatedly crossed out in red
84	206/12	100r/7	interlinear/ outer margin	as <any.> lady	inserted with caret
85	207/17	100v/6	interlinear/ outer margin	þat <she> I saw	added to line
85	208/10	100v/30-32	interlinear	thowt {And þan cam on wyth a basclard knyfe to hir syght & kytt þat precyows body d on long in þe brest} And	repeatedly crossed out in red
86	209/29	101v/14	interlinear	as meche many	expuncted by original scribe and crossed out in red
86	210/30	102r/11	interlinear	virginys to welcomyn me in þi sowle I þat	expuncted by original scribe and crossed out in red
86	212/4	102v/20	outer margin	to <þe> I tellyn	added to line
86	212/37	103r/16	interlinear	er <mokyd> japyd	"mokyd" inserted above; "japyd" crossed out

			Location	Text	Description
86	214/7	103v/23	interlinear/ outer margin	bed \<gostly\>	For	inserted with caret
88	218/8	105v/18	interlinear	be ~~displesyd~~ wyth	original cross-through duplicated in red
88	218/9	105v/19	interlinear	woldist \<be\>leuyn	superscripted and inserted with red caret
89	219/22	106r/27	interlinear	sche \<herd\> owr	insertion
BOOK TWO					
1	221/8	107r/7	interlinear	he \<be\>gan	to	inserted with caret
1	222/8	107r/35	interlinear/ outer margin	euyl \<cumpany &\> euyl	inserted with caret
2	224/25	108v/14	interlinear	had \<a\> lettyr	inserted with caret
2	226/35	109v/24	interlinear	qwiet	han\<ve\> in	"ve" written on top of "n"
3	230/8	111r/32	interlinear	for ~~me~~\<we\> may	"we" written on top of "me"
5	234/8	113r/27	interlinear	a tal\<l\> man	"l" added
6	236/27	114v/12	interlinear	whom sche	~~sche~~ myth	2nd "sche" crossed out in red
7	238/11	115r/30	interlinear	defrawdyd of	~~of~~ hir	2nd "of" crossed out in red
7	238/25	115v/8	interlinear	Inglond \<þat\> wer	superscripted insertion
7	238/25	115v/8	interlinear	~~fro þe cowrt of~~ rome	crossed out in red
7	238/37	115v/18	interlinear	man lyn\<g\> &	"g" written on top of "n"
8	242/18	117r/34	interlinear	up ~~&~~	& preseruyn	1st "&" crossed out in red

Capitulum (Chapter)	EETS page/line	MS folio/line	Location on MS folio	CONTENT	Description
9	244/5	118r/20	interlinear	pike &-swech oþer þus seke xuld a seyd as	crossed out in red
10	246/19	119r/34	interlinear	þat <þ>e cawse	superscripted insertion
10	247/21	120r/1	interlinear/ outer margin	to<þe> l hy	added to line

PRAYERS OF THE CREATURE

Capitulum (Chapter)	EETS page/line	MS folio/line	Location on MS folio	CONTENT	Description
Prayers	249/5	121r/1	interlinear	& <increse> moryn	inserted with caret
Prayers	249/6	121r/1	outer margin	Heuyn <&> l helpyn	added to line
Prayers red	249/11	121r/6	interlinear	lettyd fro l fro þi	1st "fro" crossed out in red
Prayers	250/3	121r/32	interlinear	þe pope &	crossed out in red
Prayers	250/16	121v/10	interlinear	plesyn hym <the> &	"hym" crossed out; "he" inserted above
Prayers "e"	250/21	121v/15	interlinear	haue me<y>nde þat	"y" written on top of 1st
Prayers	251/6	121v/34	interlinear	mercy <wyll> ȝefe	inserted with caret
Prayers	251/37	122r/27	interlinear/ outer margin	any <pane> l in	added to line
Prayers	252/27	122v/21	interlinear	þat <al> I	superscripted and inserted with caret
Prayers	253/3	122v/30	interlinear	& <for> perseuerawns	superscripted insertion

APPENDIX C — RUBRICATIONS — British Library MS Add. 61823

Capitulum (Chapter)	EETS page/line	MS folio/line	Location on MS folio	CONTENT	Description
PROEM					
Proem	1/1	1r/1-4	interlinear	rubric capital **H**	decorated initial - strapwork and dots
Proem	3/25	2r/26	inner margin	¶	
BOOK ONE					
Preface	5/33	3v/1-3	interlinear	rubric capital **A**	decorated initial - strapwork and dots
Preface	6/21	3v/24	outer margin	¶	
1	6/25	3v/27-29	interlinear	rubric capital **W**	solid red
1	7/19	4r/20	inner margin	¶	
2	9/7	5r/12-14	interlinear	rubric capital **A**	decorated initial - strapwork and dots
3	11/12	6r/20-22	interlinear	**ihc** inside rubric capital **O**	historiated initial
3	12/4	6v/12	outer margin	¶	
3	13/17	7r/27	inner margin	¶	
4	13/30	7v/6-8	interlinear	rubric capital **T**	solid red
5	16/27	8v/30-32	interlinear	rubric capital **T**	solid red
5	16/31	9r/1	inner margin	¶	
5	17/13	9r/18	inner margin	¶	

Capitulum (Chapter)	EETS page/line	MS folio/line	Location on MS folio	CONTENT	Description
5	17/25	9r/29	inner margin	¶	
6	18/9	9v/14-16	interlinear	rubric capital **A**	decorated initial - strapwork
7	19/24	10r/25-27	interlinear	rubric capital **A**	decorated initial - strapwork and dots
7	20/3	10v/8	outer margin	¶	
8	20/19	10v/21-23	inner margin	rubric capital **A**	decorated initial - strapwork
8	21/5	11r/9	inner margin	¶	
9	21/8	11r/11-13	interlinear	rubric capital **A**	decorated initial - strapwork, dots and circles
10	22/26	11v/21-23	interlinear	rubric capital **S**	decorated initial - strapwork
11	23/9	12r/6-8	interlinear	rubric capital **I**	decorated initial - strapwork and dots
12	25/28	13r/20-22	interlinear	rubric capital **T**	solid red
13	27/18	14r/1-3	interlinear	**ihc** in rubric capital **O**	historiated initial
13	29/19	15r/2	inner margin	¶	
14	29/27	15r/9-11	interlinear	rubric capital **T**	solid red

Page	Ref	Folio	Location	Symbol	Initial	Type
14	29/32	15r/14	inner margin	¶		
15	32/1	16r/6-8	interlinear		rubric capital **T**	solid red
16	36/4	18r/4-6	interlinear		rubric capital **T**	solid red
17	38/6	19r/9-11	interlinear		**FACE** in rubric capital **O**	historiated initial
17	38/12	19r/15	inner margin	¶		
18	41/1	20v/1-3	interlinear		rubric capital **T**	solid red
18	41/30	20v/28	outer margin	¶		
18	42/24	21r/23	inner margin	¶		
18	42/36	21v/1	outer margin	¶		
19	46/1	23r/1-3	interlinear		rubric capital **B**	decorated initial - strapwork
20	47/15	23v/13-15	interlinear		**ihc** in rubric capital **O**	historiated initial
20	47/34	23v/30	outer margin	¶		
20	48/16	24r/11	inner margin	¶		
21	48/25	24r/18-20	interlinear		rubric capital **I**	decorated initial - strapwork and circles
21	49/34	24v/25	outer margin	¶		
22	50/18	25r/8	inner margin	¶		
22	50/18	25r/8-10	interlinear		rubric capital **A**	decorated initial - strapwork and dots
22	51/10	25r/31	inner margin	¶		
22	51/18	25v/4	outer margin	¶		

Capitulum (Chapter)	EETS page/line	MS folio/line	Location on MS folio	CONTENT	Description
23	53/8	26r/18-20	interlinear	rubric capital **T**	solid red
23	53/29	26v/4	outer margin	¶	
23	54/7	26v/15	outer margin	¶	
23	54/15	26v/22	outer margin	¶	
23	54/20	26v/26	outer margin	¶	
23	54/38	27r/10	inner margin	¶	
24	55/6	27r/15-17	interlinear	rubric capital **T**	solid red
24	58/24	28v/25	interlinear	7 pen **SLASHES**	line filler
25	58/25	28v/26-28	interlinear	rubric capital **F**	decorated initial - strapwork and dots
26	60/18	29v/19-21	interlinear	?**TEARS** symbol in rubric capital **W**	historiated initial
27	63/1	31r/7-9	interlinear	**FIVE WOUNDS** in rubric capital **T**	historiated initial
28	66/18	32v/21-23	interlinear	rubric capital **A**	decorated initial - strapwork and dots
28	69/38	34r/29	inner margin	¶	
28	70/21	34v/14	outer margin	¶	
29	71/16	35r/11-13	interlinear	rubric capital **W**	decorated initial - solid red and dots

29	73/3	35v/32	outer margin	¶	
30	74/1	36r/31-33	interlinear	rubric capital A	decorated initial - strapwork
30	76/16	37v/9	outer margin	¶	
30	76/30	37v/24	outer margin	¶	
30	77/34	38r/23	inner margin	¶	
31	78/12	38v/4-6	interlinear	rubric capital T	solid red
31	78/14	38v/6-7	interlinear	Ihesus est I amor meus	red-underlined text
32	80/21	39r/17-19	interlinear	rubric capital W	solid red
32	81/3	40r/2	inner margin	¶	
32	81/5	40r/3	interlinear	seyd Benedicte &	red-underlined text
32	81/6	40r/3	interlinear	seyd Dominus I verily	red-underlined text
33	82/10	40v/4-6	interlinear	rubric capital A	decorated initial - strapwork and dots
33	83/5	40v/30	outer margin	¶	
34	84/32	41v/18-20	interlinear	rubric capital T	solid red
34	85/13	42r/3	outer margin	¶	
35	86/9	42r/32-34	interlinear	rubric capital A	decorated initial - strapwork
35	89/16	43v/34	outer margin	¶	
36	89/26	44r/7-9	interlinear	rubric capital F	decorated initial - strapwork and dots
36	89/36	44r/16	inner margin	¶	

Capitulum (Chapter)	EETS page/line	MS folio/line	Location on MS folio	CONTENT	Description
36	90/25	44v/3	outer margin	¶	
37	91/14	44v/25-27	interlinear	**ihc** in rubric capital **D** →	historiated initial - with attention-drawing line
37	91/35	45r/6	interlinear	fadyr <u>Wens-</u> l lawe	red-underlined text
38	92/28	45r/30-32	interlinear	rubric capital **A**	decorated initial - strapwork and dots
38	93/5	45v/9	outer margin	¶	
39	94/8	46r/11-13	interlinear	rubric capital **A**	decorated initial - strapwork and dots
39	95/28	46v/30	outer margin	¶	
40	96/19	47r/21-23	interlinear	rubric capital **T**	solid red
40	97/8	47v/12	outer margin	¶	
40	97/18	47v/21	outer margin	¶	
40	97/32	47v/34	outer margin	¶	
41	98/18	48r/20-22	interlinear	rubric capital **S**	solid red
41	98/26	48r/28	inner margin	¶	
41	98/32	48r/34	interlinear/ lower margin	vnqwen l chabyl <u>fyer of lofe</u> whech	red-underlined text
42	99/31	48v/14-36	interlinear	rubric capital **W**	solid red
43	102/1	49v/29-31	interlinear	**FACE** in rubric capital **O**	historiated initial

208

44	103/28	50v/18-20	interlinear	rubric capital **A**	decorated initial - strapwork and dots
44	104/26	51r/13	inner margin	¶	
45	107/25	52v/1-3	interlinear	**ihc** in rubric capital **O**	historiated initial
45	110/19	53v/18	outer margin	¶	
46	111/3	54r/2-4	interlinear	rubric capital **S**	solid red
46	111/10	54r/8	inner margin	¶	
47	112/30	54v/19-21	interlinear	rubric capital **T**	solid red
47	113/34	55r/16	interlinear	<u>Thomas Marchale</u>	red-underlined text
48	114/29	55v/9-11	interlinear	**ihc** in rubric capital **O**	historiated initial
48	115/30	56r/6	inner margin	¶	
49	117/12	56v/20-22	interlinear	rubric capital **S**	solid red
49	117/19	56v/27	outer margin	¶	
49	119/1	57v/5	outer margin	¶	
50	119/19	57v/20-22	interlinear	rubric capital **W**	solid red
50	119/27	57v/28	outer margin	¶	
51	121/1	58r/31-33	interlinear	rubric capital **A**	decorated initial - strapwork
51	121/9	58v/4	outer margin	¶	
52	123/11	59v/1-3	interlinear	rubric capital **T**	solid red
52	126/23	61r/4	outer margin	¶	
53	128/32	62r/7-9	interlinear	rubric capital **S**	solid red

Capitulum (Chapter)	EETS page/line	MS folio/line	Location on MS folio	CONTENT	Description
53	130/37	63r/15	inner margin	¶	
54	131/10	63r/24-26	interlinear	rubric capital **T**	solid red
54	131/24	63v/4	outer margin	¶	
55	135/14	65v/1-3	interlinear	rubric capital **W**	solid red
56	137/11	66v/3-5	interlinear	rubric capital **A**	decorated initial - strapwork and dots
56	137/28	66v/25	outer margin	¶	
56	138/6	67r/3	inner margin	¶	
56	138/37	67r/31	inner margin	¶	
57	139/3	67v/1-3	interlinear	rubric capital **T**	solid red
57	139/30	67v/26	outer margin	¶	
57	141/7	68v/6	outer margin	¶	
57	142/10	69r/9	inner margin	¶	
58	142/14	69r/12-14	interlinear	**ihc** in rubric capital **O**	historiated initial
58	142/21	69r/19	inner margin	¶	
59	144/5	70r/5-7	interlinear	rubric capital **T**	solid red
59	146/8	71r/6	inner margin	¶	
59	146/19	71r/16	interlinear	þis <u>peyne</u> so	red-underlined text
60	147/1	71v/1-3	interlinear	rubric capital **T**	solid red

61	148/28	72r/26-28	interlinear	rubric capital **T**		solid red
62	152/8	74r/11-13	interlinear	rubric capital **A**		decorated initial - strapwork and dots
62	153/10	74v/15	outer margin		¶	
62	154/11	75r/16	interlinear	<u>Richard Hampol, hermyte</u>		red-underlined text
62	154/12	75r/17	interlinear	<u>Incendio Amoris</u>		red-underlined text
62	154/27	75r/31	inner margin		¶	
63	154/30	75v/1-3	interlinear	rubric capital **T**		solid red
63	155/4	75v/10	outer margin		¶	
63	156/30	76r/32	inner margin		¶	
63	156/36	76v/3	outer margin		¶	
64	157/21	76v/22-24	interlinear	rubric capital **T**		solid red
64	157/24	76v/25	outer margin		¶	
64	158/26	77r/26	inner margin		¶	
65	159/21	77v/20-22	interlinear	**ihc** in rubric capital **O**		historiated initial
65	159/24	77v/23	outer margin		¶	
65	161/6	78v/2	interlinear	<u>Ihc est amor meus</u>		red-underlined text
66	161/24	78v/17-19	interlinear	rubric capital **N**		decorated initial - strapwork and ?dots
67	162/29	79r/19-21	interlinear	**FACE** in rubric capital **O**		historiated initial
67	163/10	79v/2	outer margin		¶	
67	164/25	80r/18	outer margin		¶	

Capitulum (Chapter)	EETS page/line	MS folio/line	Location on MS folio	CONTENT	Description
68	165/27	80v/22-24	interlinear	rubric capital S	solid red
68	167/11	81v/12	outer margin	¶	
69	167/16	81v/16-18	interlinear	rubric capital A	decorated initial - strapwork
69	169/6	82v/9	outer margin	¶	
70	169/18	82v/20-22	interlinear	FACE in rubric capital O	historiated initial
71	170/27	83r/26-28	interlinear	ihc in rubric capital O	historiated initial
71	171/13	83v/13	outer margin	¶	
72	172/11	84r/11-13	interlinear	rubric capital S	decorated initial - solid red and 5 dots
72	172/23	84r/22	inner margin	¶	
72	173/20	84v/18	outer margin	¶	
73	174/12	85r/7-9	interlinear	ihc in rubric capital O	historiated initial
73	175/14	85v/2	outer margin	¶	
74	176/6	85v/25-27	interlinear	rubric capital T	solid red
74	176/9	85v/28	outer margin	¶	
74	176/23	86r/7	inner margin	¶	
75	177/29	86v/11-13	interlinear	rubric capital A	decorated initial - strapwork and dots

76	179/6	87r/21-23	interlinear	rubric capital **I**	decorated initial - strapwork and dots
77	181/16	88r/25-27	interlinear	rubric capital **W**	solid red
77	182/9	88v/17	outer margin	¶	
78	184/26	89v/25-27	interlinear	rubric capital **M**	decorated initial - solid red, strapwork and dots
78	185/30	90r/24	inner margin	¶	
78	186/6	90v/6	outer margin	¶	
79	187/25	91r/20-22	interlinear	rubric capital **T**	solid red
79	188/9	91v/9	outer margin	¶	
79	190/26	92v/22	outer margin	¶	
80	191/4	93r/1-3	interlinear	rubric capital **A**	decorated initial - strapwork
80	192/24	93v/15	outer margin	¶	
81	194/25	94v/17-19	interlinear	rubric capital **W**	solid red
81	196/23	95v/10	interlinear	<u>Salue *sancta* parens</u>	red-underlined text
81	197/5	95v/25	outer margin	¶	
82	198/1	96r/19-21	interlinear	**FACE** in rubric capital **O**	historiated initial
82	198/29	96v/12	outer margin	¶	
82	199/4	96v/20	outer margin	¶	
83	200/1	97r/15-17	interlinear	rubric capital **T**	solid red
84	202/6	98r/14-16	interlinear	rubric capital **T**	solid red
84	202/22	98r/28	inner margin	¶	

Capitulum (Chapter)	EETS page/line	MS folio/line	Location on MS folio	CONTENT	Description
84	204/10	99r/11	inner margin	¶	
84	205/11	99v/10	outer margin	¶	
85	206/27	100r/19-21	interlinear	FACE in rubric capital O	historiated initial
85	207/4	100r/31	inner margin	¶	
85	207/11	100v/2	outer margin	¶	
86	209/27	101v/12-14	interlinear	FACE in rubric capital O	historiated initial
86	209/36	101v/20	outer margin	¶	
86	211/24	102v/5	outer margin	¶	
87	214/14	103v/29-31	interlinear	rubric capital T	solid red
87	215/20	104v/1	outer margin	¶	
87	215/31	104v/10	outer margin	¶	
88	216/4	104v/21-23	interlinear	rubric capital W	solid red
88	217/10	105r/22	inner margin	¶	
88	218/2	105v/14	outer margin	¶	
89	219/1	106r/8-10	interlinear	rubric capital A	decorated initial - strapwork and dots
89	220/4	106v/10	outer margin	¶	
BOOK TWO					
1	221/1	107r/1-3	interlinear	rubric capital A	decorated initial - strapwork and dots

1	221/9	107r/8	interlinear	mlo. cccc.xxxviij	red-underlined text
2	223/29	108r/17-19	interlinear	rubric capital I	decorated initial - 3 big dots
2	227/12	110r/4	inner margin	¶	
3	229/11	111r/1-3	interlinear	rubric capital T	solid red
3	230/15	111v/3	outer margin	¶	
3	230/25	111v/13	outer margin	¶	
3	230/25	111v/13	interlinear	owr Lady	red-underlined text
4	231/25	112r/7-9	interlinear	rubric capital T	decorated initial - solid red and 1 large dot
5	233/13	112v/31-33	interlinear	rubric capital W	solid red
5	235/1	113v/23	outer margin	¶	
6	235/4	113v/26-28	interlinear	rubric capital T	solid red
7	237/31	115r/13-15	interlinear	rubric capital W	solid red
7	237/31	115r/13	interlinear	¶	
8	241/26	117r/9-11	interlinear	rubric capital I	decorated initial - strap work and dots
9	243/11	117v/25-27	interlinear	rubric capital F	decorated initial - strap work
9	245/16	118v/30	outer margin	¶	
10	245/31	119r/9-11	interlinear	rubric capital F	decorated initial - strap work and dots

PRAYERS OF THE CREATURE

Capitulum (Chapter)	EETS page/line	MS folio/line	Location on MS folio	CONTENT	Description
Prayers	248/1	120r/1-3	interlinear	rubric capital **T**	solid red
Prayers	248/15	120v/13	interlinear	seyd <u>veni creator</u> | <u>spiritus</u>	red-underlined text
Prayers	248/20	120v/18	outer margin	¶	
Prayers	250/34	121v/27	outer margin	¶	
Prayers	251/19	122r/11	inner margin	¶	

216

Scribe D and the Marketing of Ricardian Literature

Kathryn Kerby-Fulton and Steven Justice

Our scribe is, of course, Doyle and Parkes' Scribe D, the fourth hand in the Trinity Gower, on which he collaborated (if that is precisely the word for the minimally co-ordinated farming-out that produced the manuscript) with the scribe of the Ellesmere and Hengwrt *Canterbury Tales* (Scribe B) and Thomas Hoccleve (Scribe E), as well as two otherwise unidentified scribes.[1] The list of the extant manuscripts in his hand includes two copies of the *Canterbury Tales* (the textually rather good Corpus 198 and the wildly eccentric Harley 7334), the Ilchester *Piers Plowman* (an early C-text bearing some important marks of proximity to the author), Trevisa's *On the Properties of Things*, and, terrifying as the thought is, eight copies of the *Confessio amantis*.[2] A further six manuscripts are known to have been written by Scribe Delta, whose hand is so nearly identical to Scribe D's that Doyle and Parkes take him to have been his apprentice; these include yet another *Confessio amantis* and three more copies of Trevisa (all *Polychronica*).[3]

Scribe D (even without any help from Delta) is responsible for the largest identifiable corpus of vernacular Ricardian literary manuscripts extant today. As has often been noticed, they are all "quality" manuscripts, created mainly, it seems, for armigerous patrons.[4] But what has not been noticed is that predominant among these patrons is a particular class of reader: parliamentarians and high-ranking civil servants associated with early Lancastrian Westminster.[5] The portfolios of these two scribes, in fact, give us a window on the tastes and interests of an audience of Westminster lawmakers of varying ranks. In this article we speculate that D's and Delta's commissions reflect demand for an evolving vernacular canon, evolving, that is, to suit the literary needs and interests of a curial culture.

Since Doyle and Parkes' landmark study identifying his hand, Scribe D has been best known for his puzzlingly enormous output of Gower manuscripts, largely made, we will suggest, for this kind of Westminster clientele. Gower, of course, had become an important icon of both literary and political good taste in Lancastrian England, and Scribe D's manuscripts can be closely associated with a number of the productions

217

of elite illuminators' workshops, especially Herman Scheerre's (the source of iconography associating Gower with a critique of Richard II's reign in at least one famous manuscript).[6] Very early in his career, Scribe D had also copied *Piers Plowman*, of course, a text also strongly associated with the legal and civil service community in Ricardian Westminster. Langland and Gower represent, in effect, the bookends of a remarkable scribal career, the trajectory of which traces the changing parliamentary and political interests of turn-of-the-century Westminster. Scribe D acted throughout his career, we would argue, as the consummate "professional reader," always working with this audience explicitly in mind.[7] This is easiest to see in the case of his Langland copying, because of his use of legal and parliamentary terminology in embryonic alliterative "interventions" (created to mend faulty alliteration in his exemplar).[8] It has been less clear (since he is known not to have "meddled" textually with his Gowers),[9] how this impulse might be traced in these later manuscripts, but as we will see, they show it as well, albeit through different, more subtle strategies. The Taylor Gower, more perhaps than any of the Gowers, suggests how politically astute both D and his clientele were. But its mysteries require some patience to unfold.

The Taylor Gower

The Taylor Gower consists of eight quires, all but the first of which are exclusively in the hand of Scribe D. The first quire is the work of two other scribes: fols. 1 and 8 are in a slightly nostalgic bastard anglicana[10] (we'll call this scribe "Scribe 1"), fols. 2-7 in an anglicana formata ("Scribe 2"). Folio 1 also contains, uniquely among Gower manuscripts, what appear to be two author portraits: in the margin of a picture of the statue from the dream of Nebuchadnezzar, a regular in the repertory of illustrated copies of the *Confessio*, is a portrait of a bearded, gray Gower; and in the initial "O" beneath, a beardless layman gestures toward a book cupboard (see fig. 1). These illustrations, as we will see, are important clues to the kind of marketing concerns that are latent in the less sensational codicological evidence elsewhere the manuscript.

Since no scrunching of text into writing space is visible to achieve the perfect jointure between the two shifts in the work of Scribes 1 and 2 (fols. 1v/2r and fols. 7v/8r) or in that between Scribe 1 and Scribe D (fols. 8v/9r), the work has been co-ordinated in some fashion. But in what fashion? The conventional layout of *Confessio* manuscripts would have left some leeway here: the two-column, 46-line format that predominates on fols. 1-8 (the work of Scribes 1 and 2) was common enough in them. In any case it would have been easy to calculate how

218

many lines each column on fols. 1 and 8 would have to contain in order to join perfectly with fol. 2 or, conversely, to calculate where fol. 2 would have to start in order to continue from fol. 1v. It would have been only a little harder to calculate where the second quire should start. The work of these three scribes could, then, have been roughly simultaneous, each having his orders on where to begin copying and on how many lines per page; they could have, but they did not.

The first reason for thinking that they did not is that, while Scribes 1 and 2 write in double-columned pages of 46 lines, Scribe D writes in double-columned pages of 45 lines.[11] This might of course have arisen through some species of communicative misfire in the original instructions to scribes, but another circumstance suggests a more interesting reason: on fols 2-7 — the inner bifolia of the first quire, and the unique contribution of our "Scribe 2" — the nearest thing to decoration is the occasional paraph mark.[12] The remaining quires — the work of Scribe D — have blue Lombard capitals with intricate penwork flourishing, the like of which does not appear on these inner bifolia of the first quire. However — and this is the striking point — the outer bifolium of quire 1 (fols. 1 and 8, the work of our "Scribe 1") also shows blue Lombard capitals with red penwork flourishing, identical with those found in the remaining quires of the work and markedly different from anything on fols. 2-7.[13] So the same person or persons did the penwork and rubrication on the elaborately formal fols. 1 and 8 and on the quires copied by Scribe D, but *not* on fols. 2-7, the work of Scribe 2. There would seem to be only one explanation for this odd state of affairs: that fols. 2-7 were already in existence before the enterprise that produced fols. 1 and 8 and the remaining quires of Taylor 5 in its present form. But since it is unlikely that Scribe 2, whenever he copied his folios, would have begun copying the *Confessio amantis* at line 185, we must suppose that fols. 2-7 were originally part of an eight-leaf quire in his hand, which, in the enterprise that produced Taylor 5, were peeled off and replaced by the work of Scribe 1, and continued by the work of Scribe D. The evidence of the decoration shared by Scribe 1 and Scribe D indicates that this enterprise was a co-ordinated project.

And it looks as though Scribe D did the co-ordinating. He has written most of the surviving catchwords. This is hardly revealing in itself, but there is one anomaly that is: Scribe D has also added catchwords, matching the first words of his assay on fol. 9r, at the bottom of 7v — not 8v, but 7v. He would have added his catchwords there, rather than at the end of the first quire, only if he had thought it important to make the note of the first words of the next quire *before fol. 8 was in his possession*. This suggests that fols. 1 and 8 were copied off the premises, and he was therefore continuing with his own stint while waiting for them.[14]

What this tells us is that, faced with (apparently) a single first quire of the *Confessio amantis*, and commissioned or wishing to make it a complete copy, Scribe D stripped off the first bifolium to send to the man we've been calling Scribe 1. (In fact, Scribe 1 probably was, or worked in the shop of, the illuminator who executed the two illustrations on 1r.) But before sending it off, he copied the final words of fol. 8v — which he was about to surrender — as catchwords at the bottom of fol. 7v — which he would have still in his possession. He could then easily, by roughly estimating the lines and then matching the catchwords against his exemplar, find where he needed to start copying. And he would likely have started copying *knowing that he would be copying all the remaining quires*, for otherwise his decision to substitute a 45- for a 46-line format would have been courting disaster.

But why did he send the outer bifolium for copying elsewhere? And, more basically, what made the *original* outer bifolium — the presumptive bifolium, now no longer extant, in the hand of Scribe 2 — unacceptable in the first place? There are two possible answers to that question.

The obvious and immediately persuasive reason for sending the outer bifolium out is that, if the minimal elaboration and decoration of fols. 2-7 is any indication, the original outer bifolium was probably none too impressive, and it would seem, from the two illustrations, the decoration, and the careful bastard anglicana of the (new) outer bifolium, that the supervisor of this project wanted some very red apples at the very front of the cart. Now this might have been the primary motive, and may have been the only motive; on the other hand, it may have been an opportunity raised by another, more politically informed motive. There is one *prima facie* reason in the first 184 lines of the *Confessio* that would likely make any scribe or any supervisor or any commissioning customer want to replace the folios containing those lines. For that portion of the Prologue, in lines 24-92, contains the dedication to Richard II in the first, and to the earl of Derby in the second, recension.[15] Now we have recently suggested that the suspicious mind might find Gower's ostentatiously precise dating of the Derby dedication to "the yeer sextethe of king Richard" — 1393 — an extremely convenient and disingenuous disguise for a revision of c. 1400, since we have only Gower's word for that date and some small reason to doubt his word.[16] If we're right, then Taylor 5 in its present form must postdate the Lancastrian revolution, so that the excision of the Ricardian dedication that we suspect occupied part of the original, discarded, bifolium might have been of some urgent consequence; this brief suggestion could easily join some other chickens that will come home to roost later in this article. We will not insist on it, but point rather to a more neutral, and less contentious proposition, which concerns Gower's own professional and entrepreneurial savvy and its neat embodiment in Taylor 5. A superb recent essay by Malcolm Parkes discusses the informal network by which owners of Gower's early works (especially the *Vox clamantis*) would learn of revisions to the text and the scribes who could enter those revisions in copies already extant.[17] Peter Nicholson, a decade ago, noticed that Gower's revision to his last great poem tended to replace excised passages with passages of the same number of lines, so that existing manuscripts could be updated with a minimum of disruption to their contents.[18] Nicholson was evidently thinking of the ease of erasure and overlining, but it would apply equally to the case of the 46-line, double-column format of the Taylor Gower: it would be easy to *recopy* a bifolium with a significant revision without indecorous compression or stretching to achieve agreements with existing and unrevised folia.

We've already said that Scribe D apparently "co-ordinated" the making of the new *Confessio* manuscript around the already extant quire 1; our coy and we hope elegant euphemism avoided the verb "supervised." But another point gives us courage to discard the euphemism, and this is the pattern of correction. Folios 2-7, and only those folios, exhibit marginal corrections and insertions. On fol. 5r, for example, the corrector has supplied the words *stant why* (Prol.577, in Macaulay's edition). It seems to us that the correction is manifestly in the hand of Scribe D: one sees in *why* both his characteristic angled hook on the descender of the *h* (one can see the same in the correction fol. 6r) and the winning, jaunty curve of his *y* descender. So Scribe D seems to have written in the corrections here. It is notable, however, that there are no such corrections, only overlinings, in the quires he himself copied; it is hard to avoid the conclusion that he was himself the supervisor, or at least the corrector. Not only did he correct fols. 2-7, but he executed the (few) corrections on his own sections, less carefully and, presumably, *currente calamo*.

Habits of codicological description lead us to speak casually and often without evidence of a "supervisor" independent of the scribes, especially when correction is executed by someone other than the main scribe or scribes. But in the case of Taylor 5, the simplest Ockhamist canons of historical explanation suggest that to speak of a supervisor apart from Scribe D himself would be to multiply entities needlessly and indeed counter-evidentially. Whatever one supposes of Middle English manuscripts generally, and of Scribe D's in particular, Taylor 5 was certainly Scribe D's own enterprise.

Scribe D, Scribe Delta, and Vernacular Texts for a Westminster Clientele

Why, one might ask, does such codicological archaeology matter? Let us quote a great scholar who has, we suspect, never in his distinguished career had occasion to look at a single Middle English manuscript: "An alternative to the scholastic library canon is not . . . to be sought in the environments linked to university culture . . . . That alternative had other sources, in the progressively less marginal presence . . . of a curial culture that . . . was largely formed outside [the university]: a culture created by laymen, notaries, judges, and chancellors . . . , following a branch of interpersonal connections and transmigrations of people and books that we have only recently begun to understand."[19] This is Armando Petrucci, describing fourteenth-century Italian humanist culture. Our attempt at a *Verfremdungseffekt* sketches, we hope, a readership that is neither an inbred coterie, nor a generalized "public," but rather a self-conscious, connected, knowing circle of committed and active, perhaps politically active, readers alert to every new development. But perhaps it founders on the details. While the analogy is a rough one (*notaries* would have a less prominent, though not a non-existent, place in an English description; the plural of *chancellors* is an embarrassment, and the *judges* has a different valence altogether in Italy from what it has in England), still, even the most self-effacing translation of Petrucci's categories to those we are most signally concerned with bears a striking resemblance to those Anne Middleton hypothesized in her classic *Speculum* essay: an audience concerned with the "middel weie," the common profit, and the "public voice," a savvy and assertively *contemporary* audience that sought the most recent and topical versions of the vernacular texts they cared for.[20]

So, it matters, at the least, that this manuscript was Scribe D's own enterprise, for it confirms what his very productiveness as a vernacular scribe, not to mention what the implications of the Ilchester *Piers* and the Harley *Canterbury Tales*, would also seem to imply: that his activity as scribe and (not to put too fine a point on it) entrepreneur of vernacular poetry presents itself to us as maybe the most sensitive register we have of the excitement and the *contemporaneity* of contemporary poetry in the later years of Richard II's reign and the earlier years of Henry IV's. Putting it that way of course begs a question: was he responding to, or helping to create or at least direct and shape, the desires of those who would be the *cognoscenti* of Ricardian writing?

The question, put thus, could take us in several directions. Among the five scribes of the Trinity Gower, Scribe D alone might, on available evidence, be thought a more or less full-time purveyor of English writing (though Scribe B's work on the Ellesmere and Hengwrt *Canterbury Tales*, and the complete version of the *Troilus* that we may assume is represented by the Hatfield fragment, might place him in the same company).[21] One might point to the aesthetic and rhetorical character of Scribe D's hand, and its relation to the hand of Scribe Delta, as well as to the difficulty Doyle and Parkes had in defining the relations of the latter to the former (was he an apprentice or a colleague?). One might suggest that these two prolific vernacular scribes were involved in a common or even competitive pursuit of an appropriate and distinctive mode of presentation, a *look*, for vernacular English poetry. One might equally notice Scribe D's comparative freedom with the texts of his Chaucer and Langland, and his comparative constraint with Gower, as Jeremy Smith has shown,[22] and the contact with, more or less proximately, that very entrepreneurial poet that his care with the Gower manuscripts implies.

One might pursue these things, and by mentioning them we obviously mean to suggest that one could do worse than to consider them. But not here. Rather, we'd like to suggest backing up, so to speak, and asking what the *oeuvre* of Scribe D, along with that of his shadow and double, Scribe Delta, might amount to as an exercise in literary entrepreneurship, in the marketing of Ricardian literature.

These two scribes present us seventeen manuscripts all told. That there are eight Gower manuscripts, two Chaucers, and one Langland may seem oddly proportioned to modern sensibilities, but the collection of authors is unsurprising. Indeed that is a problem: this collection of the three great and influential southern Ricardian poets seems so obviously *right* that one hardly thinks to reflect on it. So perhaps it is worth shifting the focus to be surprised, rather, at the four Trevisas — three *Polychronica* and one *Properties* — that outnumber even the combined strength of Chaucer and Langland on this list; and to be surprised perhaps also that the Gower and the Trevisa manuscripts dominate and, inevitably, define the corpus of these two scribes' work: Gower and Trevisa comprise twelve of the seventeen manuscripts. How does this dominance of Gower and Trevisa affect how we might understand this important moment in the creation of the Ricardian canon? And, especially, in light of what the Taylor Gower suggests about Scribe D's awareness of the market among clients interested in the emerging canon of vernacular writing?

The place to start would ideally be with Trevisa. But the difficulties he presents — he, the Oxford scholar who may or may not have had sympathetic contacts with Wyclif, who may or may not have been associated with the Wycliffite translation of the Bible, who, leaving Oxford, pursued his translations for a West-Country patron who may have been the real audience of whom the author thought or who may have been merely an occasion for accomplishing the rapid London circulation that Trevisa achieved. These difficulties and others insist that we must work far more deeply and attentively before we know how to describe Trevisa and his project.[23] But his presence in the *oeuvre* of Scribes D and Delta re-articulates the vernacular canon implied by their works, and lets us ask what *category*, besides that of vernacular writing, these authors shared, and how that category could make Scribe D want to insure the contemporaneity of his versions, as he apparently wanted to insure in the Taylor Gower. Some other aspects, both of the Taylor manuscript and of the others, might help us elaborate it.

D's concern with the *currency* of the Gower text — its inclusion of the latest and best version of the crucial dedication passage in the Prologue — may testify, *with respect to the audience*, to an attitude that regards the work as of pertinent topical interest, and maybe even as an object of topical desire: one wants the latest version. But it also testifies, *with respect to the work*, to a concern with its textual integrity, which in fact is amply witnessed by all of Scribe D's Gowers: they are careful, conservative, good texts, even preserving prominent aspects of Gower's Kentish dialect, as Jeremy Smith showed. This care with the text of Gower stands in marked contrast to his relatively free treatment of Langland in the Ilchester *Piers*, not to mention what seems the almost unrestrained meddling with Chaucer in the Harley *Canterbury Tales*.[24] We cannot say much about the textual state of his, or of Scribe Delta's Trevisas, until the difficult textual history of the *Polychronicon* is further untangled.[25] But about his care with Gower's text, unlike Langland's or Chaucer's, we can at least suggest that he treated the *Confessio*, if on the one hand as a text of contemporary and topical interest, also on the other as a *classic* or cornerstone of the vernacular canon these texts were creating.

But then what about the choice of cornerstones, the importance of Gower and Trevisa? A fine discussion by Christopher Allmand on the culture of civil lawyers in England demonstrates their very well-informed, topical interest in what we might now call "international" issues — among them, for example, the papal schism of 1378 was a more pressing interest than it seems to have been to anyone else in England — and in the problems of jurisdiction, authority, and political community raised by such issues.[26] Allmand speaks too of their books: law books, of course, canon and civil law, as well as theology. But also, he stresses, one frequently meets in their collections books of exemplary history: the *Polychronicon*, especially. (This is of course Higden's, the Latin *Polychronicon*.) We'd like to speculate that Trevisa chose the texts he would translate in order to create a canon of vernacular prose along the lines of the canon found among the culture of lawyers, topically-engaged scholars, writing-office clerks, and the like: the great reference works of Higden and Bartholomew, and tracts on issues of contemporary interest, like the friars (FitzRalph), dominion as an issue of political rule and clerical reform (the *Dialogus*), just rule and tyranny (the *De regimine*). We know that Scribe D was sensitive to the presence of such issues, certainly in the Harley *Canterbury Tales* and the Ilchester *Piers Plowman*.[27] But what we need to do is to look at little harder at D's and Delta's choice of texts. Taken together, the English *Polychronicon* and the *Confessio amantis* make a striking couple: in the reflection of the other, each looks even more clearly and powerfully to reflect a repertory of historical exemplarity. If we add Trevisa's *De proprietatibus*, which Scribe D copied, we might expand our definition of the category slightly to speak of works of *secular exemplarity* — works defining, by exemplifying, the conditions of public virtue and political efficaciousness. Frank Grady has written about *exemplarity*, secular exemplarity, as a conditioning attribute also of *Piers Plowman*, and we can say that it looks even more powerfully so when placed in, and thereby defined by, this company.

Let's say then, in this preliminary assay at the Henrician literary history of Ricardian literature, that the "project" implied by the canon of D and Delta looks like an attempt to create in the vernacular a repertory of *historical and imaginative* (as opposed to mainly discursive) works that either had a place in or were analogous with the sort of texts most commonly owned and used by those involved in the international culture of civil and canon law, the educated and often politically engaged body of men for whose professional ambition, and choice of means for its pursuit, took them through the learned laws and, most often, into episcopal and royal service.

One significant characteristic of this project, if we're even close to correct in identifying and describing it (in fact this is clearly true even if we're wrong about the character of the project), is that no one looking at these manuscripts can think that the translations and vernacular works are imagined, in their vernacular character, as condescension to the non-latinate: everything about them bespeaks a confidence not so much in the "eloquence" of the vernacular as in its capacity for intellectual, scholarly, and literary culture. We'll mention two examples here. The first and most obvious is in the quality of some of the manuscripts themselves: Princeton University Library Garrett MS 151, for example (a Scribe Delta *Polychronicon*) displays workmanship and expense (in quality of vellum, decoration, and a blue million miles of gold leaf) that points constantly toward the dignity and importance of the (vernacular) text. More interesting and complex and surprising is Scribe D's treatment of Latin: not just the Latin appurtenances to the *Confessio amantis*, but also the quotations in *Piers Plowman*. He habitually and rigorously, if that's quite the right word, avoids the hierarchy of scripts that is so common in such circumstances: though the Latin is generally set off with red ink, it appears in the same anglicana formata that characterizes his hand in the main vernacular body of the text.

Perhaps the issues and import of our guesses might be clearest if we recall one of the most cogent and influential literary-historical accounts of recent decades: Richard Green's *Poets and Princepleasers*.[28] For one can accept Green's contention that late-medieval English literature is almost entirely, in his broad but meaningful definition, "courtly" — as one cannot avoid accepting in describing Trevisa, for example — and yet now make clearer and better sense of the evidence of the London copying and circulation of such possibly "courtly" works. Whatever one feels one can say about the scribal work of D — and Delta, and Scribe B, and Hoccleve — one can certainly say that it suggests that the reading, the "reception," of Ricardian literature, even when that literature was "courtly," did not merely *happen*, did not simply perpetuate itself by its mere appeal or through an agentless market, but that it was shaped by, and around the interests of, some of the scribes to whom we owe a good many of our important texts. It is good to speak of and study the "reception" of literary works, but the term too often places a black box between the authoring of a work and its "reception" by the reader. Sometimes a black box is the best, and therefore the most honest, model one can manage. But sometimes one can look inside: and looking inside this one, we see not just reception but marketing.

Scribe D's Marketing Strategies and the Iconography of the Taylor Gower

What, then, does this marketing look like that Scribe D used to promote the new vernacular works to his clientele? We can now begin to flesh out a picture of his professional standards and tactics. We have mentioned the quiet democracy of his presentation of Latin (especially apparent to any reader who comes to D's texts after years of looking at *Piers Plowman* manuscripts). We have also mentioned his dignifying of the vernacular in his treatment of metrics: he it was who improved the alliteration in a faulty Prologue passage so skilfully that some modern critics have believed it to be Langland's, while many earlier Chaucer critics took his Harley improvements as vintage Chaucer.[29] He also imported legal terminology for the Ilchester *Piers* Prologue, and he engaged in mild, ecclesiastically correct bowdlerizing in both manuscripts, apparently with a conservative audience in mind.[30] Moreover, he was doing all this during a period that had not yet seen either the full establishment of an English literary canon or the regularization of the vernacular book trade. Doyle and Parkes have spoken of both scribes D and Delta as having "taken a prominent role in setting the pace" of that trade, particularly in the development of a hand for vernacular texts.[31] We have suggested that Scribe D was developing more than "a hand." He was, it seems, aware enough of political revisions in Gower's text to ingeniously recycle an unrevised first quire that came into his hands — and to make it a more up-market product.[32]

Taylor is an especially good instance of his talent for using illustration for enhancing the authority of his texts, and he worked for a clientele who could well afford to pay for such authority. As Jeremy Griffiths has pointed out, no other copy of the *Confessio* (except the Rosenbach, done much later, in the third quarter of the century) has an author portrait[33] — but Taylor, apparently, has two: the old man holding a book (?) in the margin of the Nebuchadnezzar picture and the young man, in the historiated initial below it, gesturing towards a book cupboard (fig. 1). According to Jean Preston, this young man could be the scribe, and we would be delighted if he were, but the same motif occurs explicitly as an author portrait in two other contemporary manuscripts, one copied by Scribe D himself. Scribe D's Trevisa, British Library Additional 27944, contains a sophisticated historiated initial of a religious, representing Bartholomeus, also gesturing toward a bookstand, very similar to the one in Taylor (fig. 2a). It is also similar to one of St. Jerome in British Library Royal I.E.IX (fig. 2b).[34] Like three of D's other Gowers, the Royal manuscript is associated with the elite illuminating shop of Herman Scheerre. It comprises the so-called "Bible of Richard II" or "Big Bible," and its miniature depicts St. Jerome as an author-translator, shown next to his Prologue.[35] This suggests that Taylor may be associated with Scheerre's workshop, too,[36] and the choice shows Scribe D to have been, unsurprisingly perhaps, a formidable critic of Gower by this point in his career. Taylor is unique among *Confessio* manuscripts in its juxtaposition of the old author with the younger, perhaps D's way of resolving a dilemma that had long confronted those deciding how to illustrate Gower's poem: whether to show the Lover as an old man (in which case to pre-empt, as John Burrow says, the revelation of his age at the end of the poem), or, as happens in the majority of manuscripts, a young man.[37] Scribe D, who, after copying the poem so many times, and writing the standard directions to illustrators so often, apparently had his own opinion by the time he produced Taylor. And he was copying for a clientele that cared about literature and politics: also done for Scheerre's workshop at about the same time as Taylor, for instance, is the Bedford Psalter and Hours (British Library Add. 42131), which associates Gower quite overtly with a critique of Richard II's reign, and which has one certain portrait of Gower (identified by an inscription), and, as Wright has argued, others, representing Gower at various ages (as, in fact, does Taylor's first folio).[38]

We do not know for certain whether D himself gave the instructions for this miniature, but Jeremy Griffiths has argued convincingly that he was responsible for the professionalizaion of the miniature presentation in the many Gower manuscripts he copied, and he certainly wrote the instructions for the miniature of the Confessor in Bodley 902, fol. 8 (fig. 3a), and similar, briefer instructions, so far unnoticed, in beside the Plimpton miniature, fol. 4v (fig. 3b).[39] It is not unlikely, then, since Taylor was demonstrably D's enterprise, that he chose — perhaps from among suggestions made by Scheerre's staff — the book-cupboard author-portrait, unique in Gower iconography.[40] To choose a pictorial motif associated with Latin authors and their prologues (Jerome and Bartholomeus) in prestigious Scheerre productions would be typical of D's campaign to enhance the authority of all the Middle English productions he copied. Together with his literary acumen, political caution and sensitivity, and his attempt to standardize and authorize everything from picture placement to metrical habits, this seems of a piece with the motivations for decisions Scribe D usually makes. And given the clientele of his workshop, this combination should not surprise. The Trinity Gower was owned by Thomas Urswick, likely the man who was Serjeant and Recorder of London, and then Chief Baron of the Exchequer, or his earlier namesake, Receiver of the County Palatine of Lancaster. Another of Scribe D's Gowers, Bodley 294, was owned by Humphrey, Duke of Gloucester, who inscribed his name in it sometime after 1414. We do not have a definite owner for Scribe D's Trevisa manuscript before the early sixteenth century, when it belonged to John Cooke, doctor of laws (admitted to Lincoln's Inn in 1519).[41] But Ralph Hanna has suggested it was likely originally made for "one of D's usual clients," perhaps one of "those great magnates who were [Sir Thomas] Berkeley's parliamentary colleagues."[42] It was for one of these, Richard Beauchamp, Earl of Warwick, that Scribe Delta's *Polychronicon*, Add. 24194, was commissioned.[43] (And we might note here that a member of Beauchamp's retinue, John Clopton, owned the fine *Piers Plowman* manuscript, now University of London, MS S.L.V.17, one of a group of heraldically marked manuscripts, Hanna suggests, that can be "inferentially linked with persons exercising legal duties in the shires.") We do not know, unfortunately, who owned the Taylor Gower (or, for that matter, the Ilchester Langland, the other of D's manuscripts that shows a Westminster ethos most vividly). But we cannot doubt that their owners would not have been out of place at a Westminster gathering of the above.

NOTES

[1] A. I. Doyle and Malcolm Parkes, "The Production of Copies of the *Canterbury Tales* and the *Confessio Amantis* in the Early Fifteenth Century," in Parkes and Andrew G. Watson, eds., *Medieval Scribes, Manuscripts, and Libraries: Essays Presented to N. R. Ker* (London, 1978), 163-210.

[2] The manuscripts, in the order mentioned, are Oxford, Corpus Christi College 198; London, British Library Harley 7334; London, University of London Senate House Library S.L.V. 88; London, British Library Additional 27944; and the eight Gower MSS: Oxford, Christchurch College 148; New York, Columbia University Plimpton 265; Oxford, Bodleian Library Bodley 902 and Bodley 294; London, British Library Egerton 1991; Oxford, Corpus College 67; Princeton University Library Taylor 5; and Cambridge, Trinity College R.3.2.

[3] The Gower is London, British Library Royal 18 C.XXII. The Trevisa MSS are Cambridge, St. John's College, H.I (204); London, British Library Additional 24194; and (likely) Princeton, Princeton University Library Garrett 151. He also is known to have written a copy of Nicholas Love's *Life of Christ* (Oxford, Brasenose College 9) and Guy de Chauliac, *Cyrurgie* (Paris, Bibl. Nat., MS anglais 25). On Scribe Delta, see Doyle and Parkes' Appendix B.

[4] Doyle and Parkes, 208.

[5] For a list of known owners, see Doyle and Parkes' Appendix C, and see also Ralph Hanna III, "Sir Thomas Berkeley and his Patronage," *Speculum* 64 (1989), 909.

[6] The Bedford Psalter and Hours, on which see Kathleen Scott, *A Survey of Manuscripts Illuminated in the British Isles: Later Gothic Manuscripts* (London, 1996) no. 54, ill. 207; on the Gower iconography, see Sylvia Wright, "The Author Portraits in the Bedford Psalter-Hours: Gower, Chaucer, and Hoccleve," *British Library Journal* 18 (1992) 190-201. (The identification of the Chaucer and Hoccleve portraits in the manuscript is, we believe, questionable, but there is at least one portrait of Gower [inscribed as such], and possibly more.)

[7] "Professional readers" refers to scribes, illustrators and correctors whose job it was to make conscious (and often interventionist) decisions about how a text should be presented to the reading public; see Kathryn Kerby-Fulton and Denise Despres, *Iconography and the Professional Reader: The Politics of Book Production in the Douce "Piers Plowman"* (Minneapolis, 1999).

[8] See Kathryn Kerby-Fulton, "'Langland in his Working Clothes'? Scribe D, Authorial Loose Revision Material and the Nature of Scribal Intervention," forthcoming in *Middle English Poetry: Texts and Traditions. Essays in Honour of Derek Pearsall*, ed. A. J. Minnis (York, 2001), 139-67.

[9] As Jeremy Smith put it, "D's variation in his Gowers is much less than in his Chaucers . . . It is possible that this state of affairs can tell us something about the literary standing of the two authors: Gower . . . a respected monument; Chaucer, with his unfinished poem ravaged by scribal intervention, a living poet"; cited from "Linguistic Features of Some Fifteenth-Century Middle English Manuscripts," in *Manuscripts and Readers in Fifteenth-Century England*, ed. Derek Pearsall (Cambridge, 1981), 112.

[10] Compare the examples of this script in Malcolm Parkes, *English Cursive Hands, 1250-1500* (London, 1979), especially plates 7-8.

[11] At least at the start of his stint. We are grateful to Sian Echard (private communication) for pointing out some inconsistencies in numbers of lines per page later in the manuscript.

[12] As on the annotation "Nabugodonosor" on fol. 4r.

[13] Similarly if less spectacularly, the red "splashing" of ordinary capitals on the folios copied by Scribe 2 follows roughly the shape of the splashed letter, while the splashing on folios 1 and 8 (Scribe 1) and quires 2 ff. (Scribe D) are vertical lines hooking right at the top.

[14] The seminal Doyle and Parkes essay, combined with the work of C. Paul Christianson (see especially his "A Community of Book Artisans in Chaucer's London," *Viator* 20 [1989] 207-18), has shown that such scribes worked in small individual quarters rather than in scriptoria, but nonetheless this does at least confirm that the bastard anglicana of fols. 1 and 8 was not just Scribe D working in a consciously more formal script. But once he had wrapped the new outer bifolium around fols. 2-7, the catchwords would no longer be where one would look for catchwords; and it is most unlikely that he would have felt the need to remind himself of the relative positions of quires 1 and 2 when he of course knew that quire 1 was the only one not in his hand. Here, we suspect, it is a matter of a professional using a common mechanism (catchwords, in this case) for a new purpose. While the catchwords on fol. 7v would be invisible *and* otiose once the new outer bifolium had been added, their presence there would help him remember *where he needed to start copying* if he still did not have fols. 1 and 8 in his possession.

[15] G. C. Macaulay, ed., *The English Works of Gower* (Oxford, 1900), vol. 1.

[16] Kathryn Kerby-Fulton and Steven Justice, "Langlandian Reading Circles and the Civil Service in London and Dublin, 1380-1427," *New Medieval Literatures* 1 (1997), 59-83.

[17] Parkes, "Patterns of Scribal Activity and Revisions of the Text in Early Copies of Works by John Gower," in *New Science Out of Old Books: Studies in Manuscripts and*

Early Printed Books in Honour of A. I. Doyle, ed. Richard Beadle and A. J. Piper (Aldershot, 1995), 82-121.

[18] Nicholson, "Poet and Scribe in the Manuscripts of Gower's *Confessio Amantis,*" *Manuscripts and Texts,* ed. Derek Pearsall (Cambridge, 1985), 130-142.

[19] Armando Petrucci, "Reading and Writing *volgare,*" in his *Writers and Readers in Medieval Italy: Studies in the History of Written Culture,* trans. Charles M. Radding (New Haven, 1995), 211.

[20] Anne Middleton, "The Idea of Public Poetry in the Reign of Richard II," *Speculum* 53 (1978), 94-114.

[21] Especially if he also worked, as Doyle cautiously suggests he might have, on the presumptive *Canterbury Tales* MS indicated by the fragment in Cambridge University Library Kk.I.3. See A. I. Doyle, "The Copyist of the Ellesmere *Canterbury Tales,*" in *The Ellesmere Chaucer: Essays in Interpretation,* ed. Martin Stevens and Daniel Woodward (San Marino, 1995), 61-63.

[22] Smith, "Linguistic Features."

[23] On Trevisa see Hanna, "Berkeley"; and David Fowler, *The Life and Times of John Trevisa, Medieval Scholar* (Seattle, 1995).

[24] See Kerby-Fulton, "Scribe D."

[25] See Hanna, "Berkeley."

[26] C. T. Allmand, "The Civil Lawyers," in *Profession, Vocation, and Culture in Later Medieval England: Essays Dedicated to the Memory of A. R. Myers,* ed. Cecil H. Clough (Liverpool, 1982), 155-80.

[27] See Kerby-Fulton, "Scribe D"; and (on Ilchester) Wendy Scase, *"Piers Plowman" and the New Anticlericalism* (Cambridge, 1989), 150, 156-58.

[28] Richard Firth Green, *Poets and Princepleasers: Literature and the English Court in the Late Middle Ages* (Toronto, 1980).

[29] See Kerby-Fulton, "Scribe D," for recent discussion, and previous bibliography.

[30] Kerby-Fulton, "Scribe D."

[31] Doyle and Parkes, "Production," 208.

[32] On recensions of Gower's later MSS see Nicholson, "Poet and Scribe," 138-42.

[33] Griffiths, "*Confessio Amantis*: The Poem and Its Pictures," in A. J. Minnis, ed., *Gower's "Confessio Amantis": Responses and Reassessments* (Cambridge, 1983), 163-78, 163.

[34] The picture occurs on fol. 229 of the Royal MS, and on fol. 8 of the Additional MS (see fig. 2). For a description of the Royal MS, see Kathleen Scott, *Later Gothic Manuscripts,* no. 26; for a descriptions of the Additional MS, see M. C. Seymour, et al., eds., *"On the Properties of Things": John Trevisa's Translations of Bartholomaeus Anglicus De Proprietatibus Rerum: A Critical Text,* 2 vols. (Oxford, 1975) 1: 13. For a discussion of the Jerome portrait, see Gereth Spriggs, "Unnoticed Bodleian Manuscripts, Illuminated by Herman Scheerre and His School," *Bodleian Library Record* 7 (1964) 193-203. For Jean Preston's remarks see *Sixty Bokes Olde and Newe,* ed. David Anderson (Knoxville, 1986), 102-103. Preston also reproduces a picture of fol. 81 of Tayler, showing Scribe D's hand.

[35] The Confessor miniatures in the three other Scribe D MSS, Bodley 294, Egerton 1991 and Corpus 67, have all been associated with the Scheerre workshop, as has

231

the Hoccleve MS, Arundel 38 (see Scott, *Later Gothic Manuscripts*, no. 50, who suggests Westminster origins). Hoccleve himself, we remember, was one of D's collaborators on the Trinity Gower. The Taylor miniatures may also be associated with Scheerre's workshop; their damaged state may account for the lack of attention they've received from art historians.

[36] Kathleen Scott notes the variety of skills apparent in books done under Scheerre's direction; see her discussion of Huntington Library HM 19913, no. 49 in *Later Gothic Manuscripts*. (This manuscript also has a Jerome author portrait, with the trademark Scheerre book cupboard motif, fol. 122.)

[37] John Burrow, "The Portrayal of Amans in *Confessio Amantis*," in Minnis, *Responses and Reassessments*, 5-31.

[38] The juxtaposition in Taylor lends credibility to Wright's thesis, although the article should be used with the caveat suggested in note 6 above.

[39] This is his current hand (or one of them), used for catchwords (e.g. Plimpton, 40v). On the illustration in Bodley 902, showing the instruction, see Spriggs, 197. Scribe D's placements Griffiths describes as lacking the authority of, for instance, Fairfax, but reflecting the professionalism evident in all D's work; see Griffiths, "*Confessio Amantis*: The Poem and Its Pictures."

[40] The scribe who copied fol. 1 of Taylor in that rather old-fashioned bastard anglicana may have been in or associated with Scheerre's workshop.

[41] Seymour, *Trevisa*, 13.

[42] Hanna, "Berkeley," 909.

[43] Hanna, 911.

FIG. 1 Two author portraits: (1) in the margin of the miniature showing the statue from the dream of Nebuchadnezzar is a figure of Gower as an old man; (2) in the initial "O" beneath is a younger Gower, gesturing toward a book cupboard. Princeton University Library, Robert H. Taylor Collection, Department of Rare Books and Special Collections, Gower Manuscript RHT 5, fol. 1r (by permission).

FIG. 2A Historiated initial showing an author portrait of Bartholemeus, gesturing toward a book cupboard, Scribe D's text of Trevisa's translation of Bartholomeus, *On the Properties of Things*, London, British Library, MS Additional 27944, early fifteenth century, fol. 8r (by permission of the British Library).

FIG. 2B   Author portrait of St. Jerome, shown gesturing to a book cupboard, London, British Library, "Bible of Richard II," MS Royal I.E.IX, fol. 229r (by permission of the British Library).

FIG. 3A Gower kneeling before the Confessor, and instructions to the illustrator in Scribe D's hand, reading *hic fiat confessor sedens et confessus coram se genuflectendo*, Oxford, Bodleian Library, MS Bodley 902, fol. 8r (by permission of the Bodleian Library, University of Oxford).

FIG. 3B Miniature of the dream of Nebuchadnezzar showing an instruction to the illustrator in Scribe D's hand, heavily cropped, the final word of which is *facienda*, New York, Columbia University, Rare Book and Manuscript Library, Plimpton MS 265, fol. 4v, re-foliated from 1v (by permission).

237

CONTRIBUTORS

CARL JAMES GRINDLEY is a visiting lecturer in Religion and Literature at the Institute of Sacred Music and Yale Divinity School. His publications have mainly been on the Renaissance reception of medieval texts, and he is presently writing a study of Cotton Caligula A.xi, which is a manuscript of *Piers Plowman*. His broader research interests concern paleography, codicology and Middle English dialectology.

MAIDIE HILMO's doctoral thesis was on "Images, Icons, and Texts: Illustrated English Literary Works from the Ruthwell Cross to the Ellesmere Chaucer." Her article on marginal illustrations concerning "Retributive Violence and the Reformist Agenda in the Illustrated Douce 104 MS of *Piers Plowman*" appeared in *Fifteenth-Century Studies*. She is also co-editor of a special issue on *The Medieval Reader* forthcoming in *Studies in Medieval and Renaissance History*.

KELLY PARSONS, a former student at the University of Victoria, is presently an independent scholar. Her poetry and reviews have appeared in various Canadian literary journals, including *The Malahat Review*. She lives in Victoria.

KATHRYN KERBY-FULTON is Professor of English Literature at University of Victoria, and Visiting Professor of Religion and Literature at the Institute of Sacred Music, Yale University. She has published *Reformist Apocalypticism and "Piers Plowman"* (Cambridge University Press, 1990), and with Steven Justice, *Written Work: Langland, Labor, and Authorship* (University of Pennsylvania Press, 1997), and with Denise Despres, *Iconography and the Professional Reader: The Politics of Book Production in the Douce "Piers Plowman"* (University of Minnesota, 1999).

STEVEN JUSTICE teaches at the University of California, Berkeley. He is author of *Writing and Rebellion: England in 1381* (1994) and co-editor, with Kathryn Kerby-Fulton, of *Written Work: Langland, Labor, and Authorship* (1997).